LI SHI MIN

FOUNDING THE TANG DYNASTY

Li Shi Min, Founding the Tang Dynasty

The Strategies that Made China the Greatest Empire in Asia

Hing Ming Hung

Algora Publishing
New York

Library of Congress Cataloging-in-Publication Data —

Hung, Hing Ming.
    Li Shi Min, Emperor Taizong of the Tang Dynasty: the emperor who made China the
greatest empire in Asia / Hung Hing Ming.
        pages cm
    Includes bibliographical references and index.
    ISBN 978-0-87586-978-0 (soft cover : alk. paper) — ISBN 978-0-87586-979-7 (hard
cover : alk. paper) — ISBN 978-0-87586-980-3 (ebook) 1. Tang Taizong, Emperor of
China, 597-649. 2. Tang Taizong, Emperor of China, 597-649—Military leadership. 3.
Emperors—China—Biography. 4.
    China—History—Tang dynasty, 618-907. 5. China—History, Military—221
B.C.-960 A.D. I. Title.
    DS749.42.T35H86 2013
    951'.017092—dc23
    [B]
                            2013005039

TABLE OF CONTENTS

INTRODUCTION

This book is about Li Shi Min (599–649), Emperor Taizong of the Tang Dynasty (618–907), who is regarded as the best emperor in Chinese history. Under his reign (626–649), China entered into a period of peace and prosperity. He made China the greatest empire in Asia of that time. He was respected by the khans of the khanates in the north and the northwest around China of that time as "Heavenly Khan." He set a very good example for the later emperors of different dynasties.

By the end of the Sui Dynasty (589–618), under the rule of the cruel emperor Yang Guang of the Sui Dynasty, rebellions broke out all over China and China was in great chaos. In 617 Li Shi Min, who was just eighteen years old, put forward a suggestion to his father Li Yuan, who was the general in charge of the military and civil affairs of Taiyuan, to march to Chang'an, the capital, while Emperor Yang Guang was far away in the east. His father accepted his suggestion and commanded the army to march from Taiyuan to Chang'an. Li Shi Min commanded an army to march ahead of the main force. Li Yuan commanded the main force and captured Chang'an. Thus Li Yuan successfully overthrew the Sui Dynasty and established the Tang Dynasty, becoming its first emperor. Li Shi Min had made the greatest contributions in overthrowing the Sui Dynasty and in establishing the Tang Dynasty.

At the beginning of the Tang Dynasty, many parts of China were still occupied by warlords and local strongmen. In 618, Li Shi Min commanded an army to march to the northwest and fought against Xue Ren Gao, the Emperor of Qin, who occupied the northwest part of China. Li Shi Min won. In 620, he carried out a northern expedition against Liu Wu Zhou, who occupied the area east of the Yellow River. He won again, and drove Liu Wu Zhou to the area of the Eastern Turkic Khanate in the north. In July 620, Li Shi Min commanded an army to march to Luoyang, the eastern capital of the Sui Dynasty, to deal with Wang Shi Chong, Emperor of Zheng. In March of the following year, Dou Jian De, the Emperor of Xia, who occupied the area north of the Yellow River, led a great army to rescue Wang Shi Chong. In May 621, Li Shi Min defeated Dou Jian De's army and captured him. In the same month Wang Shi Chong surrendered and Li Shi Min occupied Luoyang. In March 622, Li Shi Min put down the rebellion of Liu Hei Ta in the area north of the Yellow River. Li Shi Min is considered to have made the greatest contributions in the unification of China.

Li Shi Min's elder brother Li Jian Cheng, the Crown Prince, and Li Shi Min's younger brother Li Yuan Ji envied Li Shi Min because of his great accomplishments. The two brothers colluded with each other to frame Li Shi Min in front of Emperor Li Yuan, and even plotted to murder him. Urged by the ministers and generals under him, Li Shi Min laid an ambush at Xuanwu Gate of the palace and killed Li Jian Cheng and Li Yuan Ji on 4 June 626. In August 626, Emperor Li Yuan passed the throne to Li Shi Min and so he ascended the throne of the Tang Dynasty.

Emperor Li Shi Min achieved many great political and military goals. He upheld the principle of putting the interest of the people first; he practiced wise governance and showed grace to the people. He appointed wise and capable officials to responsible positions. He even appointed those who had once been hostile to him to high positions. Wei Zheng, who had been a staff under Li Jian Cheng and once advised Li Jian Cheng to get rid of Li Shi Min, was appointed to take charge of the secretariat work of the emperor. In this position Wei Zheng gave Li Shi Min much good advice. Even Li Jing, who had heard that Li Shi Min's father Li Yuan was going to rebel against the Sui Dynasty and had wanted to reveal this to Emperor Yang Guang of the Sui Dynasty, was appointed as the minister of war. He later played an important role in conquering the Eastern Turkic Khanate and Tuyuhun Khanate. Yuchi Jing De, who had once fought against Li Shi Min, was appointed great general of the Tang army. He was essential in the wars against the warlords and local strongmen. Li Shi Min had many wise ministers and generals around him. They were: Zhangsun Wu Ji, Fang Xuan Ling, Li Ji, Du Ru Hui and Chu Sui Liang. They helped Li Shi Min to make China into a great and prosperous empire and they became very famous in Chinese history. He inspired his officials to put forward proposals and followed their good advice readily. He accepted their frank criticism and he corrected his mistakes quickly. Under his reign, China was in great peace and tranquility.

At that time the army of the Eastern Turkic Khanate invaded China frequently. In 630, Emperor Li Shi Min sent armies to attack them. The armies of the Tang Dynasty won, and they captured Jiali Khan of the Eastern Turkic Khanate. The Eastern Turkic Khanate was brought to submission.

In 634, the armies of Tuyuhun Khanate invaded the northwest part of China. Emperor Li Shi Min sent armies to carry out an expedition against Tuyuhun Khanate and brought it to submission. In 639, the Kingdom of Gaochang, which was situated in northwest, turned hostile to the Tang Dynasty. Emperor Li Shi Min sent an army against them, too, and conquered the Kingdom of Gaochang. In 642, he sent armies to defeat the Xueyantuo Khanate. And that is how, under Emperor Li Shi Min, China became the largest empire in Asia.

Emperor Li Shi Min was on the throne for twenty-three years (from 626 to 649). The title of his reign was Zhenguan. This period of his reign has been referred to by historians as "The Great Period of Peace and Prosperity of the Reign of Zhenguan" ("貞觀之治").

Today there are "China Towns" in the big cities in the United States and other countries throughout the West, inhabited by overseas Chinese from China. The Chinese term for "China Town" is "Tang Ren Jie" (in Chinese characters: 唐人街), meaning "the Street (Town) of the Tang People." That means that although the overseas Chinese have left China, the land of their forefathers, they never forget that they are the descendents of the people of the Tang Dynasty.

Li Shi Min (599–649), Emperor Taizong of the Tang Dynasty

CHAPTER ONE. UNDER THE RULE OF EMPEROR YANG GUANG OF THE
SUI DYNASTY

1. The Birth of Li Shi Min

From 420 to 589, China consisted of two parts: the Southern Dynasties
(south of the Yangtze River) and the Northern Dynasties (north of the Yangtze
River).

Before the drama unfolds, we need a little background. Here is a quick re-
view of the Southern Dynasties. In 420, Emperor Sima De Wen of the Eastern
Jin Dynasty (Eastern Jin Dynasty: 317–420) abdicated and offered the throne to
Liu Yu, the Grand Commandant of the Eastern Jin Dynasty. Liu Yu ascended the
throne and established the Song Dynasty, becoming its first emperor. In 479 Liu
Zhun of the Song Dynasty abdicated and offered the throne to General Xiao Dao
Cheng. Xiao Dao Cheng ascended the throne and established the Qi Dynasty. In
501, Emperor Xiao Bao Rong of the Qi Dynasty abdicated and offered the throne
to Xiao Yan, the Grand Commandant of the Qi Dynasty. Xiao Yan ascended the
throne and established the Liang Dynasty. In 557 Emperor Xiao Fang Zhi of the
Liang Dynasty abdicated and offered the throne to Chen Ba Xian, the King of
Chen. Chen Ba Xian ascended the throne and established the Chen Dynasty.

The Northern Dynasties: In 386, Tuo Ba Gui of the Xianbei nationality, a
Mongolic people, established the Wei Dynasty in the northern part of China.
Historians refer to this dynasty as the Northern Wei Dynasty. In 534, the Northern Wei Dynasty was split into the Eastern Wei Dynasty and Western Wei Dynasty. The Emperor of the Eastern Wei Dynasty was Emperor Yuan Shan Jian.

The Emperor of the Western Wei Dynasty was Yuan Bao Ju. In 550 Emperor Yuan Shan Jian of the Eastern Wei Dynasty abdicated and offered the throne to Gao Yang, King of Qi. Gao Yang ascended the throne and established the Qi Dynasty. Historians refer to this dynasty as Northern Qi Dynasty. In 557, Emperor Yu Kuo of the Western Wei Dynasty abdicated and offered the throne to Yuwen Jue, the Grand General of the Western Wei Dynasty. Yuwen Jue ascended the throne and established the Zhou Dynasty. Historians refer to this dynasty as the Northern Zhou Dynasty. In 577, Emperor Yuwen Yong of the Northern Zhou Dynasty conquered the Northern Qi Dynasty and unified the north part of China.

In the Northern Zhou Dynasty (557–581), General Dou Yi, who married the elder sister of Emperor Yuwen Yong (who reigned from 560 to 578) of the Northern Zhou Dynasty, had a daughter. She was both wise and beautiful. Many young men came to ask Dou Yi to marry his daughter to them. Dou Yi decided to select his son-in-law by arrow shooting. He had two peacocks drawn on a wooden screen and each peacock had an eye. He declared that he would marry his daughter to the young man who could hit the two eyes of the peacocks by two arrows at a distance of a hundred feet. More than fifty young men came to try their luck, but none of them could hit the eyes of the peacocks. Then another young man came. He was given a bow and two arrows. He drew the bow calmly and let go the first arrow. The arrow hit the eye of one peacock. All the on-lookers cheered loudly. Then the young man drew the bow and let go the second arrow. The arrow flew and hit right on the eye of the other peacock. Dou Yi gladly married his daughter to the young man. The winner's name was Li Yuan, Duke of Tang. Lady Dou gave birth to four boys and one girl for Li Yuan. She died at the age of forty-five, before Li Yuan became the Emperor of the Tang Dynasty.

Li Shi Min was the second son of Li Yuan. He was born in December 599 in Wugong (now Wugong, Shaanxi Province). When he was born, two dragons were playing outside the gate of the house for three days. His elder brother was Li Jian Cheng. Li Shi Min had two younger brothers: Li Xuan Ba (who died early) and Li Yuan Ji. When Li Shi Min was four years old, a scholar visited Li Yuan. He said to Li Yuan, "You will be a very noble man, and you have a son who will be a very noble man, too." When he saw Li Shi Min, he said, "This boy looks like an emperor. When he is twenty, he will surely do great deeds to save the people and stabilize the whole realm." Li Yuan was afraid that the scholar would tell what he had said to other people and put his family in a dangerous situation. So he drew out his sword and tried to kill him, but the scholar disappeared suddenly. The given name Shi Min means "saving the people and stabilizing the realm."

2. The Establishment of the Sui Dynasty

In February 581, Emperor Yuwen Chan of the Northern Zhou Dynasty abdicated and offered the throne to Yang Jian, the Premier of the Northern Zhou Dynasty and King of Sui. Then Yang Jian ascended the throne and became the first emperor of the Sui Dynasty. His wife Lady Dugu became Empress Dugu. He appointed his eldest son Yang Yong the Crown Prince.

Portrait of Emperor Yang Jian of the Sui Dynasty

3. Yang Guang Usurps the Throne and Becomes the Second Emperor of the Sui Dynasty

Emperor Yang Jian of the Sui Dynasty had five sons. His eldest son Yang Yong was the Crown Prince, the successor to the throne. Yang Guang was Emperor Yang Jian's second son. He was made King of Jin. He did not have the right to succeed to the imperial throne. In 589, he commanded a great army to congquer the Chen Dynasty in the area south of the Yangtze River. The third son Yang Jun was made the King of Qin. The fourth son Yang Xiu was made King of Yue. The fifth son Yang Liang was made King of Han. Emperor Yang Jian was a frugal person. He did not like extravagance. But Crown Prince Yang Yong was an extravagant person. He once had his armor decorated. This led to serious criticism from his father. Emperor Yang Jian had only one wife, that is, Empress Dugu. All the princes and princesses were the children of Emperor Yang Jian and Empress

Dugu. But Crown Prince Yang Yong had many concubines. He did not love his wife Lady Yuan, but especially loved his concubine Lady Yun. Lady Yuan died suddenly. Emperor Yang Jian and Empress Dugu suspected that Crown Prince Yang Yong had sent someone to poison her. Yang Guang saw that he could make use of the divergence between his father and his brother so as to seize the throne of the Sui Dynasty. He conspired with Yang Su, a favorite minister of Emperor Yang Jian. They bought over a servant of Crown Prince Yang Yong and asked that servant to report to them all the wrong doings of Crown Prince Yang Yong. Emperor Yang Jian suspected that his heir would do harm to him. Then he ordered to arrest the officers of the guards of Crown Prince Yang Yong for further investigation. At the same time Yang Su reported all the wrong doings of the Crown Prince to Emperor Yang Jian. In October 600, Emperor Yang Jian deprived Yang Yong of the title of Crown Prince, and in November he made Yang Guang the Crown Prince. Four years later, in October 604, Emperor Yang Jian died. His posthumous title was Emperor Wen and his temple title was Gaozu. In the same month Yang Guang ascended the throne of the Sui Dynasty.

Portrait of Emperor Yang Guang of the Sui Dynasty

4. Chang'an, the Capital, and Luoyang, the Eastern Capital, of the Sui Dynasty

Chang'an, the capital of the Sui Dynasty, was situated in the area of Guan-zhong (now the area of the north part of Shaanxi Province and east part of Gansu Province). Guanzhong means the area within the four passes: Hanguguan Pass (now in Lingbao, in the western part of Henan Province) in the east, Wuguan Pass (in the southeast of Shaanxi Province) in the south, Sanguan Pass (now Dasanguan, to the south of Baoji, Shaanxi Province) in the west, Xiaoguan Pass (now northwest to Huanxian, in the eastern part of Gansu Province) in the north. Guanzhong is also called the area of Qin, because in the period of War-ring States (403 BC to 221 BC) Guanzhong was the territory of the State of Qin. Chang'an had been the capital of the Former Han Dynasty (206 BC–9 AD).

Luoyang (now Luoyang, Henan Province) was the Eastern Capital of the Sui Dynasty. Luoyang had been the capital of the Eastern Zhou Dynasty (771 BC–221 BC) and the capital of the Later Han Dynasty (25–220).

5. Construction of the Palaces in the Eastern Capital and Digging of the Canals

The capital of the Sui Dynasty was Chang'an (now Chang'an, Shaanxi Prov-ince). In March 605 Emperor Yang Guang sent Yang Su and Yuwen Kai to take charge of the construction of the Eastern Capital, Luoyang (now in Henan Prov-ince). Every month, two million able-bodied men were sent there to do hard la-bor for the construction of the palaces. Emperor Yang Guang also gave the order to transport stones of all kinds of shapes from the south of the Yangtze River and the Five Ridges (mountains across the borders of Hunan Province and Guang-dong Province) to Luoyang and to look for exotic flowers and rare trees and all kinds of rare animals all over the country to put in the gardens of the palaces in Luoyang. He mobilized a million able-bodied men in the area to the south of the Yellow River and north to the Huai River to dig the Tongji Canal. Tongji Canal started from Xiyuan (in the west of Luoyang, Henan Province) to lead water from the Luoshui River (Luo He River in Henan Province) to the Yellow River, then from Banzhu (by the side of the Yellow River in Sishui Town, Xingyang, Henan Province) to lead water from the Yellow River through Rongze (a place to the northwest of Zhengzhou, Henan Province) to Daliang (now Kaifeng, Henan Province) to take water to the Huai River (which flows from Anhui Province to the west part of Jiangsu Province). Then more than a hundred thousand able-bodied men in the area to the south of the Huai River were mobilized to dig a ca-nal from Shanyang (now Huai'an, Jiangsu Province) to Jiangdu (now Yangzhou,

Jiangsu Province) and thence to the Yangtze River. The canals were forty feet wide. Wide roads were built on both banks. Willow trees were planted along the canals. Emperor Yang Guang of the Sui Dynasty intended to travel from Luoyang to southeast China. He gave the order to have big dragon boats and about ten thousand small boats built. The overseers of the construction of the palaces in the eastern capital made the workers work very hard. The workers could not stand such hard work; four or five out of ten died. The carts carrying dead bodies out of the worksites lined up one after another on the road from Luoyang to Xingyang (now in Henan Province).

In August 605, Emperor Yang Guang started his journey to Jiangdu (now Yangzhou, Jiangsu Province). The big dragon boat and the small boats were sent to take the Emperor. The Emperor took a small boat from Luoyang through a canal to Luokou (now northeast of Gongyi, Henan Province) where he got on board the dragon boat. The dragon boat was forty-five feet high and two thousand feet long. On the first deck from the top, there were two big courts. On the second deck from the top, there were one hundred and twenty rooms, all decorated with gold and jade. On the third deck from the top, there were water pools. On the lowest deck, there were rooms for servants. The boat for Empress Xiao was a bit smaller, but was almost the same design. There were several thousand small boats following the dragon boat. Eighty thousand people were used to pull the boats. The boats lined up along the canal for a hundred kilometers.

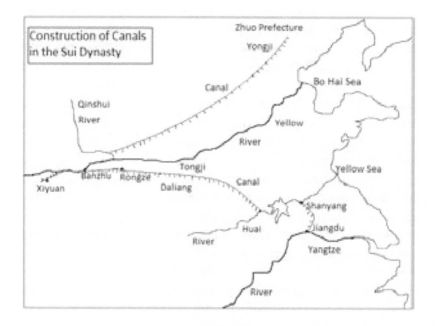

In January 608, Emperor Yang Guang issued an order to mobilize a million people to dig the Yongji Canal to lead water from the Qinshui River (now Qinhe River, which flows from southern part of Shanxi Province to the northern part of Henan Province) south to the Yellow River and north to Zhuo Prefecture (now southwest of Beijing). At that time there were not enough able-bodied men. So women were conscripted to do the hard labor.

6. The Rise of the Turks

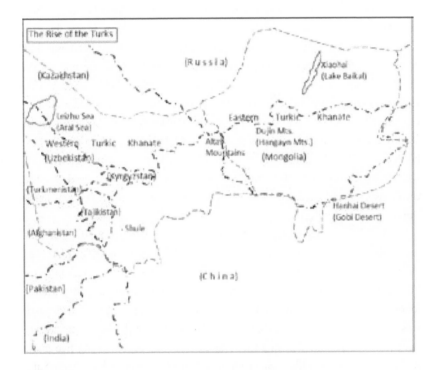

The Turks were a nomadic tribe in the Altay Mountains (a great mountain range between Xinjiang Uygur Autonomous Region of China, Mongolia and Kazakhstan). They believed that they were the descendants of a wolf. So their totem was a wolf head. They submitted themselves to the Tribe of Rouran for many generations, doing metallurgy work for Rouran. The Turks became strong in the fifth century. They defeated the Tribe of Rouran and conquered the other tribes in that area and established a vast empire with its western boundary at the Leizhu Sea (Aral Sea) in Western Asia, its southern boundary at the Hanhai Desert (now Gobi Desert) between the Inner Mongolia Autonomous Region of China and Mongolia), its north boundary at Xiaohai (now Lake Baikal, Russia), its eastern boundary to Liao Hai (now the Liao He River, Liaoning Province of

China), the southwestern boundary to Shule (now Shule in the district of Keshi, Xinjiang Uygur Autonomous Region of China). In 582, the Empire of the Turks disintegrated and split in two: the Western Turkic Khanate and the Eastern Turkic Khanate. Ashina Shetu of the Eastern Turks became Ishbara Khan. Ishbara Khan established his headquarters in the Dujin Mountain (now the eastern branch of the Hangayn Mountains in Mongolia).

The Turks had the following official ranks: the supreme ruler was Khan; the military commander of a sub tribe was Shad; the sons and brothers of a Khan were Tegins; the ministers were Yabghu (also the chief of a sub tribe); next Chur; next Yilifa; next Tudun (an official of supervision); next Irkin. In 583, Ishbara Khan commanded a great army to invade the territory of the Sui Dynasty, but it was defeated by the army of the Sui Dynasty. Then there was turmoil within the Turks. Ishbara Khan's cousin Abo Khan united with Datou Khan (who was Ishbara Khan's uncle) and attacked Ishbara Khan. In 585, Ishbara Khan submitted himself to the Sui Dynasty and the Eastern Turkic Khanate became a vassal state of the Sui Dynasty. Ishbara Khan died in 587. His younger brother Chuluohou succeeded as Yehu Khan. Yehu Khan was killed by an arrow in a battle in a western expedition. Then Ishbara Khan's eldest son Yongyulü succeeded to the throne as Dulan Khan. Ashina Rangan, another son of Ishbara Khan, was made Tuli Khan (junior khan).

In 598, Dulan Khan united with Dianque and attacked Ashina Rangan, killing all his brothers and sons and cousins—but not him. Then Dulan Khan and Dianque crossed the Yellow River and entered into the area of Yuzhou (now Yuxian, Hebei Province). Ashina Rangan got away; he rode to Chang'an with five followers to the court of the Sui Dynasty. Emperor Yang Jian of the Sui Dynasty was very glad to see him. In June that year Emperor Yang Jian sent a great army to attack Dianque and defeated the army under him. Emperor Yang Jian made Ashina Rangan Qimin Khan. Since Qimin Khan's wife had died, Emperor Yang Jian selected a girl from the royal clan of the Sui Dynasty, gave her the title of Princess Yicheng and married her to Qimin Khan. Further, Emperor Yang Jian sent a great army to attack Dulan Khan. Dulan Khan was killed by one of his subordinates. Qimin Khan recovered the power to rule the whole Eastern Turkic Khanate. Qimin Khan died in 609, and his son Ashina Duojishi succeeded to the throne and became Shibi Khan. He married his father's wife Princess Yicheng. The Eastern Turkic Khanate became strong again. However, after all that, Shibi Khan turned against the Sui Dynasty.

7. Expedition against Koguryo and the Peasant Uprisings Opposing the War against Koguryo

The Kingdom of Koguryo was situated to the northeast China. Its territory included the northern part of Korea and the area of what is now the eastern part of Liaoning Province and the eastern part of Jilin Province. Pei Ju, the minister in charge of foreign affairs, said to Emperor Yang Guang of the Sui Dynasty, "Koguryo was originally a part of the territory of China. In the Zhou Dynasty, Ji Zi was made king of that place. In the Han Dynasty and the Jin Dynasty, Koguryo was a prefecture. But now the Kingdom of Koguryo is not submitted to the rule of the Sui Dynasty. We must do our best to bring it to submission to the rule of the Sui Dynasty." Emperor Yang Guang agreed with him and made up his mind to conquer Koguryo. In February 611, Emperor Yang Guang of the Sui Dynasty issued an order to prepare for an expedition against Koguryo. Officials were sent to Donglai (now Laizhou, Shandong Province) to supervise the building of 300 sea-sailing boats. The workmen had to work in the water day and night. Many workmen died in the shipyards. In April 611, Emperor Yang Guang went to Zhuo Prefecture (the principal city of the prefecture was Ji, now Beijing). He gave the order that all the armies over the whole country should meet in Zhuo. And he also gave the order to mobilize ten thousand sailors from the Yangtze River and the Huai River. So armies all over China hurried to Zhuo from all directions. Food was transported from the grain storages in Luokoucang (now northeast of Gongyi, Henan Province) through Yongji Canal to Zhuo Prefecture. The boats transporting food lined up on the canal for five hundred kilometers. Numerous laborers were mobilized to carry military supplies to Zhuo Prefecture. And boats loaded with food and military supplies sailed north along Yongji Canal to Zhuo Prefecture. Many people died on the way. Six hundred thousand men were mobilized to push small carts to transport food to Zhuo Prefecture. Every two persons pushed a cart carrying three hectoliter of grain. But they had to travel such a long way that they ate up all the food they were transporting on their way. When they reached the destination, they did not have anything to hand over to the army. They were afraid of being punished, and so they ran away. The government imposed such heavy taxes on the people that the peasants did not have anything left. Officials pressed the peasants very hard to pay the tax.

The peasants became so poor, they could do nothing but rise up against the government. Wang Bo, an ordinary peasant in Zouping (now Zouping, Shandong Province) led the people there in an uprising against the government. They occupied Changbaishan (now in the area of Zouping, Shandong Province). He called on the people to rise against the government, and many people joined him and many people rose in many places. In December 611, Dou Jian De, a brave young man in the area to the south of the Zhangshui River (now Zhang He River, in the southern part of Hebei Province) rose in rebellion with several hundred people. At that time, Zhang Jin Cheng and Gao Shi Da rose in the area of Qinghe Prefecture (now the area around Qinghe in the southern part of Hebei Province). Dou Jian De went to join Gao Shi Da. Gao Shi Da appointed him commander of his army. Very soon, the army under Dou Jian De developed into an army of over a hundred thousand men.

When all the armies had gathered in Zhuo Prefecture (now in the area around Beijing) in January 612, Emperor Yang Guang of the Sui Dynasty commanded one million one hundred and thirty thousand men to start the war to conquer Koguryo. The army of Koguryo resisted resolutely. The army of the Sui Dynasty suffered a great setback. The first expedition ended in failure.

In January 613, Emperor Yang Guang of the Sui Dynasty gave the order to gather all the armies to Zhuo Prefecture and got ready for the second expedition against Koguryo. He personally commanded a great army across the Liao River (in Liaoning Province). He sent Yuwen Shu and General Yang Yi to march to Pyongyang (now Pyongyan, North Korea). Emperor Yang Guang of the Sui Dynasty ordered his generals to attack Liaodong (now Liaoyang, Liaoning Province) again. But the Koguryo soldiers defended the city resolutely. The Sui army attacked the city for twenty days but they could not take the city.

8. Yang Xuan Gan's Rebellion and Rebellions All Over China

Yang Xuan Gan was the son of Yang Su who had helped Yang Guang to usurp the throne of the Sui Dynasty. Yang Xuan Gan was the minister of rites. He was in charge of food supply for the expedition against Koguryo in Liyang (now Junxian, Henan Province). In June 613, Yang Xuan Gan rose in rebellion. He commanded eight thousand men to march to Luoyang, the Eastern Capital of the Sui Dynasty. The defender of the Eastern Capital was Yang Tong, King of Yue, who was the grandson of Emperor Yang Guang. He had advance warning of Yang Xuan Gan's plan to attack the Eastern Capital and was well prepared to resist the attack. Yang Xuan Gan's army grew to fifty thousand men. He won several victories but could not take the Eastern Capital. Yang You, King of Dai, was also a grandson of Emperor Yang Guang. He was in Chang'an. He sent General Wei Wen Sheng to lead forty thousand men to rescue the Eastern Capital. Emperor Yang Guang turned back from Liaodong and sent Generals Yuwen Shu and Qutu Tong with a great army to suppress Yang Xuan Gan's rebellion. Yang Xuan Gan saw that the situation was unfavorable to him and gave up the attack of the Eastern Capital. He marched his army westward. He wanted to go through Tongguan Pass (now Tongguan, Shaanxi Province) so as to enter the area of Guanzhong (the area within Hanguguan Pass, Wuguan Pass, Sanguan Pass and Xiaoguan Pass). Generals Yuwen Shu, Qutu Tong and Wei Wen Sheng pursued him. When Yang Xuan Gan's army reached Hongnong (now Lingbao, Henan Province), Yang Zhi Ji, who was the King of Cai, defended the city with determination. Yang Xuan Gan attacked the city for three days but could not take it. Yang Xuan Gan had to give up attacking the city and marched westward again. They reached Wenxiang (now to the west of Lingbao, Henan Province). The armies commanded by Yuwen Shu, Wei Wen Sheng, Lai Hu Er, and Qutu Tong caught up with Yang Xuan Gan's army in Huangtianyuan (to the west of Lingbao, Henan Province). Yang Xuan Gan deployed his army in battle formation and fought with the pursuing army. Three battles were fought in one day, and Yang Xuan Gan was defeated three times. Then a decisive battle was fought in Dongtuyuan. Yang Xuan Gan's army suffered a disastrous defeat, and Yang Xuan Gan and his younger brother Yang Ji Shan fled to Jialushu. Yang Xuan Gan knew that he could not escape and he said to his brother, "I cannot stand the insults when they execute me. You may kill me now." Yang Ji Shan drew out his sword and killed Yang Xuan Gan. Then he tried to kill himself with his own sword, but he did not die and was captured by the pursuing army and was executed later.

During Yang Xuan Gan's rebellion, Liu Yuan Jin rose in Wu (now the area around Suzhou, Jiangsu Province) in response to Yang Xuan Gan. Many peasants who would not be recruited into the army to be sent to the war against Koguryo joined him and his army grew into an army of over thirty thousand men. In September 613, Liu Yuan Jin attacked Danyang (now Nanjing, Jiangsu Province) but was defeated. Although Tu Wan Xu defeated Liu Yuan Jin many times, Liu Yuan Jin's army kept growing because after each defeat, the scattered soldiers gathered again and more poor people joined his army. So Tu Wan Xu's army got very tired. He asked permission from the Emperor to let his army to have a rest and not to have any operation until next year. The Emperor got very angry and had Tu Wan Xu investigated; he was found guilty of cowardice and was sentenced to death.

The Emperor sent Wang Shi Chong, the assistant governor of Jiangdu, with over thirty thousand soldiers to suppress Liu Yuan Jin. Wang Shi Chong started several battles with Liu Yuang Jin's army and Liu Yuan Jin was killed in a battle. Wang Shi Chong spread word that any one in Liu Yuan Jin's army who surrendered would not be killed. So within a month many of the former members of Liu Yuan Jin's army surrendered. Then one day, Wang Shi Chong had these people, thirty thousand in all, killed. When the remaining members got the news, they gathered again to fight against the government. Wang Shi Chong became a favorite of the Emperor for what he had done in the suppression of Liu Yuan Jin's uprising.

In September 613, Du Fu Wei, a young man of sixteen, and Fu Gong Shi rose in rebellion in the area to the south of the Huai River and many people joined their army.

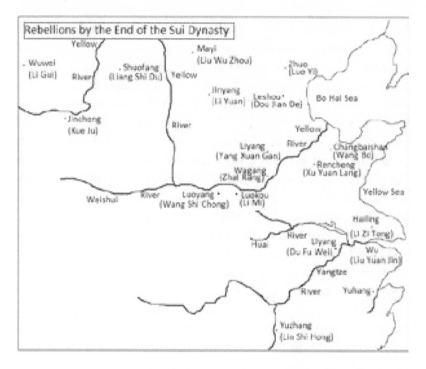

9. Emperor Yang Guang Is Besieged in Yanmen by the Turks

In August 615, Emperor Yang Guang of the Sui Dynasty was on an inspection tour to north China along the Great Wall. Shibi Khan of the Turks heard about it. He led three hundred thousand cavalrymen to carry out a surprise attack on Emperor Yang Guang. Emperor Yang Guang retreated into the city of Yanmen (now Yanmen Guan, in the northern part of Shanxi Province) in a great hurry. Then the Turks laid siege to the city of Yanmen. There were forty-one cities in Yanmen Prefecture, thirty-nine of which fell into the hands of the Turks. Arrows shot by the Turks landed right in front of Emperor Yang Guang. The Emperor could do nothing but held his grandson, crying together. An order from the Emperor was issued all over China calling on the armies to go to Yanmen to rescue him. At that time, Li Shi Min was sixteen years old. He joined the army under the command of

General Yun Ding Xing. Before the army under General Yun Ding Xing started its march, Li Shi Min said to General Yun Ding Xing, "We must prepare a lot of flags and drums so as to confuse the enemy. The reason why Shibi Khan is so bold as to have brought all his army with him to surround the Emperor is that he thinks that no relief force can come in such a short time. We must show the enemy that a great army has come. We must put up flags in an area of tens of kilometers and beat drums all night long so that the enemy will think that the relief forces have gathered. Then the Turks will lift their encirclement and leave. Otherwise, our small army will certainly be defeated." General Yun Ding Xing took his advice and when his army reached Guoxian, which was situated to the west bank of the Hutuo River, he deployed his army as Li Shi Min had suggested. The Turks' scouts immediately rode to report to Shibi Khan that great armies had gathered to rescue Emperor Yang Guang of the Sui Dynasty. At the same time Shibi Khan's wife Princess Yicheng sent a messenger to Shibi Khan, telling him that there was danger in the northern border of the Turks. The army of the Sui Dynasty rescuing Emperor Yang Guang had reached Xinkou (now Xinkou, Shanxi Province). Then Shibi Khan lifted his siege and went away.

10. Emperor Yang Guang's Trip to Jiangdu

In July 616, the newly built dragon boats made in Jiangdu (now Yangzhou, Jiangsu Province) was sent to Luoyang, the Eastern Capital. Yuwen Shu suggested that Emperor Yang Guang make a trip to Jiangdu. Emperor Yang Guang made up his mind to do just that. He ordered his grandson Yang Tong, King of Yue, to stay in Luoyang to tend to the affairs in the Eastern Capital. Some ministers tried to persuade Emperor Yang Guang not to go to Jiangdu, but Emperor Yang Guang ignored them, and even killed some of them. When the dragon boat reached Liang Prefecture (now Kaifeng, Henan Province), some local people presented a letter to Emperor Yang Guang telling him that if he made the trip to Jiangdu, he would lose his power to control China. The Emperor was so angry that he had all of them killed and continued his trip. In December 616, Emperor Yang Guang of the Sui Dynasty reached Jiangdu. From then on, he never left that place. The officials in Jiangdu area all came to meet the Emperor with all kinds of treasures. Those who brought the most valuable treasures got promotions. Wang Shi Chong, the assistant governor of Jiangdu, presented a screen with brass mirrors and was promoted governor of Jiangdu Prefecture in charge of civil and military affairs. Wang Shi Chong secretly collected beauties among the people to present to Emperor Yang Guang. From then on, he became the most favorite official of the Emperor. At that time Ge Qian, the chief of a band of more than a hundred thousand outlaws in Hejian (now Hejian, Hebei Province) occupied Hejian city and made himself King of the State of Yan. Emperor Yang Guang sent Wang Shi Chong with a great army to suppress Ge Qian. Wang Shi Chong fought with Ge Qian and killed him. But Gao Kai Dao, a general under Ge Qian, gathered the scattered soldiers under Ge Qian and occupied the area of Yan (now the northern part of Hebei Province).

Emperor Yang Guang's Trip to Jiangdu

11. Li Mi and Zhai Rang

Li Mi was a strategy planner for Yang Xuan Gan. He made many sound suggestions, but Yang Xuan Gan did not take his advice. After Yang Xuan Gan was defeated, Li Mi made his escape. In October 616, he went to join the outlaws in Wagang (in the south of Huaxian, Henan Province) led by Zhai Rang. Li Mi did a lot of work to unite the outlaws of Wagang with other groups who rose in rebellion against the rule of the Sui Dynasty. At that time, there were rumors to the effect that a person by the family name of Li would become emperor. Many people thought that Li Mi might be that person. So Zhai Rang had great faith in Li Mi. Li Mi suggested that the army of Wagang should take Xingyang (now Xingyang, Henan Province) so that the army could get sufficient food from the food storage in that area and the soldiers could have a good rest. Zhai Rang took his advice and commanded his army to attack Jindiguan (within the area of Xingyang, Henan Province) and took it. Zhai Rang took most of the counties around Xingyang. In January 617, Li Mi and Zhai Rong started a surprise attack on Luokou (now northeast of Gongyi, Henan Province) and took it. There was a great granary in Luokou in Sui Dynasty. Li Mi opened the bans to distribute food to the hungry people. And Li Mi's army got sufficient food from this food depot.

Yang Tong, King of Yue, sent Generals Liu Chang Gong and Fang Ze with twenty-seven thousand men to suppress Li Mi's army. In February 617, Li Mi and Zhai Rang defeated the army of the Sui Dynasty. More than half of the troops of the Sui Dynasty were killed in this battle. Li Mi and Zhai Rang got all the military supplies and armor. Their reputation became known far and wide. Zhai Rang suggested that Li Mi be the supreme leader of all the outlaws and be made Duke of Wei. Li Mi gladly accepted his suggestion and proclaimed himself Duke of Wei and ascended the throne. He established the Office of the Duke of Wei and the Headquarters of Marshal of the Army staffed with all kinds of officials. He appointed Zhai Rang general of the highest rank and premier. He also made Zhai Rang Duke of Dong Prefecture (now Huaxian, Henan Province). He appointed Shan Xiong Xin Left Chief General and Xu Shi Ji Right Chief General. Pei Ren Ji was the commander of the army of the Sui Dynasty defending Hulao (a pass in the West of Sishui Town, Xingyang, Henan Province). He surrendered to Li Mi with all his men and the city of Hulao. Li Mi appointed him the general of the highest rank. Qin Shu Bao and Cheng Zhi Jie joined Li Mi's army. Li Mi appointed them commanders of the cavalrymen. Outlaws in the area to the south of the Yellow River submitted themselves to the leadership of Li Mi. Li Mi's army grew into an army of over three hundred thousand men.

12. Lin Shi Hong Occupies the Area of Yuzhang Prefecture

Cao Shi Qi, the chief of a band of outlaws in the area around Boyang Lake (now in Jiangxi Province) made himself King of Yuanxing. He attacked Yuzhang Prefecture (now the area around Nanchang, Jiangxi Province) and took it. He appointed Lin Shi Hong as commander-in-chief of his army. Emperor Yang Guang ordered Liu Zi Xu with an army to suppress the rebellion. In a battle Cao Shi Qi was killed. Lin Shi Hong took command of all the army commanded by Cao Shi Qi and fought a battle against Liu Zi Xu in Pengli Lake (a lake near Pengze, Jiangxi Province). Liu Zi Xu was defeated and was killed in battle. Lin Shi Hong's army grew very quickly and very soon developed into an army of more than a hundred thousand men. In December 615, Lin Shi Hong declared himself to be emperor. The state he established was named Chu. He attacked the prefectures of Jiujiang (now Jiujiang, Jiangxi Province), Linchuan (now Linchuan, Jiangxi Province), Nankang (now Nankang, Jiangxi Province), and Yichun (now Yichun,

Jiangxi Province) and took them all. The people of those areas rose to kill the officials appointed by the Sui Government in response to Lin Shi Hong. So the vast area south to Jiujiang was under the control of Lin Shi Hong.

13. The Growth of Dou Jian De's Force

In October 616, Guo Xuan, the governor of Zhuo Prefecture (now the area of Beijing), commanded an army of ten thousand men to suppress the army led by Gao Shi Da. Gao Shi Da thought that he was not as capable as Dou Jian De, so he put all his army under the command of Dou Jian De. Dou Jian De asked Gao Shi Da to look after the food and supplies. He picked the seven thousand best fighters from the whole army. He took these seven thousand handpicked soldiers into battle against Guo Xuan. He pretended that he had had a quarrel with Gao Shi Da and he had betrayed him. He sent an envoy to tell Guo Xuan that he would surrender to Guo Xuan and would like to be the vanguard for Guo Xuan's army to attack Gao Shi Da, so as to perform meritorious services to atone for his crimes. Guo Xuan believed him and followed Dou Jian De to Changhe (now east of Dezhou, Shandong Province). When Guo Xuan was not on guard against Dou Jian De, he launched a surprise attack and killed him. Dou Jian De presented Guo Xuan's head to Gao Shi Da.

Yang Yi Chen, a general of the Sui Dynasty, who had just defeated the rebels led by Zhang Jin Cheng, commanded his army to Pingyuan (now in Shandong Province) to attack the army led by Gao Shi Da. Dou Jiang De said to Gao Shi Da, "Of all the generals of the Sui Dynasty, Yang Yi Chen is the best at the art of war. He has just won a great victory over Zhang Jin Cheng. We cannot fight with this victorious army. We'd better withdraw to avoid fighting with him. If he cannot find a chance to fight with us, he is wasting time, and his officers and men will get tired. Then we may find a chance to defeat him. Otherwise, I am afraid that you may not be a match for him." Gao Shi Da refused to take his advice. He asked Dou Jian De to stay behind to guard the camps. He himself commanded his army to meet Yang Yi Chen head-on. Several battles were fought and Gao Shi Da won all these battles. Gao Shi Da held banquets to celebrate their victories. When Dou Jian De learned of that, he said, "Gao Shi De has not yet defeated his enemy but he is already so proud. Trouble will come soon." Five days later, Yang Yi Chen inflicted a disastrous defeat on Gao Shi Da's army and killed him. Yang Yi Chen led his victorious army to attack the camps defended by Dou Jian De. The soldiers defending the camps were defeated and ran away. Dou Jian De fled with several hundred men. They reached Raoyang (now Raoyang, in the middle of Hebei Province) and found that the defenders of the city were not on guard. They took it in a surprise attack.

Since Yang Yi Chen had killed Gao Shi Da, he thought that Dou Jian De was insignificant and nothing to be worried about. So he left. Dou Jian De returned to Pingyuan after Yang Yi Chen had left. He collected the scattered soldiers and buried the dead. He held a ceremony to mourn for Gao Shi Da. His army became strong again. Many generals of the Sui army came over to him. He treated those who came over very well. Then his army developed into an army of more than a hundred thousand men. In January 617, Dou Jian De declared himself King of Changle in Leshou (now Xian Xian, Hebei Province).

14. Liu Wu Zhou's Rebellion

In 617, there was a famine in Mayi area (now Shuozhou, Shanxi Province). But Wang Ren Gong, the governor of Mayi, did not care about the life of the people in that area and would not take food from the food storage to help the people who were suffering from the famine. Liu Wu Zhou, an officer under Wang Ren Gong, was a brave and generous man. In February he united with the local forces and succeeded in killing the governor. He opened the gates to the food storages and distributed food to the poor people. He sent out envoys to the cities under the jurisdiction of the governor of Mayi. All the officials in charge of the cities expressed their submission to him. So he made himself governor of Mayi. He united with the Turks. In March he led an army to attack Loufan Prefecture (an area around Jingle, Shanxi Province) and took it. Not long later he took Dingxiang Prefecture (now Horinger, Inner Mongolia Autonomous Region). Then he declared himself emperor.

15. Xue Ju Rises in Jincheng

Xue Ju was a rich man in Jincheng (now Lanzhou, Gansu Province). In April 617, he held an uprising. He ordered his army to capture the local officials and took out food from the food storages to distribute to the poor people. He declared himself Great King of Western Qin. He made his eldest son Xue Ren Gao Duke of Qi and made his younger son Xue Ren Yue Duke of Jin. Zong Luo Hou, the leader of a group of outlaws, came over to Xue Ju. Xue Ju sent his army to occupy Xiping Prefecture (an area around Xining, Qinghai Province) and Jiaohe Prefecture (an area around Guide, Qinghai Province). Very soon his army grew to one hundred and thirty thousand men. He occupied the whole of Longxi area (the area of the west part of Gansu Province and northeast part of Qinghai Province).

16. Other Rebellions

General Liang Shi Du rose in Shuofang Prefecture (now the area around Uxin Qi, Inner Mongolia Autonomous Region). In February 617, he killed Tang Shi Zong, the governor of the prefecture. He made himself the governor of the prefecture. He united with the Turks. In March of that year, he occupied Diaoyin Prefecture (now the area around Suide, Shaanxi Province), Honghua Prefecture (now the area around Qingyang, Gansu Province) and Yan'an Prefecture (now the area around Yan'an, Shaanxi Province).

He submitted to the Turks. Then he claimed himself the Emperor of the State of Liang. Shibi Khan of the Eastern Turkic Khanate gave him a big flag on which there was a wolf head. Shibi Khan also granted him the title of Dadupijia Khan.

Luo Yi was a general of the army stationed in Zhuo Prefecture. There were a lot of grain and military supplies stored in Zhuo Prefecture for the expedition of Koguryo. In December 616, Luo Yi killed the governor of Zhuo Prefecture and distributed food to the poor people. He made himself governor of Zhuo Prefecture.

In January 617, Du Fu Wei led his army to attack Gaoyou (now in Jiangsu Province) and took it. Then he occupied Liyang Prefecture (now the area around Hexian, Anhui Province), and declared himself governor of Liyang Prefecture. He appointed Fu Gong Shi commander of his army. All the outlaws in the areas between the Huai River and the Yangtze River submitted to Du Fu Wei.

Li Zi Tong, a man of Donghai Prefecture (which is now the area around Lianyungang in the northeast part of Jiangsu Province), first joined the rebels led by Zuo Cai Xiang. Half a year later, he had an army of over ten thousand men. He found that Zuo Cai Xiang was a cruel man. So he left Zuo Cai Xiang and crossed the Huai River to join Du Fu Wei. But in September 617, Li Zi Tong tried to murder Du Fu Wei. He started a surprise attack and Du Fu Wei was wounded by him; he fell to the ground from his horse. Wang Xiong Dan, a general under Du Fu Wei, saved him and ran away into the reeds and escaped. Li Zi Tong led his army to Hailing (now Taizhou, Jiangsu Province). His army expended into an army of twenty thousand men. He declared himself general.

CHAPTER TWO. THE ESTABLISHMENT OF THE TANG DYNASTY

17. Li Yuan Becomes the General in Charge of the Military and Civil Affairs of Taiyuan

Li Yuan, Duke of Tang, was the governor of Xingyang Prefecture (now the area around Xingyang, Henan Province) and the governor of Loufan Prefecture (the area around Jingle, Shanxi Province) when Emperor Yang Guang ascended the throne of the Sui Dynasty. In 613, Li Yuan was appointed by Emperor Yang Guang commander of the guards of the palaces in Chang'an. During the rebellion of Yang Xuan Gan, he was sent by Emperor Yang Guang to Honghua Prefecture (now the area around Qingyang, Gansu Province) as the general in charge of that area. In April 616, Wei Dao Er, the chief of a group of rebels, commanded an army of a hundred thousand men to attack Taiyuan (now in Shanxi Province). Chang Wen Pan, the general in charge of the defense of that area, was killed in battle. In December, Emperor Yang Guang appointed Li Yuan commander-in-chief in charge of the military and civil affairs of Taiyuan and appointed General Wang Wei and General Gao Jun Ya as deputy commanders. They were ordered to go with an army to Taiyuan to suppress the rebellion of Wei Dao Er. On their way, they ran into Wei Dao Er in Queshugu (a valley to the west of Jiexiu, Shanxi Province). Li Yuan had only five thousand men with him and they were surrounded by Wei Dao Er's army. Li Shi Min got the news and he commanded an army of picked soldiers to rescue his father. He broke the encirclement and saved his father. And fortunately, the main force of Li Yuan's army arrived. They attacked Wei Dao Er's army from inside and outside of the encirclement and defeated him.

18. Li Yuan and Li Shi Mins' Secret Plan to Rebel against the Sui Dynasty

Li Yuan had four sons, Li Jian Cheng, Li Shi Min, Li Xuan Ba (who had died early) and Li Yuan Ji. His daughter was married to Chai Shao, the chief of the bodyguards of the crown prince of the Sui Dynasty. Li Shi Min was very brave, clever and resolute. He saw that the Sui Dynasty was declining and China was in great chaos; and he was determined to save the people from this great disorder. So he made friends with those who had great abilities. He married the daughter of General Zhangsun Cheng. Zhangsun Shun De, Zhangsun Cheng's cousin, and Liu Hong Ji had come to Jinyang (now Taiyuan) to depend on Li Yuan because they had run away to avoid being sent to the war against Koguryo. They became Li Shi Min's good friends.

Liu Wen Jing, the governor of Jinyang County (now in the Taiyuan area, Shanxi Province), and Pei Ji, the official in charge of the palace in Jinyang, were good friends. One night, they saw that there was beacon fire. Pei Ji sighed and said, "We are so poor and the whole country is in chaos. I wonder if we can survive this chaos." Liu Wen Jing laughed and said, "Nobody can tell what will happen tomorrow. If we can help each other, we don't need to worry about poverty." When Liu Wen Jing saw Li Shi Min, he knew that Li Shi Min was a special man. So he sought a chance to get close to him. He said to Pei Ji, "Li Shi Min is not an ordinary person. He is as open-minded and magnanimous as Liu Bang, the first emperor of the Han Dynasty. He is as brave and powerful as Cao Cao, Emperor Wei Wu of the Wei Dynasty. Although he is still young, he has the ability of an emperor." Pei Ji was not sure whether what Liu Wen Jing had said was true.

In April 617, Liu Wen Jing was put into prison in Taiyuan because he was related to Li Mi by marriage. Li Shi Min went to the prison to see him. Liu Wen Jing said to Li Shi Min, "Now China is in great chaos. Only the person with the ability of Liu Bang, the first emperor of the Han Dynasty, can pacify China." Li Shi Min said, "This kind of person may exist. People wonder whether this kind of person really exists only because they have not yet found him. I have come to see you not for trivial matters. I have come to discuss important matters with you. Now, please tell me what we can do in the present situation." Liu Wen Jing said, "The Emperor has made a trip to Jiangdu. The army under Li Mi has surrounded the Eastern Capital. There are rebellions everywhere and the chiefs of the rebels have armies of at least several tens of thousands of men. At present, if a really capable man makes use of the situation, it is very easy for him to get the power to rule over China. The people of Taiyuan have all gone into the city for protection against the rebels. I have been governor of Jinyang for several years and I know the local gentries very well. We can recruit a hundred thousand soldiers in no time. There is already an army of several tens of thousands of men under your father's command. If we decide to act, nobody can resist and everyone will follow. Now the defense of Guanzhong is very week. With this great army, we can march into the area of Guangzhong and seize Chang'an, the capital. Then we may issue orders to the people all over China from the capital. In less than half a year, you may get the power to rule over the whole of China." Li Shi Min said, "I agree with your idea." Li Shi Min secretly began his deployment of his followers. He did not tell his father what he was doing because he was afraid that his father would oppose it. Pei Ji was Li Yuan's good friend. Li Yuan often had long talks with Pei Ji. Liu Wen Jing wanted to ask Pei Ji to persuade Li Yuan, so, he introduced Li Shi Min to Pei Ji, and later, Pei Ji became a good friend of Li Shi Min. Li Shi Min told his secret plan to Pei Ji and asked him to find a chance to persuade Li Yuan. Pei Ji promised to do that.

The Turks attacked Mayi (now Shuozhou, Shanxi Province) in April 617. Li Yuan sent Gao Jun Ya with an army to resist the Turks. But Gao Jun Ya suffered losses in the battle with the Turks. Li Yuan was worried because he was afraid that Emperor Yang Guang would punish him for the losses in the battles with the Turks. Li Shi Min made use of the opportunity and said to Li Yuan, when there was nobody around, "The Emperor is an evil man. The people are having a terrible time. Even the areas outside the city of Jinyang have become battlefields. If you keep your loyalty to the Emperor, then since the rebels cannot be suppressed and the punishment by the Emperor for failure to complete the task is cruel, your doom will come soon. You'd better make use of the situation and do what the people want to do. We should rise with an army to overthrow the Sui Dynasty. Then the trouble will be avoided. This is the golden opportunity offered by Heaven." When Li Yuan heard these words, he was shocked. He said, "How can you say that. I will have to arrest you and send you to the county official to be investigated." He got a piece of paper and a pen ready and was going to write a report. Li Shi Min said calmly, "I have studied the present situation for some time and have come to this conclusion. I just want to tell you the truth. If you really want to arrest me and accuse me of treason, I am ready to meet my death." Li Yuan said, "How can I be so hardhearted as to accuse you. But you must be very careful not to disclose this secret to anyone else." The next day, Li Shi Min tried to persuade his father again. He said, "Now the number of outlaws has greatly increased. Outlaws are all over the country. You have been ordered by the Emperor to suppress the outlaws. Can you kill them all? Since you are not able to suppress the outlaws, there is no way for you to escape punishment by the Emperor.

Rumor has it that a person with the family name of Li will be emperor. So the whole families of Li Hun, Duke of Cheng, were killed without having committed any offence. The only offence that led to their death was that they bore the family name of Li. If you suppress all the outlaws and render outstanding services, you still will not be rewarded with anything and you'll be put in a more dangerous situation. The plan I proposed yesterday is the only way to save you from the danger you are confronting. I hope that you will not hesitate." Li Yuan said with a sigh, "I thought about your plan last night. There is something in what you said. Your plan may lead to disaster to the family or may turn our family into the family that rules over China. Whatever the result will be, I will follow your plan anyway." Actually, before Li Shi Min talked to Li Yuan, Pei Ji had found a chance to talk with Li Yuan. One day, Pei Ji, the keeper of Jinyang Palace, entertained Li Yuan in the palace. While they were drinking, they had a heart-to-heart talk. Pei Ji said, "Your second son is now secretly recruiting fighters and conspiring with other people to hold a rebellion against the Emperor. I am afraid that their conspiracy would be discovered and you will be involved and be punished by the Emperor. We must make the decision quickly. Now they have got ready to act. What do you think?" Li Yuan said, "My son is really planning to do that. Since he has begun to carry out his plan, we have to let him do what he thinks fit."

Since Li Yuan had failed to suppress the outlaws, the Emperor sent some envoys to arrest him and escort him to Jiangdu where the Emperor was staying. Li Yuan was scared. Li Shi Min and Pei Ji tried again to persuade Li Yuan to take action. Li Shi Min said, "The present Emperor is a fatuous and self-indulgent ruler. The whole country is in great chaos. It is no use for you to be devoted to the Emperor. It is only the generals under you that have failed to fulfill their duty. But you are the one to be punished. That is unfair. The situation is unfavorable for you now. You should make up your mind. The army in Jinyang is strong. There are more than sufficient food and military supplies in Jinyang. With this army and supplies, we are sure to win. Now Yang You, King of Dai, is still very young. The local forces in the area of Guanzhong have risen in rebellion. But they have not yet decided to whom they will submit themselves. If you march westward, it will be easy for you to take the area of Guanzhong and pacify that area. Why should you just wait to be punished without doing anything, like a sitting duck?" Li Yuan agreed with them and secretly made preparation to take action. But later, the Emperor sent another envoy to pardon him and put him back to his original position. Then Li Yuan postponed his action. At that time, Li Yuan's sons Li Jian Cheng and Li Yuan Ji were still in Hedong (now Puzhou Town, Yongji, Shanxi Province). That was the reason why Li Yuan delayed taking action. Liu Wen Jing said to Pei Ji, "It is said that the one who strikes first will gain the initiative. The one who strikes after his enemy has struck will be put in a passive position. Why don't you urge Li Yuan to take action sooner? You are the palace keeper for the Emperor but you entertained Li Yuan with the beauties in the palace. You have committed a crime that deserves the death penalty. I don't care if you are put to death. But by entertaining Li Yuan in the palace, you have endangered him." Pei Ji was afraid and urged Li Yuan to take action. Li Yuan asked Liu Wen Jing to make a sham order from the Emperor to recruit people in Taiyuan Prefecture, Xihe Prefecture, Yanmen Prefecture and Mayi Prefecture (these prefectures were situated in the area which is now Shanxi Province) who were over twenty and below fifty into the army so as to get ready to start an expedition against Koguryo. When the people got the information, they were very angry and more people wanted to rebel. It happened that Liu Wu Zhou killed Wang Ren Gong and occupied Fenyang Palace in Mayi. Li Shi Min said to Li Yuan, "You are the official in charge of the defense of this area but there are so many outlaws in the area under your jurisdiction that they have occupied the palace of the Emperor. If you don't take action now, trouble will come very soon." Li Yuan then summoned all the generals and officers under him and said, "Liu Wu Zhou has occupied Fenyang Palace. We have failed to stop him from doing so. We have committed a crime the punishment for which is the extinction of all our families. What shall we do?" Wang Wei and Gao Jun Ya, the deputy commanders, were very afraid and asked Li Yuan to make a decision. Li Yuan said, "All the military movements are subject to the order of the Emperor. Now the outlaws are just several hundred kilometers away but the Emperor is in Jiangdu, which is one thousand five hundred kilometers away. The way to Jiangdu is dangerous and there are outlaws on the way. We have only a small army in Jinyang. It is impossible for us to resist the strong outlaws with this small army. We are in an awkward position. I really don't know what we can do." Wang Wei said, "You are the commander of the army. If we take action after we get permission from the Emperor, it will take a long time and we may lose the best chance to suppress the outlaws. The most important thing is to suppress the outlaws. You may adopt any action at your sole discretion" Li Yuan pretended that he had to take his advice and said, "Then the most urgent thing I have to do is to recruit soldiers to expand our army." Then he ordered Li Shi Min, Liu Wen Jing, Zhangsun Shun De and Liu Hong Ji to places outside Jinyang to recruit soldiers. Within ten days, nearly ten thousand soldiers were recruited. At the same time, Li Yuan secretly sent out envoys to Hedong to call Li Jian Cheng and Li Yuan Ji to Jinyang and sent an envoy to Chang'an to call Chai Shao, his son-in-law, to Jinyang.

When Wang Wei and Gao Jun Ya saw that the armies were gathering, they suspected that Li Yuan had some conspiracy. They said to Wu Shi Yue, the general in charge of military supplies, "Zhangsun Shun De and Liu Hong Ji are both evaders of military services. They have committed a crime that deserves the death penalty. They have no right to command troops. I want to arrest them and send them to prison to be investigated." Wu Shi Yue said, "These two persons are Li Yuan's guests. If you do this, you will be in great trouble." Wang Wei and Gao Jun Ya had to give up their plan.

Liu Shi Long, the head of Jinyang Village, secretly told Li Yuan that Wang Wei and Gao Jun Ya were planning to take action against him on the day when the ceremony to pray for rain was held in the Temple of Jin Ancestors. Thus, one night in May 617, Li Yuan ordered Li Shi Min to lead some soldiers and hide outside of the city wall of Jinyang. The next morning, Li Yuan and the two conspirators, Wang Wei and Gao Jun Ya, were sitting in the government office of Jinyang attending daily affairs. Liu Wen Jing led Liu Zheng Hui, the general in charge of information, into the office. Liu Zheng Hui said that he had an information report to present to Li Yuan. Li Yuan eyed Wang Wei and Gao Jun Ya, signaling them to take the report and read it. But Liu Zheng Hui would not give the report to them, saying, "What I am going to report involves the two deputy commanders. Only the Duke of Tang can read it." Li Yuan said in great surprise, "Is that so?" Then he took the report and read it, and then he declared that Gao Jun Ya had conspired with the Turks and had induced the Turks to invade Jinyang. Gao Jun Ya shouted loudly in protest, "This is a trick by the rebels who want to have me killed." But by this time, Li Shi Min had deployed his soldiers to block all the exits. Liu Wen Jing, Zhangsun Shun De and Liu Hong Ji went up and arrested Wang Wei and Gao Jun Ya and threw them into jail. The next day, indeed, over thirty thousand Turks invaded Jinyang. The Turkish cavalrymen even attacked the north gate of the city. Li Yuan ordered Pei Ji to command the soldiers to resist the invasion. They opened all the gates wide. But the Turks did not dare to go in because they thought it was a trap. All the officers and men under Li Yuan believed that Wang Wei and Gao Jun Ya had really induced the Turks to come. Li Yuan ordered that Wang Wei and Gao Jun Ya be executed for their crime. Then Li Yuan sent General Wang Kang Da with a thousand men out of the city to fight the Turks. All of them died in battle. The people in the city were all scared. At night, Li Yuan sent some soldiers out of the city. They put up a lot of flags and beat drums loudly. The Turks thought that reinforcements were coming. So they left.

Then Li Jian Cheng and Li Yuan Ji started their journey from Hedong to Jinyang. On the way, they met with Chai Shao and they went to Jinyang together. In June 617, they reached Jinyang.

Liu Wen Jing suggested that Li Yuan establish an alliance with the Turks so as to make use of their strong soldiers and horses. Li Yuan took his advice and sent an envoy with a letter to Shibi Khan of the Eastern Turkic Khanate. The letter read, "I have raised a great army to escort the Emperor back to Chang'an from

Jiangdu. We will make peace with you and maintain a good relationship with you. I hope you will command your army to march south to bring back the Emperor and not to do any harm to the people on the way. In return for your help, I will give you a lot of money and treasure. It is up to you to make the decision." Shibi Khan got the letter and said to his ministers, "I know what kind of a person the Emperor of the Sui Dynasty is. If I escort him back to Chang'an from Jiangdu, I am sure he will punish the Duke of Tang and he will attack us. If the Duke of Tang makes himself emperor, I will help him with my army and horses in this hot summer time." So he wrote a reply letter to this effect, and the envoy deliverd the reply letter within seven days. All the generals and officers were glad to hear the intention of Shibi Khan and hoped that Li Yuan would make himself emperor. But Li Yuan would not make himself emperor. Liu Wen Jing and Pei Ji said to Li Yuan, "Although the armies have gathered, we are still in want of horses. We do not need the Turks' army, but we do need their horses. If we hesitate, Shibi Khan might change his mind and refuse to give any help." Li Yuan asked them to think of another way to solve the problem. Pei Ji suggested, "The present Emperor may be respected as Father Emperor and his grandson Yang You be made emperor of the Sui Dynasty so as to maintain the rule of the royal family. We may give an order to this effect to all the prefectures and counties to change the color of the flags from red to crimson and white. So we may show to the Turks that the present Emperor is not in power anymore." Li Yuan said, "This is as good as plugging your ears while stealing a bell. But this is the only way to solve the problem in the present situation." Li Yuan agreed with this suggestion and sent an envoy to inform Shibi Khan of their decision.

When the order was issued to the prefectures, the governor of Xihe Prefecture (now the area around Fenyang, Lingshi and Jiexiu of Shanxi Province) would not obey. Li Yuan sent Li Jian Cheng and Li Shi Min to attack that area with an army. He also sent Wen Da You, the governor of Taiyuan County, to assist them. Li Yuan said to Wen Da You, "My sons are still young. You may offer them suggestions in military affairs. I will judge whether my career will succeed by this action." At that time, most of the soldiers were new recruits and not well trained. Li Jian Cheng and Li Shi Min shared weal and woe with them. And they charged at the head of their soldiers in battle. They did not allow the soldiers to loot the people. They bought all the vegetables and fruit from the people. When a soldier stole something, Li Shi Min found out whom they had stolen from and he repaid the person; but he did not punish the soldier. So the soldier who had stolen and the person who had been robbed were both grateful to him.

When the army reached the city of Xihe (now Fenyang, Shanxi Province), they were ready to attack it, but they still let people to go into the city. Gao De Ru, the governor of Xihe, defended the city resolutely. Several days later the city fell and Gao De Ru was captured. He was brought to the gate of the camps of Li Shi Min's army. Li Shi Min said, "You arrived at your position by lying to the Emperor that you had seen the phoenix, the lucky sign. I have raised an army to punish toadies like you." Then Gao De Ru was executed, but none of his follow-ers was killed. Li Shi Min's army did not commit the slightest offence against the civilians. People resumed their normal life and daily work very quickly. All the people were glad. Then Li Jian Cheng and Li Shi Min commanded their victori-ous army back to Jinyang. It only took nine days to complete their task. Li Yuan said with great joy, "We will be invincible with the way my sons commanded the army."

Then Li Yuan decided to carry out the plan to march to Guanzhong and take Chang'an, the capital of the Sui Dynasty. Li Yuan ordered to take food from the food storages to distribute it to the poor people. More and more people joined his army. Li Yuan divided his army into two: the Left Army and the Right Army. Pei Ji and Liu Wen Jing suggested that Li Yuan be Commander-In-Chief. So the Office of the Commander-In-Chief was established. Pei Ji was appointed Chief of the General Staff; Liu Wen Jing was in charge of military affairs; Tang Jian and Wen Da Ya were in charge of the secretarial work of the Office; Wen Da Ya and his brother Wen Da You were in charge of important and confidential work; Wu Shi Yue was in charge of weapon and armor supplies; Liu Zheng Hui, Cui Shan Wei and Zhang Dao Yuan were in charge of financial affairs and civil af-fairs; Jiang Mo was the military counselor; Yin Kai Shan was in charge of Official Announcements. Zhangsun Shun De, Liu Hong Ji, Dou Cong, Wang Chang Xie, Jiang Bao Yi, and Yang Tun were appointed generals to command troops in the Left Army and the Right Army. Li Jian Cheng was made Duke of Longxi and chief commander of the Left Army; Li Shi Min was made Duke of Dunhuang and chief commander of the Right Army.

19. Li Mi's Action to Take Luoyang

In May 617, Li Mi used Luokou as a base to attack Luoyang. Chai Xiao He, one of his followers, said to Li Mi, "The area of Guanzhong is protected by the Xiao Shan Mountains and the Yellow River. In the past, Ying Zheng, the King of the State of Qin, used Guanzhong as a base to conquer the six states in the east and unified China. Liu Bang used Guanzhong as a base to unify China and established the Han Dynasty. I suggest that you ask Zhai Rang to defend Luokou and Pei Ren Ji to defend Huilou, and you personally command an army to march westward to take Chang'an. If you have taken Chang'an, the capital, you may march eastward to take Luoyang. Then you may pacify China by sending envoys with your letters to all the prefectures asking them to submit to your rule. Then the whole country will be pacified. Now the Emperor of the Sui Dynasty has lost his power to rule over China. All the powerful people are striving for it. If you don't get it first, someone else will get it. Then it will too late for regrets." Li Mi said, "This is really the best plan. I have been thinking about it for a long time. But the Emperor of the Sui Dynasty is still alive. He still has a great army. All the people under me are from the area to the east of the Xiao Shan Mountains. If I cannot take Luoyang, then no one will follow me to the area of Guanzhong. All my generals were originally outlaws. If I leave them behind, they will fight against each other. Then my great career will never be realized." Chai Xiao He then said, "Since the main force cannot march westward, I hope you will let me go west to find out the situation there." Li Mi gave him permission and sent over fifty cavalrymen to go with him. They marched to Shanxian (now in Henan Province) where more than ten thousand outlaws joined him. At that time, Li Mi's army was fighting fiercely with the Sui army in the east of Luoyang. Unfortunately Li Mi was wounded by an arrow and had to stay in camp. Yang Tong, the King of Yue, sent Duan Da and Pang Yu out of Luoyang to deploy their army in battle formation at night in the northwest of Huiluocang. Li Mi and Pei Ren Ji rode out of the camp with their army to fight with the Sui army. Li Mi's army was defeated and most of the soldiers were killed or wounded. Li Mi had to give up Huiluocang and fled back to Luokou (now northeast of Gongyi, Henan Province). When Chai Xiao He's followers got the news that Li Mi had been defeated and had retreated to Luokou, they all left him. Chai Xiao He and his cavalrymen had to turn back to join Li Mi.

20. Li Yuan's Plan to Unite with the Turks

In June 617, Shibi Khan of the Eastern Turkic Khanate sent his Prime Minister Kangqiaoli and others to Jinyang with a thousand horses. They asked Li Yuan to let them trade horses in China. In return for this favor, they would send an army to escort Li Yuan to the area of Guangzhong. Li Yuan received Kangqiaoli politely. He selected the five hundred best horses and let them take the rest back. Li Yuan's followers wanted to buy the rest of the horses with their own money. Li Yuan said to them, "The Turks have a lot of horses and they are very greedy. Later, they will come trading horses very frequently at higher prices. Then I am afraid you will not be able to afford them. I only bought half of them in order to show that we are poor and we don't need their horses urgently. Then you may buy cheaper horses later." After Kangqiaoli went back, Li Yuan sent Liu Wen Jing as his envoy to the Turks to ask for help. Before they left, Li Yuan said to Liu Wen Jing secretly, "The Turkic cavalry coming into China is harmful to the Chinese people. The reason I still want to unite with Turks is to prevent Liu

Wu Zhou from uniting with the Turks to do harm to the people on the borders. And the Turks' horses do not require many supplies. They graze in the fields. I just want the Turkic cavalrymen to show to my enemy how strong my army is. So I only need several hundred of them." Then Liu Wen Jing started his journey to the Turks. When he saw Shibi Khan, he asked him to send troops to help Li Yuan. Liu Wen Jing made an agreement with Shibi Khan to the effect that when Li Yuan succeeded in the march to Chang'an with the help of the Turks, the land and the people would belong to Li Yuan and the gold, jade and other treasures would belong to the Turks. Shibi Khan was very glad and sent his minister to tell Li Yuan that the Turks' army would be on their way soon.

21. Li Yuan's March from Taiyuan towards the Area of Guanzhong

The March from Taiyuan towards the Area of Guanzhong

In July 617, Li Yuan entrusted the defense of Taiyuan to his fourth son Li Yuan Ji and started the march to Guanzhong with an army of thirty thousand men. On 5 July 617, after a ceremony to pledge their resolution, Li Yuan commanded his army in the march. At the same time, Li Yuan officially announced to the gov-ernors of all the prefectures and counties that he had made Yang You, King of Dai, emperor of the Sui Dynasty. The chief of the Western Turks Ashina Danai also joined Li Yuan in the march to Guanzhong. On 14 July, Li Yuan reached Guhubao, which was twenty-five kilometers away from Huoyi (now Huozhou City, Shanxi Province). Yang You, the King of Dai, sent General Song Lao Sheng with twenty thousand handpicked troops to defend the city of Huoyi. General Qutu Tong stationed his army in Hedong (now Yongji, Shanxi Province) to resist Li Yuan's advance. Then it rained for days and Li Yuan's army could not move forward. Li Yuan had to send Shen Shu An with some older and weaker soldiers back to Taiyuan to fetch food to tide them over for a month.

At that time, Li Mi was in Luokou. Li Yuan wrote a letter to ask him to come over. When Li Mi got the letter, he wanted to be the leader of the alliance; he thought that his army was stronger than that of Li Yuan. He asked Zu Jun Yan to write a reply. It read, "You and I are brothers of the same family name of Li, although we are from different origins. Although I think I am not a person of virtue, still I have been elected leader of the alliance of the anti Sui Dynasty forces by the leaders of the uprisings all over China. My only intention is to unite with all the forces to make concerted efforts to overthrow the rule of the Sui Dynasty. I hope you will capture Yang You in Chang'an and kill Emperor Yang Guang." In the letter he asked Li Yuan to go to Henei (now Qinyang, Henan Province) with several thousand men so that they could meet there and establish their alliance. When Li Yuan read that, he laughed out loud and said, "Li Mi is too arrogant and extremely conceited. For now, I am concentrating my efforts on taking the area of Guanzhong. If I deny his position as the leader of the alliance bluntly, I will turn him into an enemy. So we'd better pretend to be humble and recognize him as the leader of the alliance so that he will become even prouder and block the way to Chenggao so the Sui army cannot attack me from behind; and let him fight with the Sui army in Luoyang so that the Sui army there will not come to reinforce the Sui army in Guanzhong. Then I can march westward without worrying about my rear. Once I reach Guanzhong, I will do my best to strengthen my force and defend the area with all the natural barriers while I watch Li Mi and the Sui army fighting each other. When they both are weakened, I will take advantage of their conflict." Then he asked Wen Da Ya to write back. The letter read, "Although I am a mediocre person, I have been appointed to high ranking positions in charge of important tasks. Now the Sui Dynasty is falling. I have the responsibility to save it from falling. So I have raised an army and made peace with the Turks so as to do my best to save the people of China from suffering. My purpose is to preserve the Sui Dynasty. The Chinese people are like a flock of sheep, which should be looked after by a shepherd, and no one but you has the ability to take up this great responsibility. I am already too old for this. I sincerely hope that you will realize your ambition as early as possible so as to bring peace to the Chinese people. It is my pleasure to fully support you in taking the position as the leader of the alliance. If you succeed in taking the power, and you accept me as a member of the royal family, I will be satisfied if you make me Duke of Tang. I have a lot of things to attend to, so I can not fix a date for us to meet." When Li Mi read the letter, he was extremely pleased. He showed it to his generals and officers and said, "Even the Duke of Tang supports me as the leader of the alliance. I am sure I will pacify China and secure the power to rule." From then on, Li Yuan and Li Mi sent envoys back and forth to communicate frequently.

The rain continued. Li Yuan found that their food was running out. And news came that Liu Wu Zhou and the Turks were going to attack Jinyang. Li Yuan held a meeting with his generals and officers to discuss plan for returning to Taiyuan. Pei Ji said, "Song Lao Sheng and Qutu Tong have occupied the natural barriers to resist our advance. We cannot overcome them in a short time. Although Li Mi has promised to ally with us, we still don't know what evil intention he has in his mind. The Turks are greedy and unfaithful. They are interested in nothing but material gain. Liu Wu Zhou works for Turks. Taiyuan is a big city in the north and all the families of our generals and officers are now in Taiyuan. We'd better turn back and save our base. We can always march to Guanzhong later." Li Shi Min said, "Well, now the crops in the fields are ripe. We can easily get food right here. Song Lao Sheng is a man of hot temper and we can easily defeat him and capture him in a battle. Li Mi is reluctant to part with Luokou where so much food is stored, and he has no farsighted plan. Liu Wu Zhou and the Turks seem to be in alliance, but actually there are conflicts between them. And they are suspicious of each other. Liu Wu Zhou has the ambition to take Taiyuan, but he has to deal with Mayi first. Since we have raised an army to carry out our just cause, we must plunge ahead regardless of our safety so as to save the people from the present suffering. Our task is to march to Chang'an and occupy the area of Guanzhong so as to have control over China. Now we are confronted with a very minor enemy, and we are planning to turn back. I am afraid that the army raised for our just cause might disband and all we will have is only Taiyuan. Then we are no different from any outlaws. How can we survive in this troubled time?" Li Jian Cheng supported Li Shi Min's opinion. But Li Yuan refused to listen to them and gave the order to retreat. Li Shi Min wanted to see his father to voice his opinions again, but it was already very late and Li Yuan had gone to bed and fallen asleep. Li Shi Min could not get in Li Yuan's tent, so he cried bitterly outside. Li Yuan heard the bitter cry of his son and woke up. He let Li Shin Min in and asked why he had cried so bitterly. Li Shi Min said, "We have raised an army for a just cause. If we march forward, we will win. If we turn back, our army will disband. If our army has disbanded, and our enemies take the chance to attack us, then we are doomed to perish. That's why I cried so bitterly." These words made Li Yuan realize the truth. He said, "The army has already started on its way back. What shall we do?" Li Shi Min said, "The Right Army under my command has not yet gone. Although the Left Army has started, it has not yet gone far. I would like to run after them and bring them back." Li Yuan laughed and said, "Whether my cause is successful or not depends on you. Say no more. Just do what you thnk best." Li Shi Min and Li Jian Cheng immediately rode off in the dark after the Left Army and got it to come back. And shortly later, food transported from Taiyuan arrived.

On 1 August 617, the rain stopped and it cleared up. Li Yuan ordered the soldiers to take out all the armor, weapons and military supplies to the open air to dry under the sun. In the morning of 3 August, Li Yuan's army took a mountain road to Huoyi. Li Yuan worried that Song Lao Sheng would not come out to fight. Li Shi Min said, "Song Lao Sheng is brave but he is not resourceful. If we use light cavalrymen to challenge him, he will surely come out. If he does not come out of his base, we can spread the rumor that he has secretly come over to our side. He would be afraid that this would be reported to the Emperor. In order to show that he is innocent, he has to come out to fight with us." Li Yuan said, "Your thinking is very sound." Li Yuan with several hundred cavalrymen got to a place two kilometers away from Huoyi, where they stopped and waited for the infantry to come forth. He ordered Li Shi Min and Li Jian Cheng to get close to the city wall. Li Shi Min and Li Jian Cheng with about fifty cavalrymen rode close to the city. The two brothers raised their whips pointing here and there as if they were deploying their army to lay siege to the city, and shouted some insulting words at Song Lao Sheng, who was standing at the top the city wall. Song Lao Sheng got very angry and ordered his army of thirty thousand men to go out of the city through the east gate and the south gate to fight. Li Yuan sent Yin Kai Shan to urge the main force to come quickly. When they came, Li Yuan wanted to let his officers and men to have lunch first. But Li Shi Min said, "Now is the best time to attack. We must start our attack before lunch." Li Yuan accepted his opinion and Li Yuan and Li Jian Cheng deployed the army in battle formation to the east gate, and Li Shi Min deployed his army in battle formation to the south gate, and the battle began. The battle formation under the command of Li Yuan and Li Jian Cheng was pushed back by Song Lao Sheng's army. Li Shi Min and several officers rode into the battle formation of Song Lao Sheng's army and fought through it to the rear of the formation. Li Shi Min killed over thirty enemy soldiers and the edges of his two broad swords became blunt. Blood covered his sleeves. He shook the blood off and went on fighting. The soldiers under the command of Li Yuan and Li Jian Cheng kept shouting, "We have captured Song Lao Sheng!" Song Lao Sheng's army was defeated and ran back. Li Yuan with his men charged and wanted to go into the city, but the city gate was closed before Li Yuan's army could go in. Song Lao Sheng could not get into the city either. Some of his soldiers threw down one end of a rope from the top of the city wall, and Song Lao Sheng climbed up. Lu Jun E, a sergeant, and the soldiers under him, ran to the foot of the city wall and jumped up and killed Song Lao Sheng. Then he went to see Li Yuan with the head of Song Lao Sheng. It was already dusk. Li Yuan gave the order to climb to the top of the city wall. At that time, there were no ladders to climb with. The generals, officers and men stood on one another's shoulders to form a ladder and climbed up to the top of the city wall, and took the city. Li Yuan awarded those who had rendered outstanding services in the battle to take Huoyi. The officers said that those new recruits who were originally bondservants could not be awarded equally to those who were free men. But Li Yuan said, "In the rain of arrows and stones in the battlefields, both the noblemen and the humble servants are equally exposed to death. Why should there be any difference between them when they are awarded. So they should be equally awarded if they have rendered the same services." On 4 August, Li Yuan met with the officials and people of Huoyi and gave out food to the poor. Able-bodied men were selected into the army.

On 8 August, Li Yuan took Linfen Prefecture and entered the city of Linfen (now in Shanxi Province). On 13 August, Li Yuan attacked the Prefecture of Jiang and entered the city of Jiang (now Xinjiang, Shanxi Province). On 15 August, Li Yuan reached Longmen (now Yumenkou in the northwest of Hejin, Shanxi Province) by the east bank of the Yellow River. At the same time, Liu Wen Jing and Kangqiaoli also arrived with five hundred Turkic cavalrymen and two thousand horses. Li Yuan was very glad to see that they had come late. Li Yuan said to Liu Wen Jing, "It is good timing that I have reached the Yellow River before the Turks arrived. And there are only a few Turkic soldiers but a lot of horses. This is exactly what I intended. You have done a very good job."

Xue Da Ding said to Li Yuan, "I hope you will not attack Hedong. We'd better cross the Yellow River from Longmen, and then take Yongfengcang, the food storage base. We may pacify the area of Guanzhong by sending an announcement to all the prefectures in Guanzhong." Li Yuan was about to agree with his opinion, but the generals wanted to attack Hedong first. Li Yuan appointed Xue Da Ding to a supervisory position in the office of commander-in-chief. Ren Gui, an official in charge of civil affairs in Hedong County, suggested to Li Yuan, "The local magnates in the area of Guanzhong are looking forward to your coming into the area. I worked in Pingyi for many years. I am acquainted with many of them. If you send me as your envoy to persuade them to come over, they will surely come to your side. If your army crosses the Yellow River from Liangshan and press to Hancheng and Heyang, then Xiao Zhao will submit to you and Sun Hua will come a long way to meet you. Then your army may march directly to Yongfengcang. Although you have not yet taken Chang'an, the area of Guanzhong will be under your control." Li Yuan agreed with his idea and appointed him to a high-ranking position.

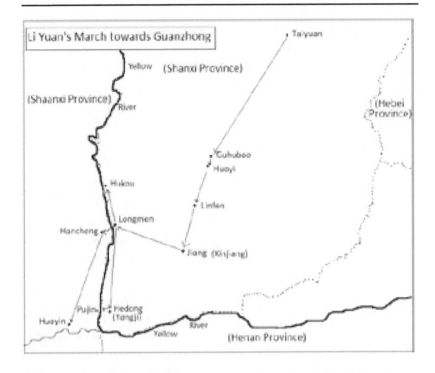

At that time, of all the outlaws in the area of Guanzhong, the strongest was Sun Hua. Li Yuan wrote a letter to Sun Hua asking him to join his cause. On 21 August, Li Yuan's army advanced to Hukou (in Jixian, Shanxi Province). People of the riverside provided their ships and boats to Li Yuan. On 24 August, Sun Hua crossed the Yellow River from the west bank to Longmen to see Li Yuan with several cavalrymen. Li Yuan warmly welcomed him. They walked into the house hand in hand and talked happily. Li Yuan highly praised Sun Hua's determination to join him, and granted him a high-ranking title, created him Duke of Wuqingxian, and appointed him governor of Pingyi Prefecture (now Dali, Shaanxi Province). Sun Hua's subordinates were all granted appropriate positions. Then Li Yuan sent Sun Hua and his men to cross the Yellow River first. Generals Wang Chang Xie, Liu Hong Ji, Chen Yan Shou, and Shi Da Nei of the Left Army and the Right Army commanded six thousand infantry men and cavalrymen to cross the Yellow River from Liangshan (Longmen) and camped on the west bank waiting for the main force. Li Yuan appointed Ren Gui as his envoy to the governors in the area of Guanzhong. Ren Gui went to Hancheng and succeeded in persuading the governor to come over.

Before Wang Chang Xie crossed the Yellow River, Li Yuan said to him, "Qutu Tong has a lot of special troops under him. Some are just twenty kilometers away from here, but they do not come to fight against us. That shows that the generals in Hedong would not follow his orders. But he has to come out to fight because he is afraid that he would be punished if he doesn't. If he comes out to attack you after you have crossed the river, I will attack Hedong; then I am sure we will take that city. If he defends the city with all his army, you may block the river to prevent him from crossing. I will attack the city of Hedong. Then he has to retreat, otherwise he will be captured." On 7 September, Qutu Tong sent General Sang Xian He with several thousand elite soldiers to cross the Yellow River by the floating bridge at night to the west bank to launch a surprise attack on the army under Wang Chang Xie, who had already crossed the Yellow River. Wang Chang Xie's army could not repel the attack and the situation was unfavorable. Sun Hua and Shi Da Nei commanded cavalrymen to move to the back of Sang Xian He's army and start an attack. Then Sang Xian He's army was defeated and he beat it back to the city of Hedong and did not dare to cross the Yellow River again. Xiao Zhao, the governor of Pingyi Prefecture, surrendered to Li Yuan.

On 10 September, Li Yuan commanded his army to lay siege to the city of Hedong. Qutu Tong stoutly defended the city. At that time, several thousand people from the area of Guanzhong were flocking to join Li Yuan's army every day. Li Yuan wanted to lead his army in the march to Chang'an. He was hesitating. Pei Ji said to Li Yuan, "Qutu Tong has a great army under his command and is protected by a strong city wall. If we circumvent this city and directly march to Chang'an and attack it, but fail to take Chang'an right away, the enemies will attack us from the front and the rear. This is very dangerous. We'd better take Hedong first, then march westward to Chang'an. The defense of Chang'an depends very much on the defense of Hedong. If we take Hedong first, it will be very easy for us to take Chang'an." Li Shi Min opposed this idea, saying, "I don't think so. Speed is precious in war. Our army has won several battles and is a victorious army; meanwhile, many people from Guanzhong have joined us. If we march boldly to Chang'an, the defenders of Chang'an won't know what to do. We have to come so quickly that the wise men do not have time to draw up their plans and the brave men do not have time to make up their resolution. In that case, we can easily take Chang'an. If we linger in front of this strongly defended city, and they draw up their plans and prepare well for our attack, then we will waste our time and those who have just joined us will be disheartened and leave us. Then we will lose. Now, many people have rebelled but they still don't know which side they will take. We must go there as soon as possible to call on them to come to our side. Qutu Tong will only take care of Hedong and himself. We don't need to worry about him."

Li Yuan took both of their counsels. He assigned several generals with an army to continue the siege of the city of Hedong. He himself led the army to march westward. On the way, many Sui officials surrendered to Li Yuan with the cities under their administration. Jin Xiao Mo, an official of Zhaoyi, surrendered with the City of Pujin (a city on the west bank of the Yellow River which was the west end of the floating bridge of boats and planks, now to the northeast of Zhaoyi, Shaanxi Province) and Zhongtan (a sandy island in the middle of the Yellow River which could be used as a connecting point for a floating bridge from the west bank and the east bank). Li Xiao Chang, the governor of Huayin (now in the east part of Shaanxi Province), surrendered to Li Yuan and handed over the food depot Yongfengcang (in the northeast of Huayin City, Shaanxi Province) to the army under Li Yuan. He made contact with the army that had crossed the Yellow River and brought them to Yongfengcang. Many governors of the counties around Chang'an also surrendered to Li Yuan.

22. The Situation in the Area to the Northwest of Guanzhong

In April 617, Xue Ju, an army officer in the area of Jincheng, held a rebellion in Jincheng (now Lanzhou, Gansu Province). In July 617, Xue Ju declared himself Emperor of Qin, his wife Empress, his son Xue Ren Gao Crown Prince. He sent his son with an army to lay siege to Tianshui (now in Gansu Province). Xue Ren Gao attacked the city and took it. Xue Ju moved to Tianshui and made Tianshui the capital of the State of Qin.

Li Gui, the general in charge of Wuwei (now in Gansu Province), got the news that Xue Ju had rebelled. He discussed the situation with Cao Zhen, Guan Jin, Liang Suo, Li Yun, and An Xiu Ren. He said, "Xue Ju will surely invade our area. The officials of the prefectures cannot resist his advance. We cannot let them come and capture us and our wives and children without doing anything. We'd better do our best to resist them and protect the area on the west of the Yellow River. Then we will decide what to do according to developments." They all agreed with him. Then they felt the need to elect a leader among them but each refused to take the leadership. Cao Zhen said, "According to the prophecy, the person with the family name of Li will become king. Now Li Gui bears the family name of Li; it is Heaven's will that he should be king." So Li Gui made himself King of Hexi Daliang.

In September 617, Xue Ju sent his general Chang Zhong Xing across the Yellow River to attack Li Gui. Li Gui and Li Yun fought against Chang Zhong Xing in Changsong (now Gulang, Gansu Province). Chang Zhong Xing's army was totally defeated. Li Gui wanted to release the captives. But Li Yun said, "We have fought very hard to win the battle and captured them. We'd better kill all of them by burying them alive." Li Gui said, "If Heaven blesses me, I will capture their chief, Xue Ju. Then they will become my subjects. If Heaven decides that

I will not succeed, it will be no use detaining them." Then he released all the captives and let them go home. Later, he attacked Zhangye (now in Gansu Province), Dunhuang (now in the west part of Gansu Province), Xiping (now Xining, Qinghai Province) and Fukan (now Linxia, Gansu Province) and took them all. Then he owned the five prefectures to the west of the Yellow River.

23. The Situation in Luoyang and Luokou

In July 617, Emperor Yang Guang sent Wang Shi Chong, the assistant governor of Jiangdu, with the elite troops in the area south to the Yangtze River to march to Luoyang. Emperor Yang Guang also ordered General Wang Long who was in the area of Qiong (now in Sichuan Province), General Wei Qi who was in Hebei (now Daming, Hebei Province), General Wang Bian who was in Henan Prefecture (now to the east of Luoyang), all commanding their troops, to Luoyang. Their task was to carry out an expedition against Li Mi. In August, Wang Shi Chong, Wei Qi, Wang Bian and the assistant governor of Henei (now Wuzhi, Henan Province) Meng Shan Yi, Dugu Wu Du (a general in charge of the army in Heyang Prefecture (now Mengxian, Henan Province)), all met in the Eastern Capital. Only Wang Long delayed. Then Yang Tong, King of Yue, sent Liu Chang Gong, the general in charge of the defense of the Eastern Capital, with all the army under him to join Wang Shi Chong. The general in charge of the defense of Yanshi (now Yanshi, Henan Province) also joined Wang Shi Chong. There were more than a hundred thousand men in this joint army. Emperor Yang Guang gave the order to the generals leading all these armies that they should be under Wang Shi Chong's command. The army under Wang Shi Chong and the army of Li Mi were confronting with each other across the Luoshui River.

24. Li Yuan Marches into Guanzhong

On 12 September 617, Li Yuan with his main force crossed the Yellow River from Hedong to Pujin through the floating bridge. On 16 September, he reached Zhaoyi (now Zhaoyi in the east of Dali, Shaanxi Province). He stayed in Changchun Palace. Thousands of the local troops and people submitted to his authority. Many people of exceptional ability came to see Li Yuan in Changchun Palace. Yu Zhi Ning, Yan Shi Gu and Li Shi Min's wife's elder brother Zhangsun Wu Ji were among them. Li Yuan received them very politely and appointed them to high ranking responsible positions. On 18 September, Li Yuan sent Li Jian Cheng, his heir apparent, Liu Wen Jing and General Wang Chang Xie with thirty thousand soldiers to station in Yongfengcang (in the northeast of Huayin City, Shaanxi Province) which was one of the most important food storages in the Sui Dynasty. Their task was to block the way from Tongguan Pass (now in the east part of

Shaanxi Province) so as to prevent the Sui army from advancing from the east. Then Li Yuan sent his second son Li Shi Min, commanding an army of about thirty thousand men, to take the area to the north of Weishui River. Zhangsun Shun De, General Liu Hong Ji, General Yin Kai Shan and other generals were under Li Shi Min's command.

When Qutu Tong got the information that Li Yuan had entered the area of Guanzhong, he appointed General Rao Jun Su as assistant governor of Hedong Prefecture and ordered him to block Puban (now Puzhou, Yongji County, Shanxi Province). He himself led an army of over thirty thousand men in quick march to Chang'an but Liu Wen Jing blocked his army's advance. At that time, General Liu Gang of the Sui army had stationed his army in Tongguan Pass. Qutu Tong wanted to join forces with him. Wang Chang Xie led his army in a surprise attack on Tongguan Pass and killed Liu Gang and took the city. Wang Chang Xie resisted Qutu Tong's army with the city of Tongguan. Qutu Tong had to retreat to a place north of the city. Li Yuan sent General Lu Shao Zong with an army to attack Hedong but could not take it.

When Li Yuan's son-in-law Chai Shao left Chang'an for Taiyuan, he said to his wife, Li Yuan's daughter, "Your father has raised an army to rebel against the Emperor. He has summoned me there. We cannot go together. But it is unsafe for you to stay in Chang'an. What shall we do?" His wife said, "You just go as quickly as you can. Don't worry about me. I am a woman. It is very easy for me to hide myself. I will think of a way out." After Chai Shao left, Chai Shao's wife went to Huxian (now in Shaanxi Province). She spent a lot of money to organize a small army. Li Yuan's cousin Li Shen Tong was originally from Chang'an. He also escaped to the mountains in Huxian. He and Shi Wan Bao raised an army to respond to Li Yuan's insurrection. He Pan Ren, a merchant doing business in the Western Regions, became an outlaw in Sizhuyuan (now in the east of Zhouzhi, Shaanxi Province). He had an army of over thirty thousand men. They kidnapped Li Gang, a minister of the Sui Government, and forced him to be a responsible official. Chai Shao's wife sent Ma San Bao to persuade He Pan Ren to join forces with Li Shen Tong. They attacked Huxian and took it. Li Shen Tong's army grew into an army of over ten thousand men. He made himself commander-in-chief of the armies in the area of Guanzhong. Chai Shao's wife sent Ma San Bao to persuade the outlaws Li Zhong Wen, Xiang Shan Zhi and Qiu Shi Li to change sides. They all agreed. The Sui army in Chang'an led several expeditions against He Pan Ren but was defeated by him. Chai Sho's wife led her army to attack Zhouzhi (now Zhouzhi, Shaanxi Province), Wugong (now Wugong, Shaanxi Province), and Shiping (now Xingping, Shaanxi Province), and took them all. Her army grew to seventy thousand men. Li Yuan's another son-in-law Duan Lun also raised an army of ten thousand men in Lantian (now Lantian, Shaanxi

Province). When Li Yuan crossed the Yellow River, Li Shen Tong, Chai Shao's wife and Duan Lun all sent envoys to meet Li Yuan. Li Yuan granted Li Shen Tong the position of Imperial Minister of State of the highest rank, and granted Li Shen Tong's son Li Dao Yan the position of an honor minister, and granted Duan Lun the position of Imperial Minister of State of the second rank. Li Yuan sent Chai Shao to Nanshan (in the area of Chang'an, Shaanxi Province) to meet his wife. He Pan Ren, Li Zhong Wen, Xiang Shan Zhi and other outlaws in the area of Guanzhong surrendered to Li Yuan. Li Yuan accepted them and wrote letters to them expressing his warm welcome, and he appointed them to some positions and put them under the command of Li Shi Min, Duke of Dunhuang.

When Wei Wen Sheng, who was the minister of justice of the Sui Dynasty and in charge of the defense of Chang'an, learned that Li Yuan was marching towards Chang'an, he was so afraid that he fell ill and could not attend to state affairs. Yang You, King of Dai, ordered General Yin Shi Shi and Gu Yi, the governor of the capital area, to go up the city wall to defend the city. On 21 September, Li Yuan reached Pujin (on the west bank of the Yellow River). On 22 September, Li Yuan crossed the Wuishui River from Linjin (now in Zhaoyi in Dali, Shaanxi Province) to Yongfengcang to see his armies in recognition of their services they had rendered. On 23 September, he returned to Changchun Palace in Zhaoyi. On 24 September, Li Yuan moved to Pingyi (now Dali, Shaanxi Province).

Wherever Li Shi Min went, the people, officials of the Sui Dynasty, and outlaws all turned over to the side of Li Yuan. Li Shi Min picked the people with greatest ability to serve in his army. He stationed his army in Jingyang (now in Shaanxi Province). His army grew into an army of ninety thousand men. Chai Shao's wife met Li Shi Min in the area to the north of the Weishui River with ten thousand professional soldiers. Her army and Chai Shao's army camped at different places and they established separate commands.

A group of outlaws of over thirty thousand men from Pingliang (now Pingliang, Gansu Province) surrounded Fufeng (now Fufeng, Shaanxi Province). The governor of Fufeng Dou Jin defended the city. The outlaws surrounded the city for several months but could not take it and they ran out of food. Qiu Shi Li sent his younger brother Qiu Xing Gong with five hundred men carrying rice and wheat and beef and wine to their camp. The chief of the outlaws, a former bondservant, went up and made a bow to Qiu Xing Gong. While the chief was bowing, Qiu Xing Gong swung his sward and killed him. Then he said to the outlaws, "You are all good people. Why should you take a bondservant as your chief? You are now known as the outlaws of the bondservant." All of the outlaws knelt down and said, "We will turn to serve you." Then Qiu Xing Gong commanding this army went to see Li Shi Min together with his brother Qiu Shi Li. Li Shi Min granted him an honorable senior position of the third rank.

Fang Xuan Ling, the commander of the army in Xicheng (now Xixian, Shanxi Province), went to see Li Shi Min at the gate of his camps. When Li Shi Min met Fang Xuan Ling, he felt as if they had been friends for a long time. Li Shi Min appointed him secretary of his command in charge of making strategic plans. Fang Xuan Ling also felt that he had met a very good friend. He did all he could to work for Li Shi Min.

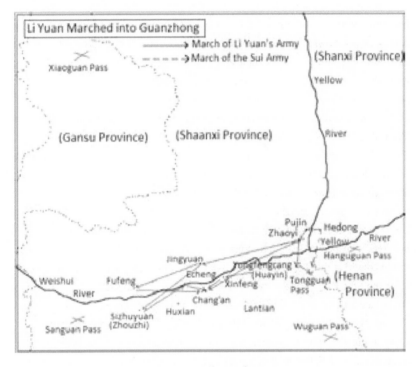

25. Li Yuan Takes Chang'an

Li Yuan ordered Liu Hong Ji and Yin Kai Shan with an army of sixty thousand men to march west to take Fufeng (now Fufeng, Shaanxi Province). After having taken Fufeng, they crossed the Weishui River and stationed their army in the old city of Chang'an. The Sui army came out of the city to fight with the army under Liu Hong Ji and Yin Kai Shan. Liu Hong Ji led his men into the battle and defeated the Sui army. At the same time, Li Shi Min commanded his army to move to Sizhuyuan (in Zhouzhi, Shaanxi Province). Li Zhong Wen, He Pan Ren and Xiang Shan Zhi with their army followed him. The army then was stationed in Echeng (the outskirt of Xianyang, where the old site of Epang Palaces is situated). The army under Li Shi Min's command grew into an army of a hundred and thirty thousand men. The army was under strict command. The army was well disciplined and they did not do any harm to the people. Li Shi Min sent an envoy from Zhouzhi to Li Yuan asking for the date on which Li Yuan would come to Chang'an. Li Yuan said, "Qutu Tong is now in the east and cannot go west. I don't need to worry about him anymore." Then he ordered Li Jian Cheng to select the best troops in Yongfengcang to march through Xinfeng (now Xinfeng Town, Lintong, Shaanxi Province) to Changle Palace (the palace of the Han Dynasty in the old city of Chang'an). Li Shi Min moved his army to the north of the old city of Chang'an and stationed his army there. On 28 September, Li Yuan maneuvered his army westward and on 3 October, reached Chang'an. His army pitched their camps to the northwest of the Chunming Gate (one of the three gates in the east part of the city wall of Chang'an). All his armies gathered around the city, more than two hundred thousand men in all. Li Yuan gave the order that all the soldiers should stay in their camps and should not do any harm to the people. Li Yuan sent several envoys to the foot of the city wall of Chang'an telling Wei Wen Sheng and others that his intention was to support the Sui Dynasty. But Wei Wen Sheng did not give any reply. On 13 October, Li Yuan gave the order to lay siege to the city of Chang'an. On October 26, Li Yuan gave the order to storm the city and also ordered that the seven temples of the Sui Dynasty should be preserved intact and the royal family of King of Dai should not be harmed. In the heat of the battlefield, Sun Hua was hit by an arrow and was killed. On 8 November, Sergeant Lei Yong Ji first got to the top of the city wall and all the troops followed and at last Li Yuan's army took the city of Chang'an.

Yang You, King of Dai, stayed in the East Palace (usually, the East Palace was the palace for the crown prince). All the attendants had deserted him. Only Yao Si Lian remained standing behind the king. When Li Yuan's soldiers arrived and were about to go into the court, Yao Si Lian shouted at them and ordered them to stop. He said, "The Duke of Tang has raised a righteous army to support the royal house of the Sui Dynasty. You must behave yourselves." All the Tang soldiers were awed and spread themselves outside the court. Li Yuan arrived and met the King of Dai in the East Palace. Then he moved the King of Dai to the rear of Daxing Palace, which was the palace for the emperor. He let Yao Si Lian help the king to the Hall of Shunyangge. Then Li Yuan returned to Changle Palace. He made twelve chapters of law and promulgated them. He abolished the harsh laws of the Sui Dynasty.

When Li Yuan entered Chang'an, Wei Wen Sheng had already died. On 10 October, Li Yuan arrested Yin Shi Shi and Gu Yi and sentenced them to death for their resistance of the righteous army. Only about ten persons were executed and Li Yuan spared all the rest. Now we come back to Li Jing, the deputy governor of Mayi (now Shuozhou, Shanxi Province). He was an enemy of Li Yuan, because when Li Yuan was in Taiyuan, Li Jing had found out about his secret plans to rebel against the Sui Dynasty. Li Jing had wanted to report the secret to Em-

peror Yang Guang of the Sui Dynasty, but on the way to Jiangdu, he found that
the way was blocked. So he had to go to Chang'an. When Chang'an fell into Li
Yuan's hands, Li Jing was arrested and sentenced to death. Before the execution,
he shouted, "You raised your army to stop the riots. Why should you kill me for
some personal hatred between us?" And Li Shi Min asked Li Yuan persistently to
spare Li Jing. Li Yuan was also moved by Li Jing's words, so he spared him. Li Shi
Min asked Li Jing to work under his command.

26. Li Yuan Makes Yang You, King of Dai, the Emperor
of the Sui Dynasty

On 15 November, Li Yuan got the imperial carriage ready and Yang You, King
of Dai, was carried in it and was pushed to Tianxing Hall to ascend the throne
of emperor of the Sui Dynasty. At that time Yang You was only thirteen years
old. The original emperor, Yang Guang, who was now far away in Jiangdu in
the eastern part of China, was respected as Father Emperor. The new emperor
entrusted all the power to Li Yuan. He offered Li Yuan a gold plated axe, which
was the symbol of power, and put him in charge of all the military and civil affairs of the whole country. He also appointed Li Yuan premier in charge of all
government decrees.

Li Yuan established the office of the premier in Wude Hall in the palace. He
appointed officials in his office. He appointed Pei Ji minister in charge of general
affairs, and Liu Wen Jing minister of war in charge of military affairs, and Li
Gang (who had been sent by He Pan Ren to see Li Yuan and had been asked by
Li Yuan to stay in the capital), general secretary of the office of premier in charge
of selection of officials, and Dou Wei minister in charge of ceremonies.

Li Yuan made his eldest son Li Jian Cheng his heir apparent, his second son
Li Shi Min Duke of Qin, and appointed him governor of the capital area, and his
third son Li Yuan Ji Duke of Qi.

In January 618, Yang You, the new Emperor of the Sui Dynasty, made Li Yuan
King of Tang. Since Li Yuan had taken Chang'an, he sent letters to the counties and prefectures in the area of Guanzhong asking them to recognize the new
government, and the governors of such counties and prefectures and chiefs of
outlaws offered their submission to the King of Tang.

27. The Confrontation between Wang Shi Chong and
Li Mi in the Area of the Eastern Capital

Wang Shi Chong commanded his army of a hundred thousand men in a con-
frontation with the army commanded by Li Mi across the Luoshui River. On
24 October 617, Wang Shi Chong crossed the river at night with his army and

camped in Heishi (in the southwest of Gongyi, Henan Province). The second day, at dawn, leaving some soldiers to guard their camp, Wang Shi Chong deployed his army in battle formation on the north bank of the river. When Li Mi got the news, he commanded his best troops to cross Luoshui River to fight. Li Mi's army was defeated. Li Mi led his best cavalrymen across to the south of the Luoshui River. The rest of his army ran to Yuecheng near the food depot in Luokou. Wang Shi Chong caught up with them and surrounded them. Li Mi and his cavalrymen rode to Heishi. The soldiers whom Wang Shi Chong had left behind to look after the camp saw that Li Mi and his cavalrymen were coming, they were shocked and lit fire signals to warn Wang Shi Chong. Wang Shi Chong saw the fire signals and had to turn back to save his own camp. Li Mi fought with Wang Shi Chong's army and defeated them. Wang Shi Chong's army suffered great losses. Three thousand soldiers under Wang Shi Chong were killed.

Since the defeat on the north bank of the Luoshui River, Wang Shi Chong stayed in his camp. Yang Tong, King of Yue, sent an envoy to see him. Wang Shi Chong felt ashamed and was afraid. He expressed his determination to do battle with Li Mi. On 8 November 617, Wang Shi Chong's army and Li Mi's Army confronted each other across Shizihe River (which is situated in the east of Gongxian, Henan Province). Li Mi's battle formation was as long as five kilometers from north to south. Zhai Rang commanded the army under him to attack Wang Shi Chong's army first but was defeated and Zhai Rang's army retreated. Wang Shi Chong commanded his army to chase Zhai Rang. Wang Bo Dang and Pei Ren Ji rode in from the side to cut Wang Shi Chong's escape route. Li Mi started his attack from the front. Wang Shi Chong was disastrously defeated and ran away to the west.

Zhai Rang's military adviser Wang Ru Xin tried to persuade Zhai Rang to make himself commander-in-chief and command the whole army, so as to take back the commanding power from Li Mi. But Zhai Rang would not listen to him. Zhai Rang's elder brother Zhai Hong said to him, "You should be the supreme ruler yourself. Why should you offer it to another person? If you don't want to be the supreme ruler, I will." Zhai Rang laughed out loud and did not care about his words. When Li Mi heard about this, he was resentful. General Cui Shi Shu had just surrendered to Li Mi with the city of Yanling (now Yanling, Henan Province). Zhai Rang kept him in custody in his own home, asking Cui Shi Shu for treasure. Cui Shi Shu did not give him what he was asking for promptly, and he was badly beaten. Zhai Rang said to Fang Yan Zao, "When you took Runan, you got a lot of treasure. You only shared it with the Duke of Wei but you did not give me any. It was I who made him Duke of Wei. Who knows what will happen in the future." Fang Yan Zao was afraid and told what Zhai Rang had said to Li Mi. Fang Yan Zao and Zheng Ting tried to persuade Li Mi to take action. They said to Li Mi, "Zhai Rang is greedy and inhumane. He does not submit to you. You'd better take action as soon as possible." Li Mi said, "Now the situation is unstable. If we start killing each other now, what will other people think of it?" Zheng Ting said, "If your hand is bitten by a poisonous snake, you have to cut your hand off resolutely because by doing so you may preserve the main body. If he acts first, it will be too late for you to regret it." Li Mi at last took their advice. On 10 November, he prepared a banquet and invited Zhai Rang. Zhai Rang came with his brother Zhai Hong, his brother's son Zhai Mo Hou, and Wang Ru Xin. Li Mi sat with Zhai Rang, Zhai Hong, Pei Ren Ji and Hao Xiao De. Shan Xiong Xin was standing in attendance. Fang Yan Zao and Zheng Ting were responsible for taking care of the officers. Li Mi said, "This banquet is intended for entertaining the very important people. The rest may leave." The officers under Li Mi had all left but the officers under Zhai Rang remained. Fang Yan Zao said to Li Mi, "It is very cold today. I hope you will allow me to prepare wine and good food for those officers who have come with the premier." Li Mi said, "As you will." Zhai Rang also said, "That would be good." Then all the officers who had come with Zhai Rang were taken out of the room. Only a warrior named Cai Jian De under Li Mi stood in attendance with a broad sword. As they were all professionally interested in archery, before the food was served, Li Mi showed a very good bow to Zhai Rang. Zhai Rang took up the bow and pulled it in full. Cai Jian De swung his broad sword and struck Zhai Rang in the neck from behind. Zhai Rang gave out a shout and fell on the couch, dead. Cai Jian De immediately killed Zhai Hong, Zhai Mo Hou and Wang Ru Xin. Xu Shi Ji heard the sound and came in and saw what was going on, but was wounded on the neck by a guard at the door. Wang Bo Dang shouted to the guard to stop him from doing more harm to Xu Shi Ji. Shan Xiong Xin was so afraid that he knelt on his knees begging for mercy. Li Mi spared him. All the men who had come with Zhai Rang were shocked and were at a total loss. Li Mi loudly announced, "We have risen in arms together in order to overthrow the brutal rule of the Emperor of the Sui Dynasty and bring peace to China. But Zhai Rang himself has committed many tyrannical acts. He has bullied and insulted his fellow officials. We cannot tolerate his tyrannical acts any more. We have decided to kill the members of his family. It has nothing to do with you." Then he helped Xu Shi Ji into his tent and treated his wound himself. The soldiers in the army under Zhai Rang's command got the news that Zhai Rang had been killed and they were ready to disband. Li Mi sent Shan Xiong Xin to calm the soldiers down. Then Li Mi rode on a horse single-handedly into the camps of Zhai Rang's army and pacified the men. Zhai Rang's army was divided into three parts and it was put under the command of Xu Shi Ji, Shan Xiong Xin and Wang Bo Dang. Zhai Rang had been cruel; Zhai Mo Hou had been suspicious and jealous, and Wang Ru Xin had been greedy. So, when they were killed, no one in Zhai Rang's army showed any sympathy to them. But this incident aroused self-suspicion among the generals and officers under Li Mi. Wang Shi Chong had predicted that Zhai Rang and Li Mi could not fare for long and anticipated that killings between Zhai Rang and Li Mi would break out, creating an opportunity for him. But when he learned that Zhai Rang had been killed and Li Mi handled things so neatly, he was disappointed. He said with a sigh, "Li Mi is clever and resolute. It is hard to predict whether he will become a dragon or a snake."

It was already December. There had been no fighting between Li Mi and Wang Shi Chong for some time. During this period, food in the Eastern Capital ran very low and the price of food ran very high. On 22 December, some soldiers under Wang Shi Chong came to surrender to Li Mi. Li Mi asked them what Wang Shi Chong was doing with his army. A sergeant said, "He is recruiting many new soldiers and has been giving good food to the soldiers. I don't know why." Li Mi said to Pei Ren Ji, "We have nearly fallen into his trap. Do you know? We have not fought with him for quite a long time. Wang Shi Chong's food is running short. Since he cannot find a chance to fight a battle with us, he has been recruiting men and giving good food to his soldiers. He must be planning to launch a surprise attack on Cangcheng in this period of time when there is no moon light at night. We must prepare for his attack." Then he ordered Hao Xiao De, Wang Bo Dang and Meng Rang with the troops under their command to lay an ambush by the side of Cangcheng, waiting to trap Wang Shi Chong's army. In the deep of night, Wang Shi Chong's army came stealthily. Wang Bo Dang first engaged in battle with them but was defeated and fell back. The troops of Wang Shi Chong were about to storm the city. Lu Ru firmly resisted the attack. Then Wang Bo Dang reorganized his men and attacked again. Wang Shi Chong's army was defeated. More than a thousand soldiers of Wang Shi Chong's army were drowned in the river.

After Wang Shi Chong's defeat by Li Mi, Yang Tong, King of Yue, came to comfort him. Wang Shi Chong complained to Yang Tong that he did not have enough men to cope with Li Mi and the men under him were very tired now after so many battles. Yang Tong put seventy thousand men under his command. With this reinforced army, Wang Shi Chong led his men into battle against Li Mi again. He defeated Li Mi in a battle on the northern bank of the Luoshui River. Then he stationed his army in the north of Gongxian (now in Henan Province). On 13 January 618, Wang Shi Chong ordered his men to build floating bridges across the Luoshui River so that his men could cross the river to attack Li Mi. Wang Shi Chong gave the order that soldiers might start crossing the river from any bridges which had been completed first. Since the bridges were not completed at the same time, some troops crossed the river earlier than the others. General Wang Bian and his men crossed the river first and reached the outer fence barriers of the camps of Li Mi's army. The soldiers in the camps were alarmed and about to collapse. But Wang Shi Chong did not know the situation was so favorable for a fierce attack. Instead, he sounded the retreat, and his army retreated in great disorder. Li Mi took advantage of this disordered retreat and led his death corps to attack and inflicted great casualties on Wang Shi Chong's army. So many of Wang Shi Chong's troops were racing for the floating bridges and so many soldiers were trying to squeeze into the bridges that more than ten thousand fell into the river and were drowned. Wang Bian died. Wang Shi Chong barely made his escape. The troops under Wang Shi Chong on the north bank of the Luoshui River were routed. Wang Shi Chong was too ashamed to go back to the Eastern Capital. He made for Heyang (now Mengxian, Henan Province) with his remaining troops. That night, there was a gale and bitterly cold rain. The soldiers forded streams and got wet. Tens of thousands of Wang Shi Chong's soldiers died on the way in the freezing weather. Only several thousand men made it to Heyang. Wang Shi Chong put himself into jail and sent an envoy to see Yang Tong, King of Yue, and asked the King of Yue to punish him for his defeat. The King of Yue pardoned him and summoned him back to the Eastern Capital. Wang Shi Chong gathered his soldiers who had fled back from the battlefield and got about ten thousand men. He stationed his troops in Hanjiacheng (in the north of Luoyang, Henan Province) and did not dare to fight against Li Mi again.

Li Mi led his victorious army in the attack of Jinyongcheng (now east part of Luoyang) and took it. Now Li Mi's army grew into an army of over three hundred thousand men. The governors of Yanshi (now Yanshi, Henan Province), Bogu (now Yiyang, Henan Province), Heyang (now Mengxian, Henan Province), and Henei (now Qinyang, Henan Province) surrendered to Li Mi with their troops and their cities. Li Mi became the most influential warlord all over China and many chiefs of outlaws such as Dou Jian De (in the area in what is now Hebei Province), Zhu Can (in the area of what is now south of Henan Province), Meng Hai Gong (in the area of what is now Caocheng and Chengwu, Shandong Province), and Xu Yuan Lang (in the area of present southwest of Shandong Province) sent envoys to suggest that Li Mi proclaim himself emperor. The generals under Li Mi also suggested that he ascend the throne. But Li Mi refused to take their advice, saying that it was not yet time to do that.

28. Qutu Tong Surrenders to Li Yuan

Qutu Tong and Liu Wen Jing confronted against each other in Tongguan area for more than a month. Qutu Tong sent Sang Xian He to launch a surprise attack on the camps of Liu Wen Jing's army at night. Liu Wen Jing and Duan Zhi Xuan fought very hard to defend their camps. Sang Xian He was defeated and fell back. Most of his soldiers were taken prisoners. Qutu Tong's force was dramatically weakened. A friend of his tried to persuade him to surrender to Li Yuan. Qutu Tong wept and said, "I have served two emperors of the same dynasty. They have treated me with great favor. How can I betray the emperor who has granted me so much favor?" Li Yuan sent a servant of his household to summon Qutu Tong to Chang'an. Qutu Tong killed that servant. When Qutu Tong learned that Chang'an had fallen into Li Yuan's hands and all his family members were under Li Yuan's custody, he left Tongguan to Sang Xian He's care and he himself led the main force to Luoyang. As soon as Qutu Tong left, Sang Xian He surrendered to Liu Wen Jing with the city of Tongguan. Liu Wen Jing sent Dou Cong commanding some light cavalrymen with Sang Xian He to run after Qutu Tong. They caught up with Qutu Tong in Chousang (in the north of Lingbao, Henan Province). Qutu Tong drew his men up in battle order. Dou Cong sent Qutu Tong's son to persuade his father to surrender. Qutu Tong cursed him loudly. "Which side have you come from? In the past, we were father and son. But from now on, you are no longer my son but my enemy." Then he ordered his men to shoot arrows at his son. But Sang Xian He shouted to the soldiers, "Now the capital has fallen to Li Yuan, the King of Tang. You are all from the area of Guanzhong. Why should you leave your own home and go to any place else?" All the soldiers under Qutu Tong laid down their weapons and surrendered. As Qutu Tong knew that he could not make his escape, he dismounted and bowed toward the southeast and cried loudly, saying, "It is not that I intentionally betray the Emperor. It is because I have lost all my force. This can be witnessed by the heavens, the earth and god." The soldiers under Dou Cong went up and arrested him. He was escorted to Chang'an. Li Yuan released him and appointed him Minister of War. Li Yuan also made him Duke of Jiang. Qutu Tong was also appointed military counselor to work under Li Shi Min in his Office of the Marshal.

29. The Death of Emperor Yang Guang of the Sui Dynasty

Since Emperor Yang Guang of the Sui Dynasty reached Jiangdu, he had led a very luxurious and dissolute life. He saw that the whole country was in great disorder and there were riots everywhere; he felt frustrated and sad. He knew that he could do nothing about it and so he spent his days drinking and often got drunk all day with beautiful girls around him. He often walked around the palaces till very late at night. He worried that his days were numbered and he could not enjoy all these beautiful scenes any more.

Seeing that Central China was in great chaos, Emperor Yang Guang did not want to go back to the north and wanted to make Jiangdu his capital. But all the ministers of his court were from the north. They were not used to the life in the south, where the weather was so humid. The valiant troops, who were intended to defend the royal family, were soldiers who followed Emperor Yang Guang to Jiangdu from the area of Guanzhong. They missed their homes very much. When they found that Emperor Yang Guang did not intend to go back to the west, many of them ran way. But most of those who had run away were caught and executed. General Sima De Kan, a general trusted by the Emperor, was appointed to command the valiant troops which were stationed in the east part of Jiangdu. Sima De Kan had a discussion with General Yuan Li and General Pei Yu Tong and made a plan to escape. Later Generals Zhao Xing Shu, Meng Bing, Niu Fang Yu, Xue Shi Liang, Tang Feng Yi, Zhang Kai, and Yang Shi Lan joined in their plan of escape. Liu Fang Yu was a good friend of Yuwen Zhi Ji, an official in charge of civil engineering. Liu Fan Yu told their escape plan to Yuwen Zhi Ji. Yuwen Zhi Ji was very glad to find out about it. Sima De Kan had agreed with the others that they would gather all their men and carry out their plan on 15 March 618. On that night, there would be full bright moon. But Yuwen Zhi Ji said to them, "Although the Emperor is bad and unpopular, his orders are to be obeyed. If you run away, you will meet the same fate as those who made their escape before. They were caught and executed. However, now the Sui Dynasty is destined to fall. Rebellions have broken out everywhere. You have gathered tens of thousands of men to carry out your plan. If you rebel against the Emperor with this great force, you will succeed in establishing the power to rule over China." Sima De Kan agreed with his idea.

Zhao Xing Shu and Xue Shi Liang suggested that Yuwen Zhi Ji's elder brother General Yuwen Hua Ji, Duke of Xu, be the leader of the action. Only after the agreement had been made did they tell Yuwen Hua Ji of their plan. Yuwen Hua Ji was a true coward. When he was told of the plan, his face turned pale and he was sweating all over. But anyway, he agreed with the plan. Sima De Kan sent Xu Hong Ren and Zhang Kai to the office of the Emperor's guards to tell their acquaintance that the emperor had learned that the valiant troops were going to rebel, that he had prepared a lot of poisoned wine, and he intended to kill all valiant troops in a banquet; and that the Emperor would stay in the south with the southerners. These words spread quickly among the soldiers and aroused great fear among them. They could not wait any longer to carry out their plan.

On 12 March 618, Sima De Kan gathered all the officers and sergeants of the valiant troops and told them of their plan of action. All the officers and sergeants said, "We will follow your instruction!" That day, it was windy and cloudy. At dusk, Sima De Kan stole horses from the royal stable and ordered his men to sharpen their weapons. At night, Pei Yu Tong was on duty in charge of the guards in the inner main hall of the palace. Tang Feng Yi was in charge of the gates of the city walls. He informed the guards in charge of each gate to close the gate but leave them unlocked. Sima De Kan gathered all his troops, totalling thirty thousand men, in the east part of the city of Jiangdu. Then he lit a fire to signal his comrades outside the city. Emperor Yang Guang saw the fire and heard noises outside the palace and asked Pei Yu Tong what was happening. Pei Yu Tong answered, "A straw shed is on fire and the people inside and outside the palace are doing their best to extinguish it." At that time, the Emperor could not get any other information from outside. So he had to believe it. Yuwen Zhi Ji and Meng Bing gathered about a thousand men outside the city. Yang Tan, King of Yan, found that rebellion had broken out and hurried to the palace to report to the Emperor, but he was detained by Pei Yu Tong and was not allowed to see the Emperor. Next day before dawn, Sima De Kan replaced all the guards at each gate who were still loyal to the Emperor with troops under Pei Yu Tong's command. Pei Yu Tong commanded several cavalrymen to Chengxiang Hall.

The Imperial Guards shouted that rebels had come. Pei Yu Tong closed all the gates but left the east gate open and drove all the guards out of the hall through that gate. When the guards left, they laid down their weapons by the gate. General Gudu Sheng asked Pei Yu Tong, "There seems to be some strange military maneuver going on. What has happened?" Pei Yu Tong said, "A rebellion has taken place. It has nothing to do with you. You'd better not take any action against it." Gudu Sheng objected loudly, "How dare you, old rebel, say that." Having no time to put on his armor, he immediately led some ten men under him to attack Pei Yu Tong and his men, but he was killed in the confusion. Sima De Kan marched at the head of an army through Xuanwu Gate to the palace. The Emperor learned that there was rebellion and changed his royal robe for a plain suit and hid himself in a room on the west of the hall. Pei Yu Tong and Yuan Li lined up their men and searched a room on the left of the hall for the Emperor. Pei Yu Tong asked where the Emperor was. One of the beauties pointed at the room on the west of the hall. Captain Linghu Xing Da drew out his broad sword and went into the room. The Emperor was found behind a curtain. He asked, "Do you intend to kill me?" Linghu Xing Da answered, "No, I dare not do that. Our intention is to escort Your Majesty back to the west." Then he helped the Emperor out of the room.

Pei Yu Tong had been a favorite of Emperor Yang Guang. When the Emperor saw him, he asked, "Are you an old friend of mine? What complaints do you have that drive you to rebel against me?" Pei Yu Tong answered, "We dare not rebel. But the officers and men long to return to the west. We just want to escort Your Majesty back to the capital." The Emperor said, "I am planning to go back to the capital. I have not yet started because I am waiting for the food provisions to arrive. Now, I have to go back with you." Pei Yu Tong assigned some soldiers to guard him. In the morning, Meng Bing met Yuwen Hua Ji with some armored horsemen. Yuwen Hua Ji was trembling so much that he could not speak. When somebody came to greet him, he just lowered his head, grabbed the saddle and said, "Thank You." When Yuwen Hua Ji reached the gate of the palace, Sima De Kan met him there and conducted him into the court and he respected Yuwen Hua Ji as the premier. Pei Yu Tong said to the Emperor, "The ministers are now in the court waiting for you to receive them." Then he led a horse to him and asked the Emperor to mount the horse and ride to the court. When the Emperor rode out of the palace, the rebels cheered loudly for their victory. Yuwen Hua Ji saw this and said to Pei Yu Tong, "There is no need to have a show of the Emperor. Take him back and have him killed as soon as possible." Then they escorted the Emperor back to the chamber hall in the palace with Sima De Kan and Pei Yu Tong at his sides, holding their swords in their hands.

The Emperor said with a sigh, "What offences have I committed that I deserve such treatment?" Ma Wen Ju said, "Your Majesty has abandoned the temples of your ancestors and made incessant tours for pleasure all the time. You carried out wars against foreign countries. You led a luxurious and dissolute life. Many able-bodied men have been killed in the wars you have started. Many ordinary people have been starved to death. People have lost the means of providing for themselves. Now outlaws are everywhere. You have appointed those who try their best to please you to important positions. You have tried your best to cover up your wrongdoings and refused to listen to good advice. How can you say that you are innocent?" The Emperor said, "I have really done a lot of harm to the ordinary people. But as for you, I have treated you all very well. You have been appointed to high-ranking positions and paid well. Why have you betrayed me? Who is the leader of this rebellion?" Sima De Kan said, "All the people throughout China hate you. Everyone is the leader in this rebellion." While this was going on, Yang Gao, King of Zhao, the Emperor's youngest son, who was only twelve yours old, was crying by the Emperor's side. Pei Yu Tong killed him with his sword. The blood of the young king spilt on the clothes of the Emperor. Pei Yu Tong wanted to kill the Emperor with his sword. But the Emperor said, "An emperor has his own way to die. You don't need to use your sword. Now bring the poisoned wine to me." But Ma Wen Ju did not allow that. He ordered Linghu Xing De to make the Emperor sit on a chair. The Emperor handed his silk kerchief over to Linghu Xing De, who made a loop round the neck of the Emperor and strangled him with it. (After Emperor Yang Guang died, he was given the posthumous name Emperor Yang, which means acting against the will of Heaven and maltreating the people.) Then they killed all the sons of the Emperor and the favorite ministers of the Emperor. Only one son of the Emperor, Yang Hao, the King of Qin, escaped death because he was a friend of Yuwen Zhi Ji. Later, Yuwen Hua Ji made Yang Hao emperor just for the purpose of signing orders.

Then Yuwen Hua Ji and all those who had taken part in the rebellion started their journey back to the west. Empress Xiao and all the concubines of Emperor Yang Guang were taken with them. The rebels robbed the people of their boats and went by waterway to Pengcheng (now Xuzhou, Jiangsu Province). Yuwen Hua Ji had an army of more than a hundred thousand men. He took Empress Xiao and the Emperor's concubines as his own wives. He led a life as luxurious as that had led by Emperor Yang Guang. When they reached Pengcheng, they could not go by boats anymore because the waterway was blocked. So they took wagons from the peasants and got two thousand of them. They carried the women and treasure on the wagons. But they ordered the soldiers to carry their armor and weapons for them. The soldiers had to carry their armor and weapons all the way. They were extremely tired. They began to complain. Sima De Kan had a secret discussion with Zhao Xing Shu and they decided to get rid of Yuwen Hua Ji. But he uncoverd their plan and acted first. Yuwen Hua Ji killed Sima De Kan. Then he moved his army west towards Luoyang, but they met with strong resistance by Li Mi and could not move further west. Yuwen Hua Ji had to move his army to Dong Prefecture (now in the area around Huaxian, Henan Province). Wang Gui, the governor of Dong Prefecture, opened the city gates and surrendered to Yuwen Hua Ji.

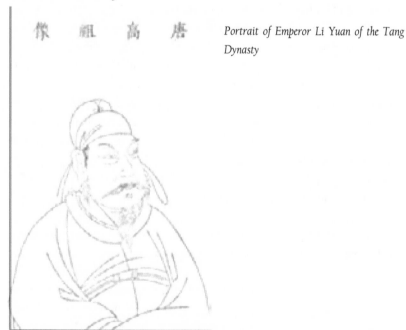

Portrait of Emperor Li Yuan of the Tang Dynasty

30. Li Yuan Becomes Emperor of the Tang Dynasty

On 15 May 618, Yang You, Emperor of the Sui Dynasty in Chang'an, stepped down from the throne and offered the throne to Li Yuan. On 21 May, Li Yuan ascended the throne and proclaimed himself Emperor of the Tang Dynasty. On 1 June, Emperor Li Yuan of the Tang Dynasty appointed Li Shi Min prime minister, Pei Ji deputy prime minister, Liu Wen Jing deputy prime minister, Dou Wei the minister in charge of the government decrees, Li Gang minister of rites, Yin Kai Shan minister of personnel, Qutu Tong minister of war, Dou Jin minister of revenue, Dugu Huai En minister of works. On 7 June, Li Yuan made his eldest son Li Jian Cheng the Crown Prince, his second son Li Shi Min the King of Qin, his fourth son Li Yuan Ji King of Qi. He also made some of his royal clansmen kings of different places. Li Yuan made Yang You, the former emperor of the Sui Dynasty who had abdicated from the throne, Duke of Xi.

31. Confrontations in the Eastern Capital Area

When news of the death of Emperor Yang Guang of the Sui Dynasty reached the Eastern Capital, Yang Tong, King of Yue, proclaimed himself Emperor of the Sui Dynasty on 25 May. He appointed Duan Da prime minister, Wang Shi Chong also prime minister, Yuan Wen Du minister in charge of government decrees, Lu Chu also minister in charge of government decrees, Huangpu Wu Yi minister of war.

The officials in the Eastern Capital were shocked to hear that Yuwen Hua Ji and his great army were marching west. A person named Gai Cong wrote a letter to Yang Tong, the new Emperor of the Sui Dynasty, suggesting that the emperor should unite with Li Mi to resist Yuwen Hua Ji. Yuan Wen Du said to Lu Chu, "We have not yet revenged ourselves on Li Mi. But our army is not strong enough to resist the advance of Yuwen Hua Ji. If we pardon Li Mi for his former offences and send him to fight with Yuwen Hua Ji, we may stay in the Eastern Capital watching them fight. If Yuwen Hua Ji is defeated, the officers and men in Li Mi's army will also be tired. We may drive a wedge between Li Mi and his generals by giving bribes to his generals. Then we may capture Li Mi easily." Lu Chu agreed with him. They appointed Gai Cong the envoy of Emperor Yang Tong to take a letter of the emperor to Li Mi.

Yuwen Hua Ji left his army's supplies and gear in Huatai (now Huaxian, Henan Province) in the care of Wang Gui. Then he led his army to march north to Liyang (now Xunxian, Henan Province). Xu Shi Ji, a general under Li Mi, was defending Liyang. When he saw that Yuwen Hua Ji's army was too strong to resist, he withdrew his army from Liyang to the west to defend Cangcheng (in the south west of Xunxian, Henan Province) where there was a huge granary.

Yuwen Hua Ji crossed the Yellow River and took Liyang. Then he dispatched an army to surround Cangcheng. Li Mi commanded two hundred thousand foot soldiers and horsemen to Qingqi (now Qixian, Henan Province) and pitched camps there. Li Mi and Xu Shi Ji contacted each other by lighting signal fires. The troops under Xu Shi Ji dug deep ditches around their camps and built high strongholds to defend themselves. The troops under Xu Shi Ji just stayed inside their camps and would not go out to fight against Yuwen Hua Ji's army. Whenever Yuwen Hua Ji launched an attack on Cangcheng, Li Mi would attack Yuwen Hua Ji's army from behind. One day Li Mi talked to Yuwen Hua Ji across the Qi He River. Li Mi said, "Your father, brothers, and sons have served the late emperor and were treated quite well by him. You have gained a lot of wealth from serving the emperor, and you enjoyed the highest rank in the government. When the emperor was guilty of misconduct and acted unreasonably, you did not do your best to persuade him to restrain himself from doing evil at the risk of your live. Instead, you have murdered him and usurped power from him. You are not a man of devotion but a traitor. Wherever you go, you will not be able to escape punishment. If you come over to my side, your descendents may survive." Yuwen Hua Ji thought for a long time in silence. Then he said, "You and I are going to kill each other. What is the use of talking so much nonsense?" Li Mi said to his followers, "Yuwen Hua Ji is such a mediocre and slow-minded person. He now has his mind on becoming an emperor. I must defeat him and drive him away." Yuwen Hua Ji had many devices built for attacking cities—catapults, battering rams, tall ladders—and was ready to storm the city of Cangcheng. But Xu Shi Ji had ordered his soldiers to dig a deep ditch around the city outside the city walls. The deep ditch prevented Yuwen Hua Ji's soldiers from getting close. Then Xu Shi Ji ordered his men to dig tunnels from the ditch outward to the positions of the enemy and sent out his soldiers through the tunnels to start an attack Yuwen Hua Ji. Yuwen Hua Ji's army was defeated and Xu Shi Ji's soldiers burned all their devices.

At that time, Li Mi had been confronting the Sui army in the East Capital for quite a long time. Now he had to resist the army under Yuwen Hua Ji from the east. So he was afraid that the Sui army in the Eastern Capital would launch raids on his army from the back. When Gai Cong came with the letter of Emperor Yang Tong of the Sui Dynasty in the Eastern Capital, he was very happy. He wrote back expressing his intention of submission to Emperor Yang Tong and requesting to be sent to annihilate Yuwen Hua Ji and his army so as to perform outstanding service to atone for the crimes he had committed before. He sent a group of soldiers to escort General Yu Hong Jian under Yuwen Hua Ji, whom Li Mi had captured in the previous battle to Emperor Yang Tong. Then he sent Li Jian and Xu Shi Yu to the Eastern Capital to see Emperor Yang Tong. Yuan Wen

Du thought that Li Mi had sincerely submitted himself to Emperor Yang Tong. So when Li Jian and Xu Shi Yu arrived, they were warmly introduced to Emperor Yang Tong. Emperor Yang Tong assigned them to high-ranking positions in the government. The Emperor made Li Mi Duke of Wei, minister of war, army marshal, and commander of the army in the east. He ordered Li Mi to annihilate Yuwen Hua Ji and his army first and come to the Eastern Capital to attend to the state affairs after he completed his task. Emperor Yang Tong appointed Xu Shi Ji Great General. The emperor wrote a letter to Li Mi praising his devotion and his ability in war and strategy, and entrusting the warfare in the east to Li Mi.

Yuan Wen Du was very glad to see that the two hostile sides had become reconciled. He held a banquet on the top of the city wall to celebrate the event. All the ministers, including Duan Da, were happy about it. Only Wang Shi Chong was unhappy. He said to Cui Chang Wen, "The Emperor has assigned senior positions to the outlaws. What does he want to do?" Yuan Wen Du suspected that Wang Shi Chong would cooperate with Yuwen Hua Ji within the Eastern Capital. From then on, there was a grudge between Yuan Wen Du and Wang Shi Chong. But outwardly, they pretended that they were still good friends.

In July, Emperor Yang Tong sent Zhang Quan and Cui Shan Fu to Li Mi with a letter, which read, "Let us forget everything that happened before today. From now on let us trust each other. I have placed in you the power to handle all the important state affairs, and the power to carry out punitive expeditions against our common enemy." When Zhang Yuan and Cui Shan Fu arrived, Li Mi knelt down to accept the letter from Emperor Yang Tong. Since there was no need to worry about the threat from the west, Li Mi led all his army to fight against Yuwen Hua Ji. He heard that Yuwen Hua Ji's food was running low. So he pretended that he would make peace with Yuwen Hua Ji. Yuwen Hua Ji was very happy and let his soldiers eat as much as they wanted because he thought that Li Mi would provide food for them. But at that time a person who had committed some offence against Li Mi defected to Yuwen Hua Ji and told him about Li Mi's trick. Yuwen Hua Ji was very angry. His food had run out. Then he led all his army across Yongji Canal. His army and Li Mi's army fought ferociously at the foot of Tongshan Mountain (within Qixian area, Henan Province). The battle lasted from eight in the morning till five in the afternoon. Li Mi was wounded by a stray arrow and fell from his horse to the ground. His men fled the battlefield in all directions. The pursuers were approaching. Only Qin Shu Bao was beside Li Mi protecting him. Qin Shu Bao gathered his men and fought desperately. At last they pressed Yuwen Hua Ji's army back. Li Mi was saved. Yuwen Hua Ji sent out foraging parties to Ji Prefecture (now Xinxiang area, Henan Province) to get food. And he sent envoys to Dong Prefecture (now Huaxian, Henan Province) to force to torture the local officials and the people until they gave food to the army. Wang Gui, who had been left in Huatai taking care of supplies, could not stand the wrongs Yuwen Hua Ji had done to the people, so he sent Xu Jing Zong to Li Mi to express his intention to change sides. Li Mi appointed Wang Gui commander of the army in Huatai (now Huaxian, Henan Province). He appointed Xu Jing Zong secretary in the Headquarters of Commander-in-Chief. Xu Jing Zong and Wei Zheng were in charge of secretarial work for Li Mi. Wei Zheng had joined Li Mi in August 617. He was a man of letters. When Yuwen Hua Ji learned that Wang Gui had defected to Li Mi, he was shocked. He led his army to march north from Ji Prefecture, intending to take the prefectures in the north, but Cheng Zhi Lue with more than ten thousand valiant troops, Fan Wen Chao with all the men under him, Zhang Tong Er with several thousand valiant troops, turned over to Li Mi. Yuwen Hua Ji had only twenty thousand men left. He led this army north to Wei Prefecture (now the area of the southeast part of Hebei Province and the northwest part of Shangdong Province). Li Mi knew that Yuwen Hua Ji was no longer a threat to him. After assigning Xu Shi Ji to stay to prevent Yuwen Hua Ji from turning back, he returned to Gongxian and the Luoyang area.

Li Mi reported every victory he had won to Emperor Yang Tong, and the officials of the court of the Sui Dynasty were cheered by every report of his victory. But Wang Shi Chong said to his subordinates, "Yuan Wen Du is only a petty official who draws up indictments. He will fall into the trap set by Li Mi. The soldiers of our army have fought against Li Mi many times. Many of their fathers and brothers have been killed by the army under Li Mi in many battles. Once Li Mi comes and is in charge of the army, all of us will be killed." His purpose was to stir up hatred among the soldiers against Li Mi. When Yuan Wen Du learned about this, he was afraid. He together with Lu Chu made up a plan to kill Wang Shi Chong. The plan was to order some soldiers to lay ambush and kill Wang Shi Chong when he came to court. But Duan Da was a coward. He was afraid that he would be implicated when the plan failed. So he sent his son-in-law to inform Wang Shi Chong of Yuan Wen Du's plan. On 15 July, at midnight, Wang Shi Chong with his soldiers raided Hanjia Gate of the palace. When Yuan Wen Du learned that Wang Shi Chong was attacking the gate, he ran to tell the emperor of the incident and deployed soldiers to defend the palace. They ordered the soldiers to shut all the gates to resist the attack by the army under Wang Shi Chong. General Baye Gang sent his men out of the walls of the palace. When he met Wang Shi Chong, he surrendered to him. General Fei Yao and Tian She fought outside the gate, but were defeated by Wang Shi Chong's army. Yuan Wen Du himself commanded the soldiers who were defending Emperor Yang Tong and he wanted to go out through Xuanwu Gate to fight with Wang Shi Chong. But the gatekeeper pretended that he could not find the key to the lock of the gate and Yuan Wen Du could not go out to fight. At dawn, Yuan Wen Du wanted to lead the soldiers out through Taiyang Gate to fight. By the time he turned back to Qianyang Hall of the palace, Wang Shi Chong had succeeded in breaking into the Taiyang Gate. Huangpu Wu Yi fled to Chang'an through a gate on the west wall of the palace. Lu Chu was captured by Wang Shi Chong's soldiers and was killed on Wang Shi Chong's order. The soldiers under Wang Shi Chong stormed the gates of Zhiwei Palace. Emperor Yang Tong sent an envoy up the wall of the Zhiwei Palace to ask why he had rebelled. Wang Shi Chong dismounted and apologized by saying, "Yuan Wen Du and Lu Chu have conspired to set me up. I request that Yuan Wen Du be killed. Then I will be willing to be punished according to the laws." Duan Da ordered General Huang Tao Shu to arrest Yuan Wen Du and to deliver him to Wang Shi Chong. While he was escorted out of the palace, Yuan Wen Du turned his head back and shouted to the Emperor, "I am going to be killed today. Your Majesty will be killed not long later!" The Emperor cried bitterly and waved him to go. As soon as he was out of Xingjiao Gate, Yuan Wen Du was killed by the soldiers under Wang Shi Chong. Duan Da gave the order in the name of the Emperor to open the gate to let Wang Shi Chong in. Wang Shi Chong sent his own soldiers to replace all the Emperor's guards. Then he went into Qianyang Hall to see the Emperor. The Emperor said to Wang Shi Chong, "You have killed important ministers of the court at your own discretion without prior report to me. Is this correct conduct on the part of a minister in the court? You are doing things at your own will because you have power in your hands. Do you have the courage to harm me?" Wang Shi Chong knelt down and said, "I was promoted by the late Emperor to this rank. I cannot repay his kindness even if I die. Yuan Wen Du had a secret plan to invite Li Mi to the Eastern Capital and do harm to the royal family. He hated me because I saw through his true intention. He intended to kill me. The situation was critical. I did not have the time to report to Your Majesty before I took action. If I cherished any evil intention of doing harm to Your Majesty, I would be punished by god and all the members of my clan would be extinguished." The Emperor believed what he had said and thought that he was still devoted to him. So he placed the power in the hands of Wang Shi Chong to handle all the civil and military affairs.

At that time, Li Mi was in Wen (now Wenxian, Henan Province) on his way to the Eastern Capital to take up his position in the court. But when he got the news that Yuan Wen Du and Lu Chu had been killed by Wang Shi Chong, he went back to Jinyong, a small city to the east of the Eastern Capital.

After Li Mi had killed Zhai Rang, he became very conceited. He did not show solicitude for his officers and men. His officers and men could not get any reward when they had rendered outstanding service. So the soldiers had some complaints. Xu Shi Ji had once made some mocking remarks about his shortcomings in a banquet. Li Mi was resentful and appointed Xu Shi Ji commander of the army stationed in Liyang. Although it was a formal appointment, it was actually a sign that they were drifting apart.

When Wang Shi Chong had seized power in the Eastern Capital, he secretly made preparations to attack Li Mi. After Li Mi had defeated Yuwen Hua Ji, many of his brave soldiers died and many of the horses of his army were killed in battle. Those who survived were very tired and many were sick. Wang Shi Chong decided to take this opportunity to destroy Li Mi. In order to encourage his soldiers, Wang Shi Chong spread the message among his troops that a sergeant named Zhang Yong Tong had seen the Duke of Zhou (the most virtuous man in the Zhou Dynasty who lived in the period before 1000 B.C.) in a dream and the Duke of Zhou had asked him to tell the people that he wanted Wang Shi Chong to launch an expedition against Li Mi. Then Wang Shi Chong had a temple to the Duke of Zhou built. Every time his army started to march to battle, they first held a ceremony in front of the temple to say their prayers. In the ceremony, he asked the "priest" or medium who communicated with the spirits of the deceased to declare that Duke of Zhou had ordered Wang Shi Chong to deal with Li Mi, and that he would achieve great success; and that otherwise the whole army would be struck by plague and all the soldiers would die. Most of the soldiers were from the area of Chu (the area south to the Yangtze River) and they were superstitious, so they all offered themselves to fight in the battlefields. Wang Shi Chong chose twenty thousand brave soldiers from all his troops. On 9 September 618, Wang Shi Chong's army started marching to the battlefields. On 10 September, his army reached Yanshi (now Yanshi, Henan Province). They pitched their camps on the southern bank of Tongji Canal. Wang Shi Chong had three floating bridges built over the canal. Li Mi left Wang Bo Dang to defend Jinyong. Li Mi himself led his select troops in the march to Yanshi and his army was stationed against Beimangshan Mountain (to the north of Luoyang, Henan Province) ready to cope with the attack by Wang Shi Chong's army. Li Mi held a military conference with all his generals. Pei Ren Ji said, "Since Wang Shi Chong has brought most of his force to fight with us, the defense of the Eastern Capital is weak. We may dispatch our troops to guard the strategic points of the roads so that the army of Wang Shi Chong cannot move east. Then we may send an army of thirty thousand men in the march west to threaten the Eastern Capital. If Wang Shi Chong returns to defend the Eastern Capital, we may stop action. If Wang Shi Chong comes again, we may advance again to threaten the Eastern Capital. Then we can have a good rest while Wang Shi Chong's men will be tired out by running back and forth. Then we are sure to score victory over him." Li Mi agreed with his idea. He said, "You are right. We have three reasons not to fight head on with Wang Shi Chong's army. First, the troops of his army are highly qualified. Second, the troops are resolute to march to our rear. Third, the troops are eager to fight because their food supply has run short. But we will just stay in strongholds and defend out city and not give a fight with them. We will preserve our strength and wait patiently for our chance. If Wang Shi Chong's troops have no chance to fight and they can go nowhere, they will be defeated within ten days." But Generals Chen Zhi Lue, Fan Wen Chao and Shan Xiong Xin all said, "There are only a few soldiers in Wang Shi Chong's army. And his troops have been defeated by us many times and have become scared. It is a rule in the art of war that if our force is double that of the enemy, we may fight a battle to defeat them. In the present situation our force is far more than double of Wang Shi Chong's force. We have an even greater chance to win the battle. Many generals from the areas of the Yangtze River and Huai River have recently joined us. They want very much to take this opportunity to render great military service. The morale in our army is high. If we lead an army like this in battle, we can overcome our enemy." Most of the generals present were excited by their words and they wanted a battle. Li Mi was confused by their suggestion and at last changed his mind and agreed with them. Pei Ren Ji tried very hard to persuade Li Mi to adopt his strategy but failed. He stamped his foot and said with a sigh, "You will regret this, one day." Wei Zheng said to Zheng Ting, who was in charge of strategic planning, "Li Mi has scored a tremendous victory over Yuwen Hua Ji but he won it at a great price. Many of his brave generals and men died in battles. The troops are very tired from fighting. It is difficult for our troops to meet Wang Shi Chong's troops in battlefields. Wang Shi Chong's food supply has run low and his troops will put up a desperate fight in order to survive. So we must not fight any battle with them at present. It would be better for us to have the soldiers dig deep ditches around our camps and build high strongholds to resist the attack by Wang Shi Chong's troops. When Wang Shi Chong has run out of food, he will have to retreat. Then we will launch a pursuit and we will be sure to win." Zhen Ting said, "Your words are just idle talk." Wei Zheng retorted by saying, "What I have suggested is the best plan. It is not at all idle talk." Then he got up from his seat and left angrily.

Cheng Zhi Jie was in command of the cavalrymen of the inner line and his soldiers were camped in Beimangshan Mountain with Li Mi. Shan Xiong Xin was in command of the cavalrymen in the outer line and camped in the north of the city of Yanshi. Wang Shi Chong sent several hundred cavalrymen across Tongji Canal to attack Shan Xiong Xin's camps. Li Mi sent Pei Xing Jian and Cheng Zhi Jie with an army to reinforce Shan Xiong Xin. Pei Xing Jian launched a charge to the enemy but was shot by an arrow and fell from his horse to the ground. Cheng Zhi Jie came to his aid. He killed several enemy soldiers and Wang Shi Chong's men retreated. Cheng Zhi Jie held Pei Xing Jian up from the ground and mounted his horse with Pei Xing Jian and rode back, but Wang Shi Chong's cavalrymen caught up with them. One of the pursuers pierced Cheng Zhi Jie with his spear. Cheng Zhi Jie turned back and broke the handle of the spear and at the same time killed the pursuer who had wounded him and then rode back in safety. At dusk both sides sounded the retreat and the soldiers turned back to their camps. Many valiant generals under Li Mi were seriously wounded in this battle. After his victory over Yuwen Hua Ji, Li Mi became proud and he underestimated the ability of Wang Shi Chong. He even did not deploy a strict watch at night against possible raids by Wang Shi Chong's army. That night, Wang Shi Chong dispatched two hundred cavalrymen to stealthily penetrate Beimangshan Mountain and conceal themselves in the valleys and beside the brooks. He ordered his soldiers to feed their horses and to sharpen their weapons. Then all his soldiers had their meal in their beds. At dawn of 10 September, before they went into battle, Wang Shi Chong's troops held a ceremony to pledge their determination to win. Wang Shi Chong said in the ceremony, "The battle today does not only decide whether we will win or lose. It is a matter of life and death. If we win, we will enjoy wealth and fame. If we lose, none of us will be able to come back alive. So today, we are not fighting for the sake of the state but actually fighting for our own lives. Let's fight bravely for victory!" In the morning, Wang Shi Chong led his men in the march to Li Mi's camps. Li Mi led his men out of the camps to meet them. Before Li Mi's troops were drawn into battle order, Wang Shi Chong ordered his men to charge. Wang Shi Chong's troops fought very bravely in and out of the battle formation of Li Mi's army.

Before the battle, Wang Shi Chong had found a man who resembled Li Mi and tied him up. When the battle was going on in great confusion, Wang Shi Chong showed the man between the battle formations of the two sides and shouted, "We have captured Li Mi!" Then all his men shouted "Long Live!" At the same time the cavalrymen who had concealed themselves in the mountain rode down quickly into the camps of Li Mi's army and set fires. Li Mi's army suffered a disastrous defeat. Li Mi's generals Zhang Tong Ren and Chen Zhi Lue surrendered to Wang Shi Chong. Li Mi rode to Luokou with about ten thousand men. That night, Wang Shi Chong laid siege to the city of Yanshi. Zhen Ting defended the city. But one of his subordinates opened the city gate and let Wang Shi Chong's army in. Li Mi's generals Pei Ren Ji, Zheng Ting, Zu Jun Yan and others were captured. After he had taken Yanshi, Wang Shi Chong directed his army to Luokou. Bing Yuan Zhen, the general in charge of the defense of Luokou, submitted to Wang Shi Chong and opened the city gate to let Wang Shi Chong into the city. Shan Xiong Xin also surrendered to Wang Shi Chong. Li Mi wanted to go to Liyang to join Xu Shi Ji. But one of his followers said to him, "On the day when you killed Zhai Rang, Xu Shi Ji was struck on the neck and was nearly killed. Today you have lost the battle and you are going to join him. Do you think that your safety may be guaranteed?" At that time, Wang Bo Dang gave up Jinyong and moved all his army to defend Heyang (now south of Mengxian, Henan Province). Li Mi went from Hulao (now in the west of Sishui Town, Xingyang, Henan Province) to Heyang to join Wang Bo Dang. Li Mi summoned all the generals to discuss what to do next. Li Mi wanted to use the area from the Yellow River north to Taihang Mountain (a mountain range between Shanxi Province and Hebei Province) as the base, which might be linked up with Liyang. From this base, Li Mi wanted to recover all the lost areas. But the generals said, "We have been defeated lately. The morale of the officers and men is very low. If we stay here, most of the officers and men will defect to Wang Shi Chong in a short time. The officers and men do not have the will and courage to fight. Then your cause may not be successful." Li Mi said, "My success depends on all the officers and men. If they do not want to fight for me, then my cause will surely fail. I will kill myself to express my apology to those who have fought for me." Then he stood up and drew out his sword and was ready to kill himself. Wang Bo Dong held him tightly preventing him from killing himself. All the generals attending the meeting cried bitterly. Then Li Mi said, "I intend to submit myself to Li Yuan, Emperor of Tang. You are welcome to go to Chang'an with me. Although I have not rendered good service to Emperor of Tang, I can guarantee that you will enjoy wealth and high rank." Liu Xie said, "You have the same ancestor as that of Li Yuan and you were once in good terms with him. Although you did not join him in the march to Guanzhong when he asked you to, you actually rendered your services by blocking the roads to Guanzhong, preventing the Sui army from getting there to fight against Li Yuan, so that Li Yuan could take Chang'an without much difficulty. You have actually contributed significantly to his success." All the generals agreed with him. Li Mi said to Wang Bo Dang, "You have a big family here to take care of. You'd better stay behind and not go with me to Chang'an." Wang Bo Dang said, "In the days when Liu Bang was confronting Xiang Yu, Xiao He, who became the premier of Han Dynasty, led his whole family to join Liu Bang. It is a pity that my brothers will not come to join you. I will resolutely go wherever you go. I will not leave you in times of difficulty. I will not regret following you even if I am killed on the battlefield." At his words, many people were moved to tears. About twenty thousand officers and men followed Li Mi to Chang'an.

When Li Mi reached Chang'an, he was warmly welcomed by Li Yuan. Li Yuan made him Duke of Xing. Li Yuan treated him as a close relative and often referred to him as "my brother." Li Mi was appointed Minister of Palace Supplies in charge of memorial ceremonies and banquets of the royal family. Not long later, some generals under Li Mi turned over to the Tang Dynasty. They were: Li Da

Yu, Liu De Wei, Jia Run Pu and Gao Ji Fu. After Li Mi left, most of the generals in charge of the defense of the cities originally under Li Mi, such as Qin Shu Bao and Cheng Zhi Jie, submitted themselves to Wang Shi Chong. Since then, Wang Shi Chong became the most powerful man in the areas of the Eastern Capital and south to the Yellow River. Emperor Yang Tong made Wang Shi Chong Duke of Zheng, and appointed him minister of war.

32. Li Shi Min's Contributions in the Expedition against Xue Ren Gao, the Emperor of Qin

In June 618, Xue Ju, the Emperor of Qin, invaded Jingzhou Prefecture (an area around Jingchuan, Gansu Province). Emperor Li Yuan of the Tang Dynasty appointed Li Shi Mi, the King of Qin, as the commander-in-chief to lead an army under eight commands to resist the advance of Xue Ju's army. Li Shi Min led his army in the march to Gaozhu (now north to Changwu, Shaanxi Province). In July, Xue Ju's army advanced to Gaozhu. Some of his troops even advanced to Binzhou (now the area of Binxian and Xunxian, Shaanxi Province) and to Qizhou (now the area of Fengxiang, Shaanxi Province). Li Shi Min ordered his officers and men to dig deep ditches and build strongholds but not to fight with the enemies. But it happened that Li Shi Min contracted malaria and was confined in bed. He entrusted the military affairs to Liu Wen Jing and Yin Kai Shan. He said to them, "Xue Ju has left his base and come a long way here. His food supply is short. His soldiers are tired. They are eager to fight. If they come to challenge for battle, you must not accept the challenge. I will defeat them when I recover." When they left Li Shi Min, Yin Kai Shan said to Liu Wen Jing, "The King of Qin has said this because he thinks that you do not have the ability to command the army against Xue Ju. If our enemies know that the king is ill, they will look down upon us. We must show our power to prevent them from attacking us." Then they drew up their army in battle orders in the southwest of Gaozhu. They thought they had more men than Xue Ju and so they were not vigilant against their enemies. Xue Ju sent some of his troops to secretly move to the rear of the Tang army and to prepare to start a surprise attack. On July 9, a battle was fought in Qianshuiyuan (in the northeast of Changwu, Shaanxi Province). The Tang army suffered a great setback. The armies under the eight commands were all defeated. Five out of ten soldiers were killed. Generals such as Murong Luo Hou, Li An Yuan, and Liu Hong Ji were killed in this battle. Li Shi Min had to return to Chang'an with his remaining army. Xue Ju occupied Gaozhu and made a show of the dead bodies of the Tang soldiers. Liu Wen Jing and Yin Kai Shi were removed from their positions as a punishment for their defeat.

In August, Xue Ju sent his son Xue Ren Gao to advance to Ningzhou (now Ningxian, Gansu Province) and lay siege to it. Xue Ren Gao's army was defeated by Hu Yan, the governor of Ningzhou, and had to retreat. Hao Yuan said to Xue Ju, "Now that the Tang army was recently defeated by our army, the people of the area of Guanzhong are shocked and that area is unstable. We must take this opportunity to march to Chang'an and take it." Xue Ju took his advice. But before he took any action, he fell seriously ill and died. His son Xue Ren Gao ascended the throne as Emperor of Qin. He stayed in the city of Xizhu (northeast of Jing-chuan, Gansu Province).

In August, Emperor Li Yuan of the Tang Dynasty appointed Li Shi Min as commander-in-chief of the army to launch an expedition against Xue Ren Gao. In November, Li Shi Min marched his army to Gaozhu (now north to Changwu, Shaanxi Province). Xue Ren Gao sent General Zong Luo Hou to resist Li Shi Min's army. Zong Luo Hou came to Li Shi Min's camps to challenge to battle. Li Shi Min ordered his officers and men to stay inside the camps and not to fight with Zong Luo Hou's army. His officers and men wanted to fight with the enemies, but Li Shi Min said, "Our army was recently defeated by our enemies. Morale is low. Our enemies are proud and look down upon us. We should shut the gates of our camps and wait for our chance. When our enemies are still prouder of themselves and our soldiers are eager to fight, we may overcome our enemies in one battle." Then he gave the order that those who dared to ask to fight would be put to death.

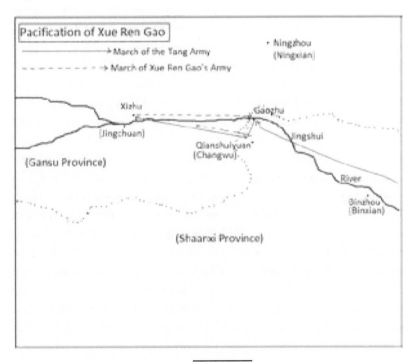

The two armies were in a stand-off with each other for sixty days. Xue Ren Gao's food supplies ran low. His general Liang Hu Lang with the soldiers under his command went to Gaozhu to surrender to Li Shi Min. Li Shi Mi learned that a good deal of discord had arisen between Xue Ren Gao and his men. So Li Shi Min ordered General Liang Shi to lead his men to pitch their camps in Qianshuiyuan to lure the enemies. When Zong Luo Hou saw that Li Shi Min's army had at last come out of their camps, he was overjoyed. He ordered all his men to charge the Tang army. But the soldiers under Liang Shi stood their ground within the advantageous natural barriers. There was no water inside the camps. The soldiers lived there without water for several days. Zong Luo Hou's army attacked fiercely. Li Shi Min estimated that Zong Luo Hou's men had got very tired from charging. Then he said to the generals around him, "Now it is time to charge." At dawn of November 7, Li Shi Min sent General Pang Yu to deploy his army in battle formation in Qianshuiyuan. Zong Luo Hou attacked Pang Yu's formation with all his troops. Pang Yu's army fought with all their might and they stood their ground with great difficulty, and the situation was very unfavorable to Pang Yu's army. At this critical moment, Li Shi Min led a great army in a surprise attack on Zong Luo Hou's army from the north of Qianshuiyuan. Zong Luo Hou commanded his army to deal with Li Shi Min's army. Li Shi Min commanded about forty valiant cavalrymen to attack Zong Luo Hou's battle formation. The Tang army attacked Zong Luo Hou's army on both sides, making loud war cries. Zong Luo Hou's army was defeated and ran away. Several thousand of Zong Luo Hou's men were killed. Li Shi Min commanded two thousand cavalrymen in the hot pursuit of the defeated army. Dou Gui tried to stop Li Shi Min by holding the reins of Li Shi Min's horse, saying, "Xue Ren Gao is still holding a city with strong walls and he still has a great army to defend the city. Although Zong Luo Hou has been defeated, we must not take them lightly and plunge ahead rashly. We'd better halt our army and make sure of the situation before we advance." Li Shi Min said, "I have thought about this for a long time. We have just won a victory. We must push on in the flush of this victory. This is a rare chance that we cannot afford to lose. Say no more, my dear uncle." Then he commanded his horsemen to ride forward at great speed. Xue Ren Gao deployed his men in front of the city wall. When Li Shi Min arrived, he occupied the other bank of Jingshui River and was ready to start an attack. Several generals under Xue Ren Gao left the battle formation and came over to surrender to Li Shi Min. Xue Ren Gao was shocked and commanded his men back into the city of Xizhu and prepared to resist Li Shi Min's army with the city walls. In dusk, Li Shi Min's main force arrived and laid siege to the city. At midnight, many of Xue Ren Gao's men got down from the city wall to surrender to the Tang army. Xue Ren Gao knew that he was at the end of his resources. The next day, Xue Ren Gao opened the city gate and surrendered to Li Shi Min.

All the generals under Li Shi Min came to express their congratulations on his great victory over Xue Ren Gao. They asked, "As soon as you won the first victory, you left the infantry behind and just commanded the cavalrymen to the city occupied by Xue Ren Gao, carrying no city assaulting devices. You pressed on to the foot of the city wall. We all thought it was impossible for you to take the city. But in the end, you succeeded. Can you tell us how?" Li Shi Min said, "All the officers and men under Zong Luo Hou's command were from the area of Long. The generals are fierce and the soldiers are brave fighters. I defeated his army by surprise attack. We did not kill or capture many of them. The main part of his army fled. If we had not pressed quickly and had let them escape into the city, Xue Ren Gao could have made use of these troops. Then it would be very difficult for us to storm the city. If we pressed very quickly to the city, leaving no chance for Zong Luo Hou's troops to enter the city to join Xue Ren Gao, most of Zong Luo Hou's soldiers would flee back to the area of Long. Xizhu's defense was weak. Xue Ren Gao was scared. He did not have the time to think of a good way to defend the city when we arrived at the foot of the city. That is the reason why we have overcome him." At his words, all the generals were convinced by Li Shi Min's wisdom.

Baitiwu, the horse that carried Li Shi Min in the battle against Xue Ren Gao

Li Shi Min put Xue Ren Gao's brothers, Zong Luo Hou and Zhai Chang Sun, in command of the soldiers who had surrendered, and even went hunting with them, showing no sign of distrust. They were in awe of him, and grateful, and were willing to serve him heart and soul. Emperor Li Yuan of the Tang Dynasty sent an envoy to Li Shi Min to convey his order that Xue Ren Gao and all his followers be executed because many of the Tang officers and men had been killed by Xue Ju and Xue Ren Gao. Li Mi tried to persuade Emperor Li Yuan by saying, "Xue Ju and his son Xue Ren Gao killed many innocent people. That is why they have been destroyed. Your Majesty should show mercy and kindness to the people who have surrendered and submitted to Your Majesty." Emperor Li Yuan accepted his advice and changed his order to the effect that only the chief plotters should be executed, while all the rest were to be granted pardons. Emperor Li Yuan sent Li Mi to Binzhou (now Binxian, Shaanxi Province) to welcome Li Shi Min. When Li Mi saw Li Shi Min, he was greatly surprised. He said to Yin Kai Shan, "He is a true hero. He is the only person who can pacify the whole realm." On November 22, Li Shi Min came back to Chang'an with his victorious army. Li Shi Min was warmly welcomed by the ministers of the Tang Dynasty.

33. Xu Shi Ji Comes Over to the Tang Dynasty

When Li Mi went to Chang'an with his followers, Xu Shi Ji remained in Liyang area, holding that area for Li Mi. Wei Zheng, one of the followers of Li Mi to Chang'an made a suggestion to Emperor Li Yuan of the Tang Dynasty to send him to pacify the area in the eastern area. Emperor Li Yuan appointed Wei Zheng as the envoy to the east to persuade the local lords in the east to come over to the Tang Dynasty. Wei Zheng went to Liyang and sent a letter to Xu Shi Ji to ask him to go over to the Tang Dynasty. Xu Shi Ji accepted his suggestion and made up his mind to go over to the Tang Dynasty. He said to his assistant Guo Xiao Ke, "The people and lands of this area belong to Li Mi, the original Duke of Wei. If I present the people and lands of this area to the Emperor of the Tang Dynasty in my name, people will think that I use the property of my former master to earn favor from the Emperor of the Tang Dynasty for myself. I do not want to leave such an impression on other people and I will be ashamed of myself if I do this. I should prepare a book listing the number of households, people and horses and lands of each county in this area and present it to Li Mi, Duke of Wei, so that Li Mi may present it to the Emperor of the Tang Dynasty." Xu Shi Ji sent Guo Xiao Ke to Chang'an to see the Emperor of the Tang Dynasty. When the Emperor received Guo Xiao Ke, Guo Xiao Ke did not present the book of the number of people and lands of the area of Liyang, but only gave a secret book to Li Mi. The

Emperor of the Tang Dynasty wondered why Guo Xiao Ke had not presented him the book with the number of people and lands of Liyang area under the jurisdiction of Xu Shi Ji since he had decided to change sides. Guo Xiao Ke told the Emperor that Xu Shi Ji did not want to give the Emperor the impression that Xu Shi Ji had owned that area and presented the area to the Emperor so as to earn favor from the Emperor; the area belonged to Li Mi, the Duke of Wei; he had given the book to Li Mi so that Li Mi could present it to the Emperor himself. After the Emperor understood his intention, he gave very high praise to Xu Shi Ji. He said, "Xu Shi Ji never forgets the kindness of his former master. He does not want to earn favor from the Emperor with his former master's property. He is really a devoted person." The Emperor granted the royal family name of Li to Xu Shi Ji. So Xu Shi Ji was renamed as Li Shi Ji. Later the second word "Shi" in his name was deleted. So his name became Li Ji.

34. The Death of Li Mi

Li Mi was not satisfied with the treatment by the Emperor of the Tang Dynasty after he had arrived Chang'an. He was put in charge of banquets given by the royal family. He felt insulted. After one banquet, he talked with General Wang Bo Dang. Wang Bo Dang was also unhappy about his treatment by the Emperor, so he said to Li Mi, "Now everything depends on your plan. You still have great power. Xu Shi Ji is now in control of Liyang area, and Zhang Shan Xiang is now in control of Xiangcheng. Vast areas to the east of Xiaoshan Mountain are under the control of the generals formerly under you. There are not many armies in the area to the south of the Yellow River. You don't need to stay in this position for long." Li Mi was glad at his words.

One day, Li Mi said to the Emperor, "I have been here for quite a long time and Your Majesty has treated me kindly. I have been in the capital for a long time without doing any service to Your Majesty. Now many generals to the east of the Xiaoshan Mountain are formerly under my command. If Your Majesty sends me to that area to gather all of them together, under the great support of the Tang Dynasty, it will be very easy for me to defeat Wang Shi Chong." The Emperor knew that most of the generals formerly under Li Mi had not submitted to Wang Shi Chong, so he was about to agree with Li Mi's suggestion. But when the Emperor discussed this matter with his ministers, most of them were against the suggestion. They said, "Li Mi is a very cunning and treacherous man. If Your Majesty lets him go back to the the area to the east of the Xiaoshan Mountain, it would be releasing a harnessed tiger back to the wild mountains. He will not come back anymore." The Emperor said, "Whether a man can be an emperor is at Heaven's will. It is not at any person's own will. If he betrays and leaves me, I will let him go. If he goes to the east and fights with Wang Shi Chong, that is fine. I will benefit from their fighting with each other."

So the Emperor decided to send Li Mi to the east to gather his former subordinates. Li Mi asked the Emperor to let Jia Run Pu go with him. The Emperor agreed. Before they left the capital, the Emperor invited them to dinner. The Emperor proposed a toast, saying, "Now we three are drinking a toast to express that we shall work closely towards the same goal. I hope you will achieve great success in this mission. You have made a very solemn promise. I hope you will keep your promise. Some of my ministers were strongly against your going back to the east. But I have faith in you. I will not listen to words that harm the relation between you and me." Li Mi and Jia Run Pu knelt down to accept their mission from the Emperor. Wang Bo Dang was also sent as the deputy of Li Mi.

When Li Mi reached Huazhou (now Weinan, Shaanxi Province), the Emperor ordered him to leave half of the army to defend Huazhou and lead the other half to go out of Hanguguan Pass into the east. Zhang Bao De, chief secretary of the army, was afraid that Li Mi would run away and he would be punished for this. So he wrote a secret report to the Emperor saying that he was sure that Li Mi would betray the Emperor. When the Emperor got the report, he changed his mind. In order not to scare Li Mi, the Emperor gave the order that the army should go on its mission, but Li Mi should go back to the capital to take up some other mission. Li Mi got the order when he reached Chousang (now in the north of Lingbao, Henan Province). Li Mi said to Jia Run Pu, "The Emperor has sent me to carry out the mission, but now suddenly calls me back without any reason. The Emperor once said that some of his ministers were strongly against my going on the mission. Some ministers must have succeeded in telling to the Emperor some slanderous words against me. If I go back to Chang'an, I will surely be killed. It would be better for us to attack and take Taolin County. We may take the army and the food stored in Taolin County to go north across the Yellow River. When we reach the north of the Yellow River, the Tang army cannot catch up with us. When we reach Liyang and join forces with Xu Shi Ji, we will achieve our goal. What do you think?" Jia Run Pu said, "The Emperor has been very kind to you. And it is very clear that the whole country will belong to the Li family. The whole country will be unified as one. You have submitted yourself to the Emperor. Why should you turn against him? Ren Gui and Shi Wan Bao are now generals in charge of Xiongzhou and Guzhou. If you rebel in the morning, their army will arrive here in the evening. Even if you take the city of Taolin, you don't have the time to muster your troops. Once you are declared a traitor, nobody will be on your side. I think you'd better obey the order and go back to the capital to see the Emperor, to show that you have no intention to rebel. You will prove yourself true to the Emperor. You may wait for another chance to accomplish your ambition to recover the area to the east of the Xiaoshan Mountain." Li Mi said angrily, "The Emperor of the Tang Dynasty has humiliated me by appointing me the minister in charge of royal banquets. It is in the book of prophecy that the Li Family will be emperor. I also bear the family name of Li. I also have the chance to be emperor. The Emperor of the Tang Dynasty has not killed me, but instead, he has let me go out of his control. This shows that it is Heaven's will that I should be emperor. The Emperor of the Tang Dynasty owns the area of Guanzhong. I will own the area to the east of the Xiaoshan Mountain. Heaven has granted this area to me. I should take this gift from Heaven. Why should I give this gift to others? You are my best friend. Why should you give such a suggestion? If you disagree with me, I will kill you before I go on with my journey." Jia Run Pu said, with tears in his eyes, "Although your name is also in the book of prophecy, it seems that Heaven has appointed Li Yuan emperor. Your chances are very dim. You went over to the Emperor of the Tang Dynasty when you had been defeated by Wang Shi Chong. Now the whole country is divided into many parts and occupied by those who have great armies. This time, if you betray the Emperor, you will have no one to depend on. No one will commit himself to you. After you killed Zhai Rang, the generals under you all said that you were an ungrateful person. No one will hand the army under him over to you. The generals are all afraid that you will take the military power from them, and they will resist you. You have lost your area of influence. You will have no place to stay. Since I am your close friend, I have spoken very frankly. I hope you will think about it." Li Mi was so angry that he raised his sword and was about to kill Jia Run Pu. Wang Bo Dang and others begged him to spare Jia Run Pu. Li Mi at last let Jia Run Pu go. Jia Run Pu went to Xiongzhou (now Yiyang, Henan Province). Wang Bo Dang also tried to persuade Li Mi to give up his plan, but Li Mi would not listen to him. Wang Bo Dang said, "I am your true follower. I will not change my mind even if death threatens ahead. If you would not listen to me, then I will have to die with you. But even if I die, that does not do much good to your course."

Li Mi killed the envoy sent by the Emperor of the Tang Dynasty. On December 30, Li Mi reached Taolin. He wrote to the governor of Taolin that the Emperor had called him back to the capital and he wanted to leave his family members in the county city. Li Mi had several brave soldiers put on women's clothes in disguise as his wife and concubines. When they entered the city, they took off their women's clothes, started a surprise attack and took the city. Then they drove all the soldiers in the city and carried all the food stored in the city to go east very quickly towards Nan Shan Mountain (in the area of Shanxian, Henan Province). At the same time, he wrote a letter to Zhang Shan Xiang, his former subordinate who was at that time in control of Yizhou (now Xiangcheng, Henan Province), asking him to come to help him.

General Shi Wan Bao, who was in charge of Xiongzhou, discussed the situation with the army commander Sheng Yan Shi. Shi Wan Bao said, "Li Mi is a brave man. Wang Bo Dang is also a brave man. They have rebelled against the Emperor. It is difficult to stop them." Sheng Yan Shi said with a smile, "If you send me with several thousand men, I will kill them and bring their heads to you." Shi Wan Bao asked, "What strategy will you use?" Sheng Yan Shi said, "It is a secret. I cannot tell you at present." Then he commanded his army into Xiong'ershan Mountain (to the south of Yiyang, Henan Province). He laid an ambush along a road. He deployed archers in high places on both sides of the road, and soldiers who carried swords and spears hid themselves in the valley by a brook. He gave the order that when half of Li Mi's men crossed the brook, all the archers should shoot their arrows and the soldiers hiding in the valley should attack Li Mi's soldiers. One of the officers asked Sheng Yan Shi, "I hear that Li Mi is going east towards Luozhou. But you have led us to the south of Xiong'ershan Mountain. Can you tell me why?" Sheng Yan Shi said, "Li Mi declares that he is going to the east to Luozhou, but his true intention is to go south to Xiangcheng to join force with Zhang Shan Xiang. If Li Mi enters the valley and we pursue him from behind, we cannot spread out our force because the path is narrow. If he just sends one person to protect his rear, we can do nothing about it. Now we have entered the valley first and occupied the vital places. I am sure we will kill Li Mi this time."

Li Mi's army marched through the area of Shanzhou (now Shanxian, Henan Province) without resistance. Then he led his army to turn south into Xiong'ershan Mountain. Li Mi thought that there would not be any trouble for the rest of the journey since they had come into the mountain. But when his army came to the south of the mountain into the valley, Sheng Yan Shi's army suddenly attacked. Li Mi and Wang Bo Dang were both killed. Sheng Yan Shi sent the heads of Li Mi and Wang Bo Dang to Chang'an, the capital. For his service, Sheng Yan Shi was made Duke of Geguo.

At that time, Li Ji was in Liyang. The Emperor of the Tang Dynasty sent an envoy with Li Mi's head to Liyang. The envoy showed the head of Li Mi to Li Ji and told him how Li Mi had rebelled against the Emperor of the Tang Dynasty. Li Ji cried bitterly and bowed to Li Mi's head. He sent a letter to the Emperor asking permission to bury Li Mi's dead body. The Emperor gave the order to send Li Mi's dead body to Liyang. Li Ji put Li Mi's head and body together and held a mourning ceremony. Li Ji was dressed in white as if he was mourning for his monarch. Li Mi was buried in the south of Liyangshan Mountain.

35. Wang Shi Chong Declares Himself Emperor of Zheng

Since Li Mi left the area of Luoshui River, Wang Shi Chong became the most powerful man in that area. He occupied Luoyang, the Eastern capital of the Sui Dynasty. Yang Tong, the Emperor of the Sui Dynasty, was under his control. Wang Shi Chong had a great army and a lot of followers. Yang Tong knew that Wang Shi Chong was ambitious; Wang Shi Chong would someday depose him and ascend the throne himself. Although Yang Tong knew Wang Zhi Chong's ambition, he could do nothing about it, because he had no army.

On 19 January 619, Wang Shi Chong invaded the area of Guzhou (now Xin'an, Henan Province). Wang Shi Chong appointed Qin Shu Bao and Cheng Zhi Jie as generals. But Qin Shu Bao and Cheng Zhi Jie knew that Wang Shi Chong was a treacherous man. Cheng Zhi Jie said to Qin Shu Bao, "Wang Shi Chong is a narrow-minded man. He likes to utter imprecations. He is more like a witch than a ruler. He is not a monarch who can pacify the present chaos." They made up their minds to turn over to the Emperor of the Tang Dynasty. Wang Shi Chong's army and the Tang army fought in Jiuju (now a place to the north of Yiyang, Hanan Province). Qin Shu Bao and Cheng Zhi Jie were in the battle formation. They rode out of their formation with several followers to Wang Shi Chong. They got down from their horses and bowed to Wang Shi Chong and said, "We are grateful for the kindness shown to us. We really want to render service to repay your kindness. But you are always suspicious of us, and believe slanderous talk. You are not the master for whom we should render our service. We have come to say farewell to you." After saying that, they jumped up their horses and rode very quickly to the side of the Tang army. The Emperor of the Tang Dynasty was very glad that Qin Shu Bao and Cheng Zhi Jie had come over. He placed them under the command of Li Shi Min, King of Qin. Li Shi Min had heard about them for a long time. Li Shi Min appointed Qin Shu Bao as commander-in-chief of the cavalry, and Cheng Zhi Jie as commander-in-chief of the third army of the left wing. At that time, Generals Li Jun Xian and Liu Tian An under Wang Shi Chong also resented Wang Shi Chong. They also went over to the Tang Dynasty. Li Shi Min appointed Li Jun Xian as a member of the general staff, Liu Tian An as commander-in-chief of the fourth army of the right wing.

When Wang Shi Chong led his army and all his supporters to attack Xin'an (now in Henan Province), he was actually carrying out his plan to usurp the throne of the Sui Dynasty. He thought that he was powerful enough to usurp the throne, so he took all his supporters to Xin'an to discuss how to force the present emperor to step down from the throne and let him ascend it. Li Shi Ying was strongly against this idea. He said, "Now many lords have come to join you because you are powerful enough to revitalize the Sui Dynasty. If you now declare a plan to ascend the throne, I am afraid that all these lords will be disappointed and will leave you." Wang Shi Chong said, "You are right." Wei Jie and Yang Xu said, "It is very clear that the rule of the Sui Dynasty has come to an end. Ascending the throne is a special matter. You should make the decision by yourself. It is not necessary to discuss this matter with others." Yue De Yong said, "Heaven has shown signs that the change of dynasty will occur this year. If you don't seize the chance and act timely, you will lose the chance to be the emperor." Wang Shi Chong agreed with their ideas. They decided that as the first step to the throne, Wang Shi Chong should send somebody to see the Emperor of the Sui Dynasty to ask him to grant Wang Shi Chong the nine symbols of supreme power (horses and carriage, embroidered robes, bows and arrows, guards, musical instruments, gates painted red, battle axe and so on).

Duan Da was sent to see Emperor Yang Tong of the Sui Dynasty to ask him to grant Wang Shi Chong the nine symbols of power. Emperor Yang Tong said, "The Duke of Zheng has been rewarded for his service of defeating Li Mi. He has been promoted to the minister of war. Recently, he has not rendered great service. There is no reason to grant him anything." Duan Da said, "The Duke of Zheng wants them." Emperor Yang Tong stared at Duan Da and said, "Do as you like." On 12 March 619, Duan Da declared in the name of Emperor Yang Tong of the Sui Dynasty that Wang Shi Chong was appointed premier. Wang Shi Chong was made King of Zheng and was granted the nine symbols of power.

On 2 April 619, Wang Shi Chong sent Duan Da to see Emperor Yang Tong again. Duan Da said to the Emperor, "Now the King of Zheng is very powerful. It is destined that the King of Zheng will be the emperor. We hope your Majesty will give up the throne and let the King of Zheng have it." Emperor Yang Tong said angrily, "The Sui Dynasty was established by my great grandfather. If this dynasty should last, you are forbidden to say such things. If it is the end of this dynasty, the King of Zheng may just take the throne. It is not necessary to ask me to give up the throne and let him have it."

On 5 April 619, Wang Shi Chong declared that Emperor Yang Tong of the Sui Dynasty had agreed to give up the throne and let Wang Shi Chong ascend it. At the same time, he sent his elder brother Wang Shi Yun to put Emperor Yang Tong of the Sui Dynasty under house arrest. On 6 April, Wang Shi Chong ascended the throne of the Zheng Dynasty. On April 10, he made his son Wang Xuan Ying crown prince, his second son Wang Xuan Shu King of Han. He made his elder brother Wang Shi Yun King of Qi. His brothers were all made kings. Those who had helped him ascend the throne, such as Duan Da, Yun Ding Xing, Zhang Jin and Du Yan, were given high-ranking positions.

Some generals did not like Wang Shi Chong. They conspired to overthrow him and put the former Sui emperor back to the throne. Their conspiracy was discovered and they were all put to death. Wang Shi Yun said to Wang Shi Chong, "Some generals conspired to rebel because the deposed emperor of the Sui Dynasty is still alive. We'd better kill the deposed Emperor." Wang Shi Chong agreed with him. Wang Shi Chong sent Wang Ren Ze to carry out this task. Wang Ren Ze went to the place where the deposed emperor was kept and ordered the deposed emperor to drink a bowl of poisoned wine. The deposed emperor said, "Please ask the King of Zheng to spare my life. He once said that he would treat me well." But his request was turned down. Then he begged them to let him say farewell to his mother. This request was turned down too. Then he spread a sheet of cloth on the floor and burned incense. He knelt down and said his prayer: "I wish from now on, if I am reborn, I should not be born in a royal family." Then he took the bowl and drank up the poisoned wine. The poisoned wine was not enough to kill him. So they strangled him to death with a rope round his neck.

36. Dou Jian De Declares Himself Emperor of Xia

After Yuwen Hua Ji was defeated by Li Mi, he ran away to Liaocheng (now in the west part of Shandong Province), taking with him Empress Xiao, wife of Emperor Yang Guang of the Sui Dynasty. He used the treasures he had taken from the palace in Jiangdu to buy over Wang Bo, the head of the local forces, to help him defend Liaocheng.

Dou Jian De said to his subordinates, "We are subjects of the Sui Dynasty. The Emperor of the Sui Dynasty is our monarch. Now Yuwen Hua Ji has killed our monarch, so he is our enemy. We must carry out an expedition against him." So Dou Jian De raised a great army to march to Liaocheng.

In February 619, Dou Jian De and Yuwen Hua Ji fought several battles outside Liaocheng. Dou Jian De defeated Yuwen Hua Ji, who retreated into Liaocheng. Dou Jian De ordered his army to storm the city. Wang Bo opened the city gates and let the army in. Dou Jian De went into the city and captured Yuwen Hua Ji. Then he went to see Empress Xiao, and said a few words of consolation. He also captured Yang Zheng Dao, the grandson of Emperor Yang Guang of the Sui Dynasty. He held a grand ceremony to mourn for the late emperor. Then he arrested those who had actively taken part in killing Emperor Yang Guang of the Sui Dynasty, such as Yuwen Zhi Ji, and killed them. He brought Yuwen Hua Ji and his sons back to Xiangguo (now Xingtai, Hebei Province), his capital, and executed them there.

In September 619, Dou Jian De marched his army southward to invade Xiang-zhou (now Anyang, Henan Province). Li Shen Tong, King of Huai'an and the governor of the area to the north of the Yellow River (who had been sent by Emperor

Li Yuan of the Tang Dynasty to bring order to the area north of the Yellow River in October 618), could not resist the attack by Dou Jian De. He had to retreat to Liyang. After Dou Jian De had taken Xiangzhou, he attacked Liyang (now Xunx-ian, Henan Province). Li Ji, the commander-in-chief of the Tang army in Liyang, could not withstand the attack by Dou Jian De's army and the city of Liyang fell, too. Li Ji, Li Shen Tong and Princess Tong'an (who was the younger sister of Emperor Li Yuan of the Tang Dynasty), were captured. Dou Jian De treated Li Shen Tong and Princess Tong'an kindly. He put them in very good houses and treated them as guests. He released Li Ji and appointed him commander-in-chief of the army in Liyang. But in January 620 Li Ji ran away to Chang'an, the capital of the Tang Dynasty.

At that time, Dou Jian De was friendly with Wang Shi Chong. But when Wang Chong ascended the throne in Luoyang and murdered Emperor Yang Tong of the Sui Dynasty, Dou Jian De severed all relations with Wang Shi Chong, and declared himself Emperor of Xia.

37. The Situation in the Eastern Turkic Khanate

In February 619, Shibi Khan commanded a great army to cross the Yellow River and reached Xiazhou (now Uxin Qi, Inner Mongolia Autonomous Region; in Sui Dynasty it was Shuofang). Liang Shi Du led an army to join forces with Shibi Khan. They planned to invade Taiyuan (now the area around Taiyuan, Shanxi Province). But Shibi Khan died that month. His son Ashina Shibobi was still very young and could not be made khan; instead, he was made Nibu Shad (chief of a sub tribe) and was sent to the east part of the Eastern Turkic Khanate (near the area of Beijing). Shibi Khan's younger brother Ashina Silifu was made Chuluo Khan. Then Chuluo Khan took Shibi Khan's wife Princess Yicheng as his own wife. Chuluo Khan knew that Empress Xiao, wife of Emperor Yang Guang of the Sui Dynasty, and Yang Zheng Dao, the grandson of Emperor Yang Guang of the Sui Dynasty, were in the hands of Dou Jian De, and in February 620, he sent an army to Mingzhou to get Empress Xiao and Yang Zheng Dao and escort them to the Eastern Turkic Khanate. Dou Jian De did not dare to refuse to let them go. So Empress Xiao and Yang Zheng Dao were escorted to the court of Chuluo Khan.

In June of that year, Chuluo Khan died. Princess Yicheng did not make Chu-luo Khan's son Aoshe Shad khan, because Aoshe Shad was a weak man. She made Chuluo Khan's younger brother Ashina Duobi khan, and he became Jiali Khan. After Ashina Duobi became Jiali Khan, he took Princess Yicheng as his wife, thus ensuring she would continue to be honored and provided for, according to the social customs of the Turks in those days. At the same time Jiali Khan made his nephew Ashina Shibobi a junior khan. So Ashina Shibobi became Tuli Khan.

38. The Death of Liu Wen Jing

Liu Wen Jing, the minister of civil affairs, thought that he had greater ability than Pei Ji and had made greater contributions in the establishment of the Tang Dynasty than Pei Ji. But Pei Ji held an official position much higher than his. So Liu Wen Jing hated Pei Ji very much. Whenever Emperor Li Yuan held court to discuss state matters, Liu Wen Jing was always against any suggestion put forward by Pei Ji and he insulted Pei Ji several times publicly. One day in September 619, he was drinking wine with his brother Liu Wen Qi. When he was half drunk, he drew out his sword and struck it on a pillar, saying, "I will cut off Pei Ji's head someday." It happens that Liu Wen Jing's house was haunted. One night, Liu Wen Jing's brother Liu Wen Qi invited necromancers to the house to drive out the spirits. They performed their sorcery, waving their swords with their hair in disarray. One of Liu Wen Jing's concubines who had been out of favor lately secretly told her elder brother that Liu Wen Jing was plotting a rebellion and urged him to tell the Emperor. The Emperor issued an order to arrest Liu Wen Jing and throw him into jail. The Emperor sent Pei Ji and Xiao Yu to interrogate him. In the interrogation, Liu Wen Jing said, "When we held the uprising in Jinyang, I was appointed the officer in charge of military supplies. I felt disgraced. Now Pei Ji holds the position of a premier. He has grand houses. My contributions are no less than those of Pei Ji. But I have a much lower rank and have such a miserable house I cannot protect my mother from the wind and rain. I am very unhappy about it. So I uttered a few words of complaint when I was drunk." After the Emperor got the report, he said to the ministers at court, "From what Liu Wen Jing has said, it is clear that he is planning a rebellion." Li Gang and Xiao Yu said that Liu Wen Jing had no such intention. Li Shi Min protected Liu Wen Jing, saying, "It is Liu Wen Jing who first made the plan in Jinyang to hold an uprising again the Sui Dynasty. Pei Ji was told of the plan only later. But when we had taken Chang'an and taken control, Liu Wen Jing was appointed a position much lower than that of Pei Ji. He did have some complaints, but he has no intention of starting a rebellion." Pei Ji said to the Emperor, "Liu Wen Jing is really a resourceful man. He has greater strategic abilities than anyone else. But he is treacherous. Now the situation is still unstable. If we do not kill him today and spare him this time, he will cause trouble later." The Emperor thought for a long time. At last he took Pei Ji's advice. Liu Wen Jin and his brother Liu Wen Qi were executed on the same day.

39. Li Shi Min Defeats Liu Wu Zhou

After Liu Wu Zhou became governor of Mayi (now Shuozhou, in the north part of Shanxi Province), he began expanding his territory. In April 619, he colluded with the Turks and marched southward to invade Bingzhou (now the area around Taiyuan, Shanxi Province). His army and the Turkic army were stationed in Huangsheling (in the north of Yuci, Shanxi Province). Li Yuan Ji, the fourth son of Li Yuan, was the chief commander of Taiyang area. Li Yuan Ji ordered General Zhang Da to attack Liu Wu Zhou's army in Huangsheling with some infantry. General Zhang Da refused to go because he thought there was no chance of succeeding against Liu Wu Zhou's strong army with such a small force. But Li Yuan Ji made him go. As soon as the battle began, all the soldiers under Zhang Da were killed, and Zhang Da was captured by Liu Wu Zhou. Zhang Da was very angry with Li Yuan Ji, so he switched sides and led Liu Wu Zhou's army to attack Yuci. Very soon, Yuci fell into the hands of Liu Wu Zhou. On 18 April, Liu Wu Zhou's army laid siege to the city of Bingzhou (now in the area around Taiyuan, Shanxi Province) but was repulsed by the army under Li Yuan Ji. On 19 May, Liu Wu Zhou's army attacked Pingyao (now Pingyao, Shanxi Province) and took it.

Song Jin Gang, a leader of a band of rebels in Yizhou (now Yixian, Hebei Province), was defeated by Dou Jian De. He led four thousand men to join Liu Wu Zhou. Liu Wu Zhou knew that Song Jin Gang was very good at the art of war, so he made him King of Song and entrusted him with military affairs. He gave half of his property to him. Song Jin Gang was so grateful to Liu Wu Zhou that he divorced his wife and married Liu Wu Zhou's sister. He succeeded in persuading Liu Wu Zhou to take Jinyang. Liu Wu Zhou appointed Song Jin Gang chief commander of the southern expedition army. In June 619, Song Jin Gang led an army of thirty thousand men to invade Bingzhou; Liu Wu Zhou led an army to invade Jiezhou (now Jiexiu, Shanxi Province) and took it. The Emperor of the Tang Dynasty ordered Li Zhong Wen to attack Liu Wu Zhou. Liu Wu Zhou and Huang Zi Ying led an army to Queshugu (in the south of Jiexiu, Shanxi Province). Liu Wu Zhou sent his horsemen to challenge Li Zhong Wen. Li Zhong Wen sent his army to fight with Liu Wu Zhou's horsemen. As soon as the two armies met, the horsemen retreated. Li Zhong Wen and his army gave hot pursuit, but were ambushed. The Tang army was defeated, and Li Zhong Wen was captured. But Li Zhong Wen managed to escape and returned to Chang'an, the capital of the Tang Dynasty. And the Emperor of the Tang Dynasty sent him to fight with Liu Wu Zhou again.

The Emperor of the Tang Dynasty was worried about Liu Wu Zhou's invasion. Pei Ji, the premier, offered to take charge. The Emperor, much relieved, appointed Pei Ji commander-in-chief of Jinzhou area (now Linfen, Shanxi Province) to conduct the expedition against Liu Wu Zhou.

On 12 September 619, Pei Ji reached Jiexiu. Song Jin Gang defended the city of Jiexiu against the Tang army. Pei Ji stationed his army in Dusuoyuan (in the Mianshan Mountain, southwest to Jiexiu, Shanxi Province). His soldiers got their drinking water from streams flowing from the mountain. Song Jin Gang sent soldiers to block the upper part of the streams so that no water could flow downstream. With no more drinking water, Pei Ji moved his army to a different place where they could get water. While Pei Ji's army was underway, Song Jin Gang led his army to attack them. Pei Ji's army was in great disorder, and soon they fled from the battlefield. Pei Ji lost all the army and fled to Jinzhou alone. He wrote a letter to the Emperor of the Tang Dynasty asking to be punished for his defeat. But the Emperor did not blame him; instead, the Emperor put him in charge of the defense of Hedong (now the area of the whole Shanxi Province).

Liu Wu Zhou's army marched towards Jinyang (Taiyuan, Shanxi Province). Li Yuan Ji, who was responsible for the defense of the city, was very afraid and decided to run away. He said to General Liu De Wei, "I will lead the strongest soldiers out of the city to fight with Liu Wu Zhou's army. You will stay in the city with the weaker soldiers to defend the city." At night on 16 September 619,

Li Yuan Ji led the army out of the city, bringing his wife and concubines and children with him. He fled all the way to Chang'an. As soon as Li Yuan Ji left, the city of Taiyuan fell into Liu Wu Zhou's hands.

After he had occupied Taiyang, Liu Wu Zhou sent Song Jin Gang to attack Jinzhou (now Linfen, Shanxi Province). Song Jin Gang soon took Jinzhou. Then he pressed to Jiangzhou (now Xinjiang, Shanxi Province) and took Longmen (now in Shanxi Province). Longmen was situated on the east bank of the Yellow River. If Song Jin Gang's army crossed the Yellow River, Chang'an, the capital of the Tang Dynasty, would be in danger. And to make the situation worse, Wang Xing Ben, an enemy of the Tang Dynasty, had occupied Pufan (now Puzhou, Shanxi Province), a place just beside the Yellow River. Wang Xing Ben united with Song Jin Gang, becoming a great threat to the Tang Dynasty.

In October 619, Liu Wu Zhou and Song Jin Gang attacked Kuaizhou (now Yicheng, Shanxi Province) and took it. Pei Ji, the commander-in-chief of the Tang army in Jin area (now Shanxi Province), was a coward. He did not have the ability to command the Tang army to fight against Liu Wu Zhou's powerful army. He ordered all the people in those areas to leave their homes and withdraw into the cities and fortresses, and he ordered the Tang soldiers to burn all the properties the people had left behind. The people in those areas were outraged. Under the leadership of Lu Chong Mao, the people of Xiaxian (now Xiaxian, Shanxi Province) rose up against the Tang Dynasty and took the city. The Emperor of the Tang Dynasty ordered Li Xiao Ji, King of Yong'an, to lead an army to suppress the rebellion.

These rapid developments threw the Emperor of the Tang Dynasty into great panic. He issued an imperial order to give up the land to the east of the Yellow River. The imperial order read, "Liu Wu Zhou's army is very powerful. It is very difficult for our army to resist it. We will have to give up the areas east of the Yellow River and concentrate all our army to defend the area of Guanzhong." Li Shi Min presented a memorandum to his father, the Emperor of the Tang Dynasty, which read, "Taiyuan is the base of the Tang Dynasty. The areas to the east of the Yellow River are rich. The capital depends on many supplies from those areas. I will feel uneasy if we give up those areas. If Your Majesty puts thirty thousand men under my command, I will defeat Liu Wu Zhou and recover the areas occupied by him." The Emperor agreed with him and put all the men he could mobilize under Li Shi Min's command. On 20 October, the Emperor of the Tang Dynasty went to Huayin (now Huayin, Shaanxi Province). He held a ceremony in Changchun Palace to see Li Shi Min off on his mission to conquer Liu Wu Zhou.

In November 619, Li Shi Min commanded his army to march across the Yellow River from a place near Longmen (now in Shanxi Province) while the Yellow River was frozen. He stationed his army in Bobi (in the southwest of Xinjiang,

Shanxi Province), confronting with Song Jin Gang's army. At that time, as all the food storages had been looted, the army under Li Shi Min could not get supplies from these depots. Most of the people in that area had withdrawn into cities or fortresses in order to avoid Song Jin Gang's army. So Li Shi Min's army could not get food from the local people, either. Li Shi Min issued an announcement telling the local people that he was leading an army to fight against Song Jin Gang. When the people knew that Li Shi Min had come, they all came back to their homes. Then Li Shi Min bought food from the people, so his army got their supplies. And then Li Shi Min ordered his army to stay within the camps and not to fight with the enemy.

One day, Li Shi Min with several horsemen went out to reconnoiter the enemy encampment. When they got close to the enemy camps, they all spread out. Only one guard was with him. After reconnoitering, Li Shi Min went up a hill with his guard and there they lay down and fell asleep. Song Jin Gang's men saw them and came out of their camps to catch them. Li Shi Min and his guard were sleeping so hard that they did not know that the enemy soldiers were approaching. It happened that a rat being chased by a snake hit the guard in the face and the guard woke up. He was shocked to see that the enemy soldiers were so close. He woke Li Shi Min and they jumped on their horses and took off, but soon the enemy soldiers caught up with them. Li Shi Min drew his bow and shot one of his long arrows at the enemy general. The general was killed, and the soldiers had to give up the pursuit.

Lü Chong Mao, a local man of Xiaxian (now Xiaxian, Shanxi Province), killed the governor of Xiaxian and organized an army to rebel against the Tang Dynasty. He declared himself King of Wei. The Emperor of the Tang Dynasty sent Li Xiao Ji, King of Yong'an, to command an army to suppress the rebellion. Yu Jun, the commander-in-chief of the Tang army in Shanzhou (now Shanxian, Henan Province) was under the command of Li Xiao Ji. In late December 619, the army of the Tang Dynasty commanded by Li Xiao Ji attacked Xiaxian. Lü Chong Mao asked Song Jin Gang for help. Song Jin Gang sent General Yuchi Jing De and General Xun Xiang to rescue him. They led an army secretly and quickly to Xiaxian and attacked and defeated the Tang army under Li Xiao Ji. Li Xiao Ji was captured. He tried to escape, but was killed. Having defeated the Tang army, Yuchi Jing De and Xun Xiang were on their way back to Kuaizhou. Li Shi Min sent Generals Yin Kai Shan and Qin Shu Bao to attack the army under Yuchi Jing De and Xun Xiang on their way back. A battle was fought in Meiliangchuan (in the south of Wenxi, Shanxi Province). Yuchi Jing De and Xun Xiangs' army was defeated. Yuchi Jing De and Xun Xiang ran back to Kuaizhou (now Yicheng, Shanxi Province).

Not long later, Yuchi Jing De and Xun Xiang led an army to rescue Wang Xing Ben in Pufan. Li Shi Min personally led three thousand men through small roads to make a shortcut to Anyi (now Yuncheng, Shanxi Province) and attacked the army under Yuchi Jing De and Xun Xiang on their way to Pufan. The Tang army defeated the enemy. All the soldiers under Yuchi Jing De and Xun Xiang were captured. Only Yuchi Jing De and Xun Xiang escaped back to Kuaizhou. Li Shi Min led the victorious army back to Bobi.

Pei Ji was defeated by Liu Wu Zhou's army many times and was not able to stabilize the situation in the Jin area (now Shanxi Province). The Emperor of the Tang Dynasty was very angry. So he called him back to Chang'an and scolded him severely for his defeat. Then the Emperor handed him over to the minister of justice for further investigation of his crimes. But not much later, the Emperor changed his mind and released Pei Ji, and treated him kindly as before.

The officers and men of the Tang army stayed in their camps for quite a long time. They were getting impatient. Some of the generals went to see Li Shi Min to ask him to let them go and fight Song Jin Gang's army. Li Shi Min explained, "Song Jin Gang has led a great army far away from his base to this place. His generals and soldiers are brave. Liu Wu Zhou has occupied Taiyuan. Song Jin Gang has provided strong protection for Liu Wu Zhou. But his army does not have much food. They are subsisting by looting. His food supply is low. He wants to fight a decisive battle before he runs out of food. We, on the other hand, have sufficient food supplies. We can wait till he runs out of food and the morale of his army runs low. Then we can dispatch troops to the areas of Fen and Xi to threaten his rear. When he runs out of food, he has to withdraw. We must wait till that moment has come."

In January 620, General Qin Wu Tong of the Tang army attacked Wang Xing Ben in Pufan (now in the area of Puzhou, Shanxi Province). Wang Xing Ben came out of the city to fight, but he was defeated and had to withdraw into the city. Soon thereafter, his army ran out of food and there were no reinforcements. He wanted to make a breakthrough and run away, but no one would follow him. So on 14 January, he opened the city gate to surrender. On 17 January, the Emperor of the Tang Dynasty came to Puzhou (now Puzhou, Shanxi Province). Wang Xing Ben was executed on that day. Li Shi Min came to Puzhou to see the Emperor of the Tang Dynasty. Song Jin Gang led his army to lay siege to the city of Jiangzhou. On 29 January, the Emperor of the Tang Dynasty left Puzhou for Chang'an.

On 14 April 620, Song Jin Gang ran out of food and began to retreat to the north. Li Shi Min ordered his army to pursue them. Li Shi Min caught up with Xun Xiang's army in Lüzhou (now Huozhou, Shanxi Province) and defeated it. Li Shi Min led his victorious army in a continued pursuit of the defeated enemy.

They went after them for one day and one night without any rest, covering a distance of a hundred kilometers. They fought eight battles along the way and won great victories. When they reached Gaobiling (in the south of Lingshi, Shanxi Province), General Liu Hong Ji stopped Li Shi Min's horse, saying, "Your Highness has defeated the enemy and pursued the enemy here. You have rendered great service. I think it is too dangerous to penetrate too deep into the enemy rear. You'd better take care of yourself. The soldiers are now hungry and tired. We may stay here till the food convoy arrives and the soldiers have eaten. Then we may continue our pursuit." Li Shi Min said, "Song Jin Gang is now at the end of his resources and has run away. His officers and men do not have the fighting spirit. Such chances are hard to come by, but easy to lose. I must take this advantage of our victory to destroy the enemy completely. If we stay here and let Song Jin Gang catch his breath and make a plan to cope with us, then it will be impossible to destroy him. I am determined to sacrifice myself for the country. I will do my best even in the face of danger." After saying that, he urged his horse to gallop forward. His officers and men had to follow him. They caught up with Song Jin Gang in Queshugu (in the southwest of Jiexiu, Shanxi Province). Eight battles were fought in one day and Li Shi Min's army won all of them. They killed and captured tens of thousands of soldiers. At night, they pitched camps in the west part of Queshugu. Li Shi Min had not eaten for two days and had kept his armor on for three days. There was only one goat left, and Li Shi Min shared the goat with all his officers and men.

On 23 March 620, Li Shi Min led his army to Jiexiu. Song Jin Gang still had twenty thousand men. He deployed his men outside the south gate of the city from north to south. Li Shi Min sent Li Ji to attack the enemy battle formation, but the attack was not successful. Li Shi Min led his cavalrymen to attack the enemy formation from behind the formation and defeated the enemy. Three thousand of Song Jin Gang's men were killed. Song Jin Gang fled. Li Shi Min and his cavalrymen pursued the enemy for more than twenty kilometers. Li Shi Min reached Zhangnanbao, a stronghold still held by the Tang army. The generals holding the fortress did not know that it was Li Shi Min, so they did not let him in. Li Shi Min took off his helmet to show that he was really Li Shi Min. The defenders cheered loudly, and many of them were so happy that they shed tears because they had been in the enemy rear for quite a long time and still held the stronghold for the Tang Dynasty. They opened the gate to let Li Shi Min and his men in. Li Shi Min's followers told the general that Li Shi Min had not had food for several days. The general immediately prepared food for Li Shi Min and his men.

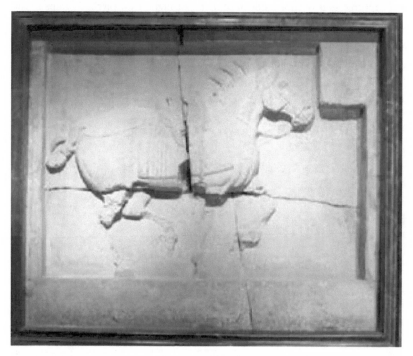

Teqinbiao, the horse that carried Li Shi Min in the battle against Song Jin Gang

After Song Jin Gang left Jiexiu, Yuchi Jing De and Xun Xiang gathered all the soldiers left behind to defend the city of Jiexiu. Li Shi Min sent Li Dao Zong and Yuwen Shi Ji to persuade Yuchi Jing De and Xun Xiang to surrender. And indeed, Yuchi Jing De and Xun Xiang surrendered and presented the cities of Jiexiu and Yong'an (now Huozhou, Shanxi Province) to Li Shi Min. When Yuchi Jing De surrendered, Li Shi Min was very pleased. He appointed Yuchi Jing De general in command of the eight thousand men originally under him. The army under Yuchi Jing De camped among the camps of the other armies under Li Shin Min. Qutu Tong was worried that Yuchi Jing De would rebel; he told Li Shi Min of his worries, but Li Shi Min would not listen to him.

When Liu Wu Zhou got the news that Song Jin Gong had been defeated, he gave up Bingzhou (the area of Taiyuan, Shanxi Province) and ran away to the area under the rule of the Turks. Song Jin Gang gathered all the army left by Liu Wu Zhou and wanted to fight against Li Shi Min, but the soldiers would not fight anymore. So Song Jin Gong also ran into the area of the Turks, but very soon they killed him. Not long later, Liu Wu Zhou was also killed by the Turks.

Li Shi Min marched his army northward and recovered Jinyang (Taiyuan) and Bingzhou. The whole area to the east of the Yellow River was under control. The Emperor of the Tang Dynasty appointed Li Zhong Wen commander-in-chief of the army in Bingzhou. By the end of May, Li Shi Min returned to Chang'an.

40. Li Shi Min Conquers Wang Shi Chong and Dou Jian De

The Emperor of the Tang Dynasty decided to attack Wang Shi Chong. On 1 July 620, the Emperor of the Tang Dynasty appointed Li Shi Min commander-in-chief of all the armies sent to attack Wang Shi Chong.

On 21 July, Li Shi Min reached Xin'an (now Xin'an, Henan Province). Wang Shi Chong sent Wang Hong Lie, King of Wi, to defend Xiangyang (now Xiangcheng, Henan Province), Wang Xing Ben, King of Jing, to defend Hulao (now in the west of Sishui Town, Xingyang, Henan Province), Wang Tai, King of Song, to defend Huaizhou (also called Henei, now Qinyang, Henan Province), Wang Shi Yun, King of Qi, to defend the south city of Luoyang, Wang Shi Wei, King of Chu, to defend the city proper, Wang Xuan Ying, the crown prince, to defend the east city, Wang Xuan Shu, King of Han, to defend Hanjiacheng, Wang Dao Xun, King of Lu, to defend Yaoyicheng. Wang Shi Chong led all the generals and soldiers, thirty thousand in all, to cope with the attack by the Tang army.

General Luo Shi Xin of the Tang army led the vanguards to lay siege to Cijian (now in a place to the west of Luoyang, Henan Province). Wang Shi Chong led thirty thousand men to rescue the city. On 28 July, Li Shi Min led some cavalrymen to reconnoiter Wang Shi Chong's camps. Incidentally, Li Shi Min and his small force met with a great army led by Wang Shi Chong himself. Wang Shi Chong's army surrounded Li Shi Min and his few troops. Li Shi Min drew his bow to shoot and killed many of Wang Shi Chong's officers and men and captured one of Wang Shi Chong's generals. Wang Shi Chong had to retreat. Li Shi Min went back to his own camp. The next morning, Li Shi Min led fifty thousand men to Cijian. Wang Shi Chong had to withdraw from Cijian back to Luoyang. Li Shi Min ordered general Shi Wan Bao to march from Yiyang (now in Henan Province) to Longmen, General Liu De Wei to attack Henei (now Qin-yang, Henan Province), General Wang Jun Kuo to block the food supply line in Luokou (now northeast of Gongyi, Henan Province), General Huang Jun Han to attack Huiluocheng (now Yanshi, Henan Province) from Heyin (now Mengjin, Henan Province). Li Shi Min's great army was stationed in Beimang (Beimang-shan Mountain, which is situated to the north of Luoyang, Henan Province).

On 14 August 620, General Huang Jun Han sent his army to attack Huiluo-cheng and took it. Wang Shi Chong sent his son Wang Ying Xuan, the crown prince, to retake Huiluocheng, but he failed to recapture it. Since Huiluocheng was quite close to the city of Luoyang, Wang Shi Chong ordered his soldiers to build a half-moon shaped fortress to the west of Huiluocheng. He left some troops there to defend it.

Wang Shi Chong deployed his army in battle formation near Qingcheng For-tress, which was situated in the northwest of Luoyang. Li Shi Min also deployed his army in battle formation nearby. Wang Shi Chong called across the stream to Li Shi Min, "Since the fall the Sui Dynasty, your father Li Yuan has become the Emperor of the Tang Dynasty in the area of Guanzhong, and I have become the Emperor of Zheng in the area south to the Yellow River. I have never in-vaded your territory in the west. But you have raised a great army to invade my territory in the east. You have come a long way here and your supply lines are stretched. The outcome of this war is still pending." Li Shi Min called back, "All the people across the realm have submitted to the Emperor of the Tang Dynasty. But you have refused to submit and prevented the people here from submitting to the Tang Dynasty. The people in the east are longing for the army of the Tang Dynasty to come. Now the righteous and courageous troops from Guanzhong are doing their best to save the people in the east. We have carried out an ex-pedition against you. If you surrender, I am sure you may still enjoy wealth and rank. If you intend to resist our army, then it is no use talking anymore." Wang Shi Chong said, "Shall we stop fighting each other and have a peace talk?" Li Shi Min answered, "I have got the order to take the Eastern Capital. I have not been authorized to negotiate peace with you." The two armies confronted with each other till night fell.

In order to concentrate all the strength to defeat Wang Shi Chong, the Emperor of the Tang Dynasty sent an envoy to Dou Jian De to establish a friendly relationship with him. Dou Jian De agreed. In order to show his sincerity, he released Princess Tong'an and sent guards to escort her back to Chang'an. Princess Tong'an was the younger sister of the Emperor of the Tang Dynasty. Princess Tong'an, together with Li Shen Tong, King of Huai'an, and Wei Zheng, had been captured as early as October 619, when Dou Jian De attacked Liyang (now Xunxian, Henan Province).

On 17 August 620, General Shi Wan Bao attacked Ganquan Fortress. On the same day, Li Shi Min sent General Wang Jun Kuo to attack Huanyuan (a pass in Huanyuan Mountain in Goushi, Henan Province). Wang Jun Kuo took Huanyuan. Wang Shi Chong sent General Wei Yin to attack Wang Jun Kuo. Wang Jun Kuo pretended to be defeated and withdrew. Wei Yin gave pursuit, but was ambushed and was defeated. Wang Jun Kuo pursued Wei Yin to Guancheng (now Zhengzhou, Henan Province), then turned back to Huanyuan.

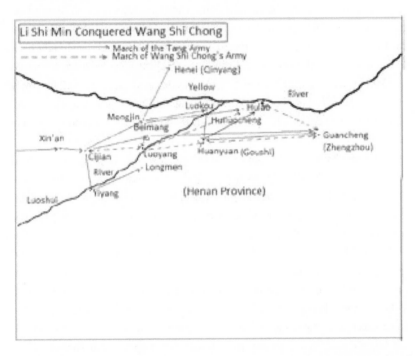

Xun Xiang, the general who together with Yuchi Jing De had surrendered to Li Shi Min after Song Jin Gang had been defeated, betrayed the Tang Dynasty and ran away. The Generals suspected that Yuchi Jing De would also defect and run away, so they put him in prison. Qutu Tong and Yin Kai Shan said to Li Shi Min, "Yuchi Jing De is a fierce general. Now that he has been put in prison, he must be very angry. If he is released, he will cause trouble in the future. We'd better kill him." Li Shi Min said, "No, I don't think so. If he had intended to defect, he would have done it before Xun Xiang." He ordered that Yuchi Jing De be set free immediately. He invited Yuchi Jing De into his tent and gave him a lot of gold. He said, "You and I are alike in temperament and should trust each other. I hope you will forget this unhappy incident. I never listen to slanderous words, and never kill faithful people. If you really want to leave, I will help you with this gold. After all, we have worked together for some time."

On 21 August, Li Shi Min went on an inspection tour of the battlefield with five hundred cavalrymen. Then they went up the tomb of Emperor Xuanwu of the Wei Dynasty in Beimang Mountain to the north of Luoyang. Suddenly, Wang Shi Chong appeared with more than ten thousand men; they surrounded Li Shi Min and his men. Shan Xiong Xin rode toward Li Shi Min with his spear pointing at him. At this critical moment, Yuchi Jing De jumped on his horse, shouting. With his spear, Yuchi Jing De struck Shan Xiong Xin off his horse. Wang Shi Chong's army backed off a little bit. Yuchi Jing De protected Li Shi Min and broke through the encirclement. Then they led the cavalrymen to attack Wang Shi Chong's army. They rode into the enemy battle formation from the front and fought through to the back of the formation, and then fought back to the front. They did this several times. Later, Qutu Tong led a great army to join in the battle. Wang Shi Chong's army was defeated and he himself narrowly escaped. Chen Zhi Lue, a commander of Wang Shi Chong's army, was captured. More than a thousand of his men were killed and more than six thousand were captured.

After the battle, Li Shi Min exclaimed to Yuchi Jing De, "You have repaid me so soon!" Li Shi Min rewarded him handsomely with gold and silver. From then on, Yuchi Jing De became Li Shi Min's most favorite general. Yuchi Jing De was very good at dodging spears. In battle, he would ride into the enemy battle formation solo, several enemy generals tried to kill him with their spears. But every time, he successfully dodged their spears and did not get hurt. He could grab spears from the hands of enemy fighters and kill them with their own weapons. Li Yuan Ji, King of Qi, was very good at fighting on horseback with a spear. When he got to know that Yuchi Jing De was good at dodging spears, he wanted to have a contest. He requested that the spearheads should be removed, but Yuchi Jing De said, "I will remove the point from my spear. Your Highness does not need to remove yours." In the contest, Li Yuan Ji tried with all his skill to hit Yuchi Jing De, but he could never hit him. Li Shi Min asked Yuchi Jing De, "Which is more difficult, to dodge a spear or to grab the spear from the hands of the enemy?" Yuchi Jing De said, "It is more difficult to grab the spear from the enemy." Then Li Shi Min asked Yuchi Jing De to grab the spear from Li Yuan Ji's hands. Li Yuan Ji went at him again but still could not hit Yuchi Jing De; while

Yuchi Jing De grabbed the spear from Li Yuan Ji's hands three times. Outwardly, Li Yuan Ji highly praised Yuchi Jing De, but inwardly, he resented him.

The war against Wang Shi Chong went on successfully. On 15 October 620, General Luo Shi Xin attacked Xiashi Fortress which was situated nine kilometers northwest of Luoyang, and took it. Then he laid siege to Qianjin Fortress which was situated in the north of Luoyang. The defenders of Qianjin cursed Luo Shi Xin. At night, Luo Shi Xin ordered a hundred soldiers to slip toward the foot of the fortress, carrying thirty babies. Then they made the babies cry. One of the soldiers said loudly, "We have come from the Eastern Capital to join General Luo Shi Xin." Not long later, one of the men at the foot of the fortress cried, "This is Qianjin Fortress. We have come to the wrong place!" Then they left. The defenders thought that Luo Shi Xin's men had left and that the people who had just come were really just refugees from the Eastern Capital. So they decided to go out to pursue Luo Shi Xin's army. But as soon as they opened the city gate and went out of the fortress, the soldiers under Luo Shi Xin who had secluded themselves nearby rushed into the fortress and took it.

Yang Qing, the commander of Wang Shi Chong's army in Guancheng (now Zhengzhou, Henan Province) decided to surrender to the Tang Dynasty. He sent an envoy to see Li Shi Min. Then Li Shi Min sent Li Ji to take over the city of Guancheng. At that time, Wang Shi Chong's eldest son Wang Xuan Ying was in Hulao (now in the west of Sishui Town, Xingyang, Henan Province). When he got news that Yang Qing had surrendered to the Tang Dynasty, he commanded a great army to Guancheng but was defeated by the army under Li Ji. Wang Xuan Ying had to go back to Hulao.

Wang Shi Chong saw that the situation was very unfavorable to him. He sent an envoy to Dou Jian De for help although Dou Jian De was his enemy because Wang Shi Chong had invaded Liyang (now Xunxian, Henan Province), which belonged to Dou Jian De, and in retaliation, Dou Jian De had taken Yinzhou (now Anyang, Henan Province), which belonged to Wang Shi Chong. At first, Dou Jian De would not rescue Wang Shi Chong, but Liu Bin, a member of his staff, said, "Now the whole country is in great chaos. The Tang Dynasty has got the area of Guanzhong. The Zheng Dynasty has got the area to the south of the Yellow River. The Xia Dynasty has got the area to the north of the Yellow River. These three Dynasties are almost equally strong. They are like the three legs of a tripod. But the Tang army is attacking the Zheng Dynasty, and since this autumn, the Tang army has grown stronger and stronger, and the territory of the Zheng Dynasty has been greatly reduced. The Zheng Dynasty will not be able to withstand them, and someday it will be destroyed. If the Zheng Dynasty is destroyed, the Xia Dynasty alone will not be able to stand against the Tang Dynasty. It is better to give up the hatred between Your Majesty and the Emperor of the Zheng

Dynasty and send our army to rescue Wang Shi Chong. If the Xia Dynasty army attacks the Tang army from outside, and the army of the Zheng Dynasty attacks it from inside, then we are sure to defeat the Tang army. After the Tang army retreats, we may wait for the situation to change. If conditions permit, we may defeat the Zheng Dynasty. Then we may use the armies of the two dynasties to attack the Tang Dynasty. Then we may unify the whole country." Dou Jian De took his advice. In January 621, Dou Jian De sent an envoy to Wang Shi Chong, telling him that he had promised to send an army to rescue him. At the same time, Dou Jian De sent an envoy to Li Shi Min asking him to withdraw all the army surrounding Luoyang to Tongguan Pass and return the lands to Wang Shi Chong. Li Shi Min detained the envoy sent by Dou Jian De and did not give any reply. Wang Shi Chong sent his brother's son Wang Wan and Zhangsun An Shi with gifts of gold and jade to Dou Jian De to urge him to rescue Luoyang.

Li Shi Min chose about one thousand of his bravest cavalrymen. All of them were dressed in black and wore black armor. He divided these one thousand men into several detachments. He appointed Qin Shu Bao, Cheng Zhi Jie, Yuchi Jing De and Zhai Chang Sun as commanders. In every battle, Li Shi Min put on black armor and led them in a vanguard. They could break all enemy resistance. On 28 January 621, Qutu Tong and Dou Gui were leading some troops on patrol of the camps in Beimang Mountain. Wang Shi Chong launched a sudden attack on them. Qutu Tong and Dou Gui could not resist the attack and retreated. Li Shi Min led his black armored detachments to rescue them. Wang Shi Chong's army was defeated. The Tang army captured the commander of Wang Shi Chong's cavalrymen. Six thousand of Wang Shi Chong's men were killed or captured in this battle, but Wang Shi Chong escaped. He rode back to Luoyang.

On 3 February, Wang Shi Chong's crown prince Wang Xuan Ying led an army of six thousand men to escort a food convoy from Hulao (now in the west of Sishui Town, Xingyang, Henan Province) to Luoyang. Li Shi Min sent General Li Jun Xian to attack him on the way. Li Jun Xian defeated the army escorting the convoy. Wang Xuan Ying had a very narrow escape.

Li Shi Min thought it was time to attack Luoyang city. He sent Yuwen Shi Ji to the Emperor of the Tang Dynasty to ask permission to launch the operation. The Emperor said, "Go back and tell the King of Qin that the purpose of attacking Luoyang is to end the war. When Luoyang is taken, all the public properties should be sealed. The jade objects and silk fabrics should be distributed among the officers and men."

On 13 February 621, Li Shi Min moved his army to Qingcheng Fortress which was situated in Xiyuan, a royal park to the west of Luoyang. Before Li Shi Min's army could establish their camps and build barricades, Wang Shi Chong led twenty thousand men out of the west gate of Luoyang and arrayed his army along the Gushui River to oppose the Tang army. All the Tang generals were afraid because they were not ready to fight. Li Shi Min deployed his special troops in Beimang Mountain. Then he went up the tomb of Emperor Xuanwu of the Wei Dynasty to inspect the situation. He said to the generals around him, "Now Wang Shi Chong is in a very difficult situation. He has dispatched all the army he could gather for a desperate fight. If we defeat him today, he will not dare to send any army out of the city to fight with us." Then he ordered Qutu Tong to lead five thousand men across Gushui River to attack Wang Shi Chong's battle formation. He told Qutu Tong to make a smoke signal as soon as his army started fighting. When Li Shi Min saw the smoke, he led his special troops to ride southward to join in the fighting. Li Shi Min wanted to know how strong the enemy formation was. He led about thirty cavalrymen and rode into the enemy formation. They entered from the front and slashed through to the back of the formation, then fought back to the front. Wang Shi Chong's soldiers were overcome with fear and ran away. But when Li Shi Min was fighting, he lost contact with the others. Only General Qiu Xing Gong was with him. Wang Shi Chong's cavalrymen were pursuing them. Suddenly, Li Shi Min's horse was struck by an arrow and could not gallop any more. Qiu Xing Gong turned back and drew his bow. He shot down several pursuers, and Wang Shi Chong's cavalrymen fell back for some time. Qiu Xing Gong jumped dawn from his horse and let Li Shi Min mount the horse. He walked with his long knife in his hand in front of the horse. He jumped this way and that, shouting loudly. He killed several enemy soldiers. Thus Li Shi Min and Qiu Xing Gong made their breakthrough. Wang Shi Chong was also fighting valiantly. His troops were scattered, then they gathered again. The battle went on from eight in the morning till noon. Then Wang Shi Chong withdrew his army into the city. Li Shi Min ordered his men to pursue the enemy till they reached the city wall. Then Li Shi Min laid siege to the city. In this battle, seven thousand men under Wang Shi Chong were killed or captured.

The city of Luoyang was heavily defended. There were stone launchers, which could catapult twenty-kilo stones for a distance of two hundred feet. The defenders put eight bows together forming a wheel which could shoot arrows as big as axes for a distance of five hundred feet. Li Shi Min's army attacked the city day and night for ten days, but their attacks were not successful. The officers and men of the Tang army were worn out and wanted go back. Even General Liu Hong Ji suggested to Li Shi Min that they withdraw from Luoyang and go back. Li Shi Min said, "We have come here with a great army. We must defeat Wang Shi Chong once and for all. The cities in the east have all been submitted to us. Luoyang is isolated. It cannot resist our attack for a long time. Victory will belong to us. Why should we give up the attack and go back when we are on the brink of victory?" Then he issued an order to the army, "If Luoyang is not taken, the army will not go back. Anyone who dares to mention turning back will be put to death." From then on, no one dared to say anything about this. The Emperor of the Tang Dynasty heard how the war was gong, and secretly sent a message to Li Shi Min urging him to withdraw the army. Li Shi Min wrote a memorandum to the Emperor telling him that Luoyang would surely be taken. Then he sent Feng De Yi, one of his staff officers, to Chang'an to present an analysis of the situation to the Emperor. Feng De Yi said to the Emperor, "Although Wang Shi Chong has occupied a vast area, the people are not willing to obey him. His orders are only effective in the city of Luoyang. Wang Shi Chong is now at the end of his resources. The city of Luoyang will be taken sooner or later. If we withdraw now, Wang Shi Chong will revitalize and unite with other warlords. Then it will be more difficult for us to conquer him." Then, the Emperor gave the consent to continue the siege of Luoyang. Li Shi Min wrote a letter to Wang Shi Chong, telling him what would be waiting for him if he would not surrender, but Wang Shi Chong did not give any reply.

On 30 February, Shen Yue, the commander of the army under Wang Shi Chong in Guancheng (now Zhengzhou, Henan Province) surrendered the city to General Li Ji. That night, General Wang Jun Kuo sprang a surprise attack on Hulao (now in the west of Sishui Town, Xingyang, Henan Province) and took it. Wang Xing Ben, King of Jing made by Wang Shi Chong, was captured.

Saluzi, the horse that carried Li Shi Min in the battle against Wang Shi Chong; General Qiu Xing Gong was pulling out an arrow that had hit the horse

Since the Tang army had laid siege to the city of Luoyang, no food supplies could be transported into that city. The food ran out, and many people died of hunger. Even high-ranking officials were starving and many of them died.

In November 620, Dou Jian De led his army to cross the Yellow River to the area of Caozhou (now Caoxian, in the southwest of Shandong Province) to attack Meng Hai Gong, the leader of a peasant uprising in the area of Caozhou. In February 621, Meng Hai Gong was captured by Dou Jian De's army. Then Meng Hai Gong surrendered to Dou Jian De. In March 621, Dou Jian De left General Fan Yuan to defend Caozhou and he himself led a great army to rescue Wang Shi Chong. Dou Jian De's army reached Huazhou (now Huaxian, Henan Province). Han Hong, Wang Shi Chong's general defending Huazhou, opened the city gate to let Dou Jian De's army into the city. On 24 March 621, he took Guanzhou (in the area of Zhengzhou, Henan Province). Then he occupied Xingyang (now Xingyang, Henan Province) and Yangzhai (now Yuzhou, Henan Province). His army marched along the Yellow River, and at the same time, his ships loaded with food supply sailed up the Yellow River. Wang Shi Chong's younger brother Wang Shi Bian sent General Guo Shi Heng to lead several thousand men to join force with Dou Jian De's army. There were more than a hundred thousand men in Dou Jian De's army. Dou Jian De stationed his army in Chenggao (now Sishui Town, Xingyang, Henan Province). Then he sent an envoy to Wang Shi Chong to tell Wang Shi Chong that he had come to rescue him.

Dou Jian De sent an envoy to Li Shi Min in January 621 demanding Li Shi Min to withdraw his army to Tongguan Pass and return the lands to Wang Shi Chong. Li Shi Min gathered all his generals together to discuss the situation. Many generals held the opinion that they should avoid fighting with Dou Jian De. But Guo Xiao Ke said, "Now Wang Shi Chong is in a great difficult situation. He will soon be captured. Dou Jian De has come all the way to rescue him. It is the will of Heaven that Dou Jian De and Wang Shi Chong should be destroyed together. We should take advantage of the natural barrier in Hulao to resist Dou Jian De. When there is opportunity, we may send an army to defeat him." Then Xue Shou, one of Li Shi Min's staff officers, said, "Now Wang Shi Chong is defending Luoyang, the Eastern Capital. He still has a lot in his treasury. His soldiers are brave ones chosen from the eastern area. What he needs is food. We have blocked his food supply. This is the reason why he cannot fight with us. And this is the reason why he cannot stand fast for very long. Dou Jian De has come a long way here with his great army to rescue Wang Shi Chong. His soldiers are also brave fighters. They will fight desperately with us. If we let Dou Jiang De's army reach here so they can join with Wang Shi Chong's army, and let the food from the north arrive in Luoyang, it will be disastrous for us. That would be just the beginning of the war. And I cannot see when it will end. The day of reunification for the whole country will never come. Now I think our plan should be this. We can split our army in two; one of them will continue the siege to Luoyang, digging deep ditches and building strong camps. If Wang Shi Chong comes out for a battle, they should stay in camp and not fight. Your Highness will lead the best troops to take Chenggao. When Dou Jian De comes, Your Highness will fight him. Once Dou Jian De is defeated, Wang Shi Chong will be defeated. I think, within twenty days, these two chiefs will be captured." Li Shi Min highly praised their suggestions. Xiao Yu, Qutu Tong and Feng De Yi said, "Our soldiers have been fighting for a long time and they are all very tired. Wang Shi Chong is now defending Luoyang resolutely with the high walls of this city. We cannot take this city in a short time. Dou Jian De has just defeated Meng Hai Gong. He is now taking his victorious army to fight with us. We are being attacked from the front and the rear. We'd better withdraw to Xin'an and wait for the right chance to come." Li Shi Min said, "Wang Shi Chong's army is now disheartened and they have run out of food. There is dissension and discord among Wang Shi Chong and his generals and ministers. We don't need to attack the city and we may just sit and wait, and the city will fall into our hands. Dou Jian De has just defeated Meng Hai Gong. His generals are proud and his soldiers are tired. We may use the natural barriers in Hulao to prevent Dou Jian De from going to Luoyang. If he dares to fight us, we can easily defeat him. If he hesitates and stops advancing, then within a month Wang Shi Chong will collapse and Luoyang will fall into our hands. The strength of our army will be doubled. Then we will be able to overcome two enemies at the same time. On the other hand, if we don't act immediately and let Dou Jian De take Hulao, then the two armies will join forces and will become very powerful. Then there will be no chance for us to defeat them. I have made up my mind." Qutu Tong asked for permission to raise the siege of Luoyang and withdraw the army to strategic points to wait for the situation to change. But Li Shi Min refused to give permission. He divided the army into two equal halves. One half was under the command of Li Yuan Ji, King of Qi. This half of the army would continue the siege of Luoyang. Qutu Tong was assigned to assist Li Yuan Ji. On 24 March 621 Li Shi Min led three thousand five hundred brave soldiers to march eastward to Hulao Pass. They left Luoyang at noon. They passed Beimang Mountain to Heyang (now Mengxian, Henan Province). Then they turned to Gongxian (now northeast of Gongyi, Henan Province). When Li Shi Min's army started their march, Wang Shi Chong was at the top of the city wall and saw the army leaving. He did not know where that army was going, so he did not send his army out to fight.

Qingzhui, the horse that carried Li Shi Min in the battle against Dou Jian De

On 25 March, Li Shi Min entered Hulao (a pass in the West of Sishui Town, Xingyang, Henan Province). On 26 March, Li Shi Min led five hundred cavalry-men to ride to a place ten kilometers east of Hulao to reconnoiter Dou Jian De's army camps. On the way, he spread his cavalrymen along both sides of the road, in hiding. He appointed Li Ji, Cheng Zhi Jie, and Qin Shu Bao to command these cavalrymen. Li Shi Min went forward just with four cavalrymen. He said to Yuchi Jing De, "I will use my bow, and you will use your spear. We can fend off a million enemy soldiers with my bow and your spear." But some time later, he said, "The best plan is that we should turn back when the enemy soldiers see us." They rode on till they were a thousand meters away from the enemy camps. Li Shi Min saw a group of Dou Jian De's troops, and he shouted, "I am Li Shi Min." Then he drew his bow and shot an arrow. The general commanding that group of troops was killed. Dou Jian De sent six thousand cavalrymen to run after Li Shi Min. The cavalrymen with Li Shi Min were afraid when they saw so many enemy soldiers coming after them. Li Shi Min said to them, "You just ride on. Yuchi Jing De and I will protect the rear." Then they turned back and rode slowly. When the enemy got close to them, Li Shi Min shot one of his arrows and killed one more enemy soldier. The enemy stopped advancing for a moment. Then Li Shi Min retreated again. Then the enemy advanced and got close again. Li Shi Min drew his bow again and killed one more enemy soldier. They repeated this several times until the enemy entered the place where the ambush had been laid. Li Ji, Cheng Zhi Jie and Qin Shu Bao led the cavalrymen to spring upon the enemy. They killed six hundred enemy soldiers, and captured two of their generals.

After the battle, Li Shi Min wrote a letter to Dou Jian De: "The areas of Zhao and Wei belonged to the Tang Dynasty. Now you have occupied these areas. But since you have treated Li Shen Tong, King of Huai'an, quite politely and you have sent envoys to escort Princess Tong'an back to Chang'an, we have given up the hatred between us. Recently, you have become friendly with Wang Shi Chong. You have gone back on your own words. Wang Shi Chong will be destroyed sooner or later. You have led all your army to rescue him. You have acted in the interest of other people. You have wasted a lot of resources for the interest of other people. This is not a clever policy. The battle today is just a clash of the vanguards. We have blocked your way to rescue Wang Shi Chong. You will not be able to accomplish your task. We hope you will stop advancing. You will regret if you don't listen to my advice."

Dou Jian De's army was blocked in front of Hulao for almost a month and could not move a step further. The officers and men under him were longing for home. Ling Jing, one of his ministers, said to Dou Jian De, "I suggest that the whole army of Your Majesty should cross the Yellow River and take Huaizhou and Heyang. Troops may be sent to defend these cities. Then the main force may pass Taihang Mountain and enter the area of Shangdang. Then Your Majesty may take the areas of Fen and Jin; then our army may advance to Pujin. We have three advantages by doing this: firstly, we will march in areas without much defense, so we are sure to win; secondly, we may expand our territory and have more population, and we may be strengthened; thirdly, the Tang Dynasty which occupies the area of Guanzhong will be threatened, and the Emperor of the Tang Dynasty will have to raise siege from Luoyang and withdraw his army to defend the area of Guanzhong. This is by far the best plan." Dou Jian De was going to take his advice, but Wang Shi Chong's envoys came one after another, urging Dou Jian De to relieve Luoyang. Wang Wan and Zhangsun An Shi begged Dou Jian De to relieve Luoyang everyday. They bribed the generals under Dou Jian De to prevent Dou Jian De from accepting the plan suggested by Ling Jing. The Generals said to Dou Jian De, "Ling Jing is a scholar. He does not know much about military affairs. Your Majesty should not take his advice." Then Dou Jian De said to Ling Jing, "Now the generals are very resolute to fight. I have decided to fight a decisive battle with Li Shi Min. With their resolute fighting spirit, I will be sure to win." Ling Jing argued fiercely. Dou Jian De was furious and ordered his guards to throw him out. Then Dou Jian De's wife said to him, "There may be something in Ling Jing's suggestion. Now the defense of the area of Guanzhong is weak. If Your Majesty leads your army into the Taihang Mountain from Fukou Passes into Taihang Mountain, and unites with the Turks to attack the area of Guanzhong, the Emperor of the Tang Dynasty has to raise the siege from Luoyang and withdraw his army to defend Guanzhong. Our army has stayed here for a long time. The soldiers are tired and so much food and materials have been wasted. If we continue like this, it is impossible for us to win." Dou Jian De said, "I have come to rescue the Zheng Dynasty because it is in a perilous situation. If I go away now, others would say that I am afraid of the enemy and I would be breaking my promise to rescue Wang Shi Chong. I will not do that." Dou Jian De decided to fight a decisive battle with the Tang army.

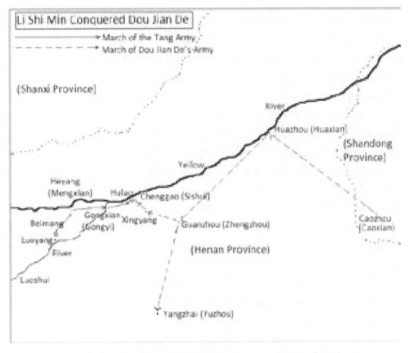

A spy reported to Li Shi Min, "Dou Jian De must know that the Tang army has run out of fodder for the horses. And the horses have to be put to the pastureland north of the Yellow River. Dou Jian De has decided to make use of this opportunity to start a surprise attack to Hulao." On 1 May, Li Shi Min made a tour to the future battlefield and reconnoitered the enemy camps. Then he left a thousand horses on o the green island in the Yellow River so that the enemy would believe that the Tang army had really run out of feed for the horses and the horses could not be used in battle.

In the morning of 2 May, Dou Jian De led all his army to battle. He deployed his army in battle formation from the southern bank of the Yellow River to the eastern bank of Sishui River. The battle formation was as long as ten kilometers. The whole battle formation advanced to the beat of drums towards the city of Hulao. The Generals of the Tang army were intimidated by the sight of such a great battle formation. Li Shi Min rode up a hill with the generals to watch. He said to the generals, "Dou Jian De's soldiers are from the north of the Yellow Rive. They have never fought with really strong enemies. Now they are going to attack this natural barrier, but the soldiers are talking and laughing loudly. This shows that they are not disciplined. The army is deployed very close to the city. This shows that they have underestimated our ability. We will just stay inside the city and will not fight with them. Then their courage will drop. When the soldiers stay in battle formation for a long time, they will become hungry and thirsty. Then they will retreat. When they retreat, we will go after them. Then we are sure to win. I can predict that we will defeat our enemy as soon as noon is past."

Dou Jian De really did take the Tang army lightly. He sent three hundred cavalrymen across the Sishui River. The cavalrymen stopped at a place just five hundred meters away from the camps of the Tang army. They sent an envoy to Li Shi Min asking him to send several hundred of his best men to spar with them. Li Shi Min let Wang Jun Kuo with two hundred soldiers with spears to compete with them. The two sides played the game for some time, and then they went back to their own camps. Wang Wan rode the horse that had originally belonged to Emperor Yang Guang of the Sui Dynasty. The horse's armor was made of gold. It blazed in the sun. Wang Wan sat on the horse in front of the whole army to show off. Li Shi Min observed, "That is really a good horse." Yuchi Jing De asked Li Shi Min to let him get the horse for him. Li Shi Min stopped him. He said, "I will not sacrifice a warrior for a horse." But Yuchi Jing De would not listen, and with two cavalrymen he rode to the enemy formation. Soon after, they captured Wang Wan and the horse and rode back. Meanwhile, Li Shi Min sent soldiers to bring back the horses grazing on the island in the Yellow Rive. He would start the attack when the horses were brought back.

Dou Jian De's battle formation had been deployed since seven in the morning. By noon, the soldiers were tired and hungry. They sat on the ground, and they fought among themselves for drinking water. They did not want to march forward. They just wanted to retreat. Li Shi Min saw that it was time to start the attack. He ordered Yuwen Shi Ji to lead three hundred cavalrymen to ride past the west wing of the enemy formation and then turn south. Before they started, Li Shi Min said to Yuwen Shi Ji, "When you pass the enemy formation, see if the formation stays unmoved. If so, then you should lead the troops back. If the formation moves, you should attack them from the east." When Yuwen Shi Ji and his men rode to the enemy battle formation, it moved. At that time, the horses which had been left on the island in the Yellow River were brought back, and Li Shi Min immediately ordered his army to charge. He rode at the head of the cavalry, and the main force followed them. They crossed the Sishui River and then charged the enemy.

At that time, Dou Jian De and his ministers were holding morning court. When the Tang warriors suddenly appeared, the ministers were in great panic and ran towards Dou Jian De. Dou Jian De sent for the cavalrymen to repel the attack, but the ministers blocked their way so that the cavalrymen could not carry out their task. Dou Jian De ordered the ministers to withdraw, but the Tang army had already arrived. The two armies met and a terrible fight began. The dust rose high. Li Shi Min led Shi Da Nai, Cheng Zhi Jie, and Qin Shu Bao carrying a big banner, rolled up, with a big character of "Tang" on it, and rode into the enemy formation from the front and sliced their way through to the back of the formation. Then they unrolled the flag and the big emblem of "Tang" was seen flying at the back of Dou Jian De's battle formation. When Dou Jian De's troops saw that, they lost heart and began to run away. The Tang army pursued them for fifteen kilometers. They killed three thousand. Dou Jian De was wounded by a spear and rode with great pain. Generals Bai Shi Rang and Yang Wu Wei of the Tang army rode after him. Dou Jian De fell from his horse. General Bai Shi Rang raised his spear and was about to kill him. Dou Jian De shouted, "Don't kill me! I am King of Xia. You will be rich if you take me prisoner." General Yang Wu Wei got off his horse and bound him up, put him on the back of his spare horse and brought him before Li Shi Min. Li Shi Min said angrily, "I was on an expedition against Wang Shi Chong. It was none of your business. Why have you come all the way here to attack my army?" Dou Jian De said, trembling, "I have come here in order to save you the trouble of going all the away to get me." Fifty thousand of Dou Jian De's men were captured. Li Shi Min released them and sent them home on that day.

On 8 May, Dou Jian De, Wang Wan, Zhangsun An Shi and Guo Shi Heng were put in cages on wagons and driven to the foot of the city wall of Luoyang. Wang Shi Chong was at the top of the city wall. Wang Shi Chong and Dou Jian De talked over the wall with tears in their eyes. Li Shi Min let Zhangsun An Shi go into the city of Luoyang to tell Wang Shi Chong how Dou Jian De had been defeated. Wang Shi Chong called all his generals together to discuss what to do next. Wang Shi Chong expressed his intention to make a breakthrough and get to Xiangyang (now Xiangcheng, Henan Province) in the south. But the generals said, "Our survival depends on the King of Xia. But now the King of Xia has been captured. Even if we might succeed in making a breakthrough, we could not achieve anything." While they were hesitating, Li Shi Min sent an envoy to tell Wang Shi Chong that if he surrendered, Li Shi Min would spare his life. So on 9 May, Wang Shi Chong was dressed in white, with his son, the crown prince,

and his ministers, and went to the gate of the camps of Li Shi Min's army to surrender. Li Shi Min received him politely. Wang Shi Chong knelt down with his
head to the ground, covered with sweat. Li Shi Min sent his army into Luoyang
to maintain order and prevent any looting.

On 10 May, Li Shi Min entered the palace in Luoyang. He sent Fang Xuan
Ling to collect the documents and books of the Sui Dynasty from the administration department, but he could not get anything because all of them had been
destroyed. Li Shi Min sent Xiao Yu and Dou Gui to seal all the storage houses
and collect all the gold and silk to grant to the generals and officers. He ordered
the arrest of more than ten generals and ministers of the Zheng Dynasty who had
committed serious crimes, such as Duan Da, Shan Xiong Xin, Guo Shi Heng and
Zhu Can. Li Ji was a good friend of Shan Xiong Xin. Li Ji went to see Li Shi Min.
He said to Li Shi Min that Shan Xiong Xin was a brave general. He begged Li Shi
Min to spare Shan Xiong Xin's life. But Li Shi Min refused. Then Shan Xiong Xin,
Duan Da and the others were executed on the bank of Luoshui River.

Shifachi, the horse that carried Li Shi Min in the battle against Dou Jian De at Hulao

On 9 July Li Shi Min with his victorious army went back to Chang'an, the
capital of the Tang Dynasty. Li Shi Min rode at the head of his army, wearing
armor made of gold. Twenty-five generals, including Li Yuan Ji, King of Qi, Li Ji,
Cheng Zhi Jie, Yuchi Jing De, Qin Shu Bao, followed him. In the army, there were
ten thousand cavalrymen and thirty thousand foot soldiers wearing armor. They

marched into the capital to the beating of the drums. Li Shi Min presented Dou Jian De and Wang Shi Chong and other captives and the small cart and other things that had been used by the emperors of the Sui Dynasty to the Emperor of the Tang Dynasty in the ancestral temple. The Emperor of the Tang Dynasty held a grand banquet to entertain Li Shi Min and all the generals who had rendered outstanding service in the battles in overcoming Dou Jian De and Wang Shi Chong. Considering that no one had ever made such great contributions as those rendered by Li Shi Min, Emperor Li Yuan of the Tang Dynasty granted Li Shi Min the title of Grand General of Heavenly Strategies. Li Shi Min enjoyed the rank higher than any kings and dukes.

When Wang Shi Chong was brought before the Emperor of the Tang Dynasty, the Emperor blamed him for resisting the Tang army. Wang Shi Chong said, "I should be killed for that, but the King of Qin has promised to spare my life." So the Emperor set Wang Shi Chong, his sons, his brothers and nephews free, and sent them into exile in the area of Shu (now Sichuan Province). Dou Jian De was executed in the market place.

On 12 July, Wang Shi Chong and his elder brother Wang Shi Yun were staying in an official guest house in Yongzhou (an area around Xi'an, Shaanxi Province) waiting for the escorts to take them to the area of Shu (now Sichuan Province). Dugu Xiu De, the governor of Dingzhou (now Dingzhou, Hebei Province), led his brothers to the house where Wang Shi Chong was staying. When they arrived, Dugu Xiu De pretended that he had an order from the Emperor to Wang Shi Chong. He called outside the house, "The Emperor has an order to the King of Zheng!" Wang Shi Chong and his brother Wang Shi Yun came out of the house in a great hurry. When they came out of the house, Dugu Xiu De swung his sword and killed Wang Shi Chong and Wang Shi Yun. Dugu Xiu De killed Wang Shi Chong to revenge his father Dugu Ji, whom Wang Shi Chong had killed in January 619. When the Emperor heard of this, he dismissed Dugu Xiu De from the office of the Governor of Dingzhou.

41. Li Shi Min Pacifies the Rebellions of Liu Hei Ta and Xu Yuan Lang

After Dou Jian De was defeated, many of his generals went hiding in the area to the north of the Yellow River. They bullied the local people and brought great suffering to the people there. The local officials of the Tang Dynasty punished them severely. So the former generals under Dou Jian De were afraid. At that time, the Emperor summoned Fan Yuan, Dong Kang Mai, and Gao Ya Xian to Chang'an. They were all former generals under Dou Jian De. Fan Yuan discussed this matter with Dong Kang Mai and Gao Ya Xian. Fan Yuan said, "Wang Shi

Chong surrendered to the Tang Dynasty with the city of Luoyang. His generals and ministers such as Duan Da and Shan Xiong Xin were executed. If we go to Chang'an, we will certainly meet the same fate. We have experienced a hundred battles in these ten years. We should have been killed long ago. Life is not important to us anymore. We must do something with the rest of our lives. The King of Xia captured Li Shen Tong, the cousin of the present Emperor of the Tang Dynasty; he treated Li Shen Tong kindly and released him. But when Dou Jian De was captured by the Tang army, he was executed immediately. The King of Xia has been very kind to us. We must revenge him. Otherwise we will be very ashamed to face the people." So they decided to hold a rebellion again. They practiced divination and the divination showed that the rebellion would be successful if it was led by a man by the family name of Liu. So they went to Zhangnan (now in Linzhang, Hebei Province) to see Liu Ya, a former general under Dou Jian De. They told him of their plan for a rebellion and asked him to be the leader. Liu Ya said, "Peace and order has just been restored in the realm. I intend to spend the rest of my life tilling the land and growing crops. I don't want to stir up trouble anymore." They were very angry and killed him lest he reveal their secret plan. Liu Hei Ta, a former general under Dou Jian De, was also living in Zhangnan. Fan Yuan, Dong Kang Mai and Gao Ya Xian went to visit him. When they found him, he was working in his vegetable garden. Gao Ya Xian told him of their plans and asked him to be the leader of the rebellion. Liu Hei Ta agreed with them readily. Liu Hei Ta immediately killed a cow and had it cooked. They discussed the details of their plan while they were eating and drinking. Liu Hei Ta had been one of the bravest generals under Dou Jian De. He organized an army of about a hundred men. On 19 July 621 Liu Hei Ta led his army to attack the county city of Zhangnan and took it.

When the Emperor of the Tang Dynasty got news of Liu Hei Ta's rebellion, he ordered the establishment of army commands in Mingzhou (now Yongnian, Hebei Province), Weizhou (now Daming, Hebei Province), Jizhou (now Hengshui, Hebei Province), and Dingzhou (now Dingzhou, Hebei Province). The Emperor sent Li Shen Tong, King of Huai'an, to suppress the rebellion.

On 12 August, Liu Hei Ta took Shuxian (now in the area of Xiajin, Shandong Province). Quan Wei, the Governor of Weizhou (now Daming, Hebei Province), led an army to fight with Liu Hei Ta's army. Liu Hei Ta's army defeated Quan Wei's army. Quan Wei was killed in battle. Liu Hei Ta took over Quan Wei's soldiers and equipment. Some of the former generals and officers under Dou Jian De came to join Liu Hei Ta's army. Liu Hei Ta's army expanded into an army of two thousand men. Then Liu Hei Ta had a platform built in Zhangnan. A grand ceremony was held there to mourn for Dou Jian De and to pledge their determination to hold a rebellion. In the ceremony, Liu Hei Ta made himself commander-in-chief of the army. The Emperor of the Tang Dynasty sent General Qin Wu Tong with three thousand men in Guanzhong and General Li Xuan Tong, commander-in-chief of the army in the area of Dingzhou (now Dingzhou, Hebei Province), to attack Liu Hei Ta's army.

Xu Yuan Lang, a former leader of a group of outlaws in Yanzhou (now in Shandong Province), had submitted himself to the Tang Dynasty and had been bade commander-in-chief of the army in the area of Yanzhou and was made Duke of Lu Prefecture by the Emperor of the Tang Dynasty. When he got the news that Liu Hei Ta had rebelled against the Tang Dynasty, he secretly united with Liu Hei Ta. On 26 August, Xu Yuan Lang rebelled in Rencheng (now Jining, Shandong Province). Liu Hei Ta made Xu Yuan Lang commander-in-chief of the rebellion army in Rencheng. The local gentry of Yanzhou (now Yanzhou, Shandong Province), Yunzhou (now Yuncheng, Shandong Province), Chenzhou (now Huaiyang, Hernan Province), Qizhou (now Qixian, Henan Province), Yizhou (now Ruzhou, Henan Province), Luozhou (now in the northeast of Luoyang, Henan Province), Daizhou (now Wucheng, Shandong Province) and Caozhou (now Caoxian, Shandong Province) responded to Xu Yuan Lang's rebellion. Then Xu Yuan Lang occupied Chuqiu (now a place in the east of Huaxian, Henan Province). On 7 September, Xu Yuan Lang declared himself King of Lu.

In September 621 Li Shen Tong commanded an army from Guanzhong to Jizhou (now Hengshui, Hebei Province) to join force with Li Yi, commander-in-chief of the Tang Army in Youzhou (now in the southwest of Beijing). Li Yi's original name was Luo Yi. When rebellions against the Sui Dynasty rose everywhere, Luo Yi pacified the area of Zhuo Prefecture (now the area of Beijing). When Li Yuan became Emperor of the Tang Dynasty, Luo Yi submitted to the Tang Dynasty. The Emperor of the Tang Dynasty granted him the royal family name of Li. So Luo Yi became Li Yi. Fifty thousand Tang troops in Xingzhou (now Xingtai, Hebei Province), Mingzhou (now Yongnian, Hebei Province), Xiangzhou (now Anyang, Henan Province), Weizhou (now Daming, Hebei Province), Hengzhou (now Zhengding, Hebei Province) and Zhaozhou (now Zhaoxian, Hebei Province) were mobilized to fight against Liu Hei Ta's army. The Tang army under Li Shen Tong and the army under Liu Hei Ta fought to the south of the city of Raoyang (now Raoyang, Hebei Province). The army under Li Shen Tong greatly outnumbered the army uder Liu Hei Ta. Li Shen Tong's battle formation was as long as five Kilometers. Liu Hei Ta had to deploy his army in single column along the bank of Rao River to oppose the Tang army. That day, there was a wind storm. At first, the strong wind was favorable for the Tang army, and Li Shen Tong took the advantage to charge Liu Hei Ta's army. But suddenly, the direction of the wind changed and blew hard against the Tang army. Liu Hei Ta immediately started a counter-attack and defeated the Tang army. Li Shen Tong lost two thirds of his men. Li Yi was fighting on the west wing and he defeated Gao Ya Xian. But when he heard that Li Shen Tong had suffered great losses, he retreated to Gaocheng (now in Hebei Province). Liu Hei Ta won a great victory over the Tang army. Then he attacked Li Yi in Gaocheng. Li Yi was defeated and went back to Youzhou. Liu Hei Ta's army became a very strong army.

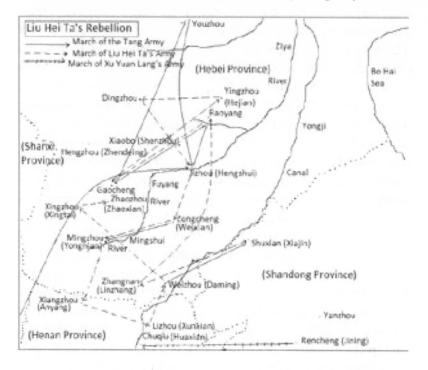

In December 621, Liu Hei Ta occupied Yingzhou (now Hejian, Hebei Province). On 19 September, Liu Hei Ta occupied Dingzhou (now Dingzhou, Hebei Province). Li Xuan Tong, commander-in-chief of the Tang army in Dingzhou, was captured by Liu Hei Ta. Liu Hei Ta tried his best to pursuade Li Xuan Tong to surrender, but Li Xuan Tong refused. In the prison, the jail keepers entertained him with meat and wine. Li Xuan Tong asked one of them to lend him his sword so he could show them a sword dance. While he was dancing, he killed himself with the sword.

On 3 December, Liu Hei Ta occupied Jizhou (now Hengshui, Hebei Province). Liu Hei Ta sent letters to the former generals and officers under Dou Jian De in Zhaozhou (now Zhaoxian, Hebei Province) and Weizhou (now Daming, Hebei Province) calling on them to rise against the Tang Dynasty. The former generals and officers under Dou Jian De killed the local officials of the Tang Dynasty to respond to Liu Hei Ta. Then Liu Hei Ta commanded a great army of over thirty thousand men to march toward Zongcheng (now Weixian, Hebei

Province). At that time Li Ji, the commander-in-chief of the army in the area of Lizhou (now the area around Xunxian, Henan Province) stationed his army in Zongcheng. When he saw that the army of Liu Hei Ta was too strong for him to resist, he gave up Zongcheng and retreated to Mingzhou (now Yongnian, Hebei Province). On 12 December Liu Hei Ta pursued the Tang army under Li Ji. The Tang army was defeated. About five thousand Tang soldiers were killed. Li Ji had a narrow escape. On 14 December the local gentry of Mingzhou took the city from inside and presented the city to Liu Hei Ta. Ten days later Liu Hei Tang commanded his army to attack Xiangzhou (now Anyang, Henan Province) and took it. Then Liu Hei Ta marched his army to the south and took Lizhou (now Xunxian, Henan Province) and Weizhou (Daming, Hebei Province). So within half a year, Liu Hei Ta recovered the area formerly occupied by Dou Jian De. Then Liu Hei Ta took Xingzhou (now Xingtai, Hebei Province) and Zhaozhou (now Zhaoxian, Hebei Province).

On 1 January 622 Liu Hei Ta declared himself King of Handong. He made Mingzhou his capital. He appointed Fan Yuan premier, Dong Kang Mai minister of war, Gao Ya Xian commander of the right army.

The Emperor of the Tang Dynasty decided to send Li Shi Min, King of Qin, and Li Yuan Ji, King of Qi, to pacify the rebellion of Liu Hei Ta. On 8 January 622 Li Shi Min marched his army to Huojia (now Huojia, Henan Province). Liu Hei Ta gave up Xiangzhou (now Anyang, Henan Provence) and retreated to Mingzhou, the capital of his kingdom. Then Li Shi Min took Xiangzhou and marched to Feixiang (Now Feixiang, Hebei Province). He stationed his army along the Mingshui River to threaten Mingzhou, Liu Hei Ta's capital.

Li Yi, the commander-in-chief of the army of the Tang Dynasty stationed in Youzhou (now the area around Beijing) led an army of forty thousand men to march southward to join force with Li Shi Min. Liu Hei Ta got the information and decided to intercept Li Yi's army. He appointed his premier Fan Yuan commander of an army of ten thousand men to defend his capital. On 27 January 622 Liu Hei Ta led a great army to march northward to meet the army led by Li Yi. That night, Liu Hei Ta's army camped in Shahe (now Shahe, Hebei Province). The governor of Yongning County (near Mingzhou) Cheng Ming Zhen led a team of soldiers with sixty big drums to the bank of Mingshui River one kilometer away from Mingzhou. They beat the drums with great force. The drums made such thundering sound that the houses shook and tiles on the roofs were shaken to the ground. Fan Yuan was so afraid that he sent a messenger to tell Liu Hei Ta that Mingzhou was in great danger. Liu Hei Ta sent his younger brother Liu Shi Shan and Zhang Jun Li with ten thousand men to continue their march to the north to intercept Li Yi's army. He turned back immediately with the main force to rescue Mingzhou.

On 30 January, Li Yi's army and Liu Hei Ta's army led by Liu Shi Shan and Zhang Jun Li fought on the bank of Xuhe River (a river flew through the northeast of Baoding, Hebei Province). Li Yi won a great victory in that battle. Eight thousand men under Liu Shi Shan and Zhang Jun Li were killed or captured. Li Yi marched southward and occupied vast areas under the rule of Liu Hei Ta.

Li Xuan Huo, a native of Mingshui County (now Quzhou, Hebei Province), took the county city and surrendered to Li Shi Min. Li Shi Min sent Wang Jun Kuo with one thousand five hundred cavalrymen into the city to defend it. In February, on his way back to Mingzhou, Liu Hei Ta decided to attack Mingshui County. When Liu Hei Ta's army reached Lieren (to the north of Feixiang, Hebei Province), Li Shi Min sent general Qin Shu Bao to attack Liu Hei Ta's army and defeated it. On 17 February Li Shi Min took Xingzhou (now Xingtai, Hebei Province).

Li Yi comannded his army to march southward and took Dingzhou (now Dingzhou, Hebei Province), Lianzhou (now Gaocheng, Hebei Province), Luanzhou (now Luancheng, Hebei Province), and Zhaozhou (now Zhaoxian, Hebei Province). Then Li Yi commanded his army to march towards Mingzhou to join force with Li Shi Min.

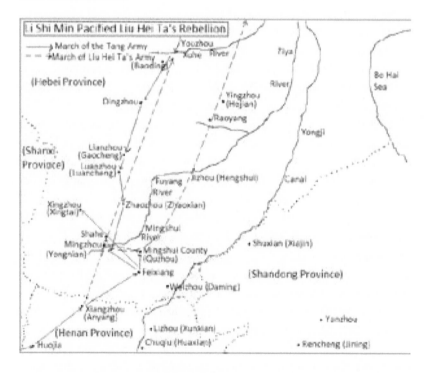

Liu Hei Ta's army attacked Mingshui County fiercely. There was a moat of fifty feet wide around the city wall. Liu Hei Ta ordered his soldiers to dig two tunnels to the city. Li Shi Min tried three times to lead his troops to reinforce the defenders in the city but they were driven back. Li Shi Min was anxious. He was afraid that General Wang Jun Kuo could not stand up to the attack by the enemy. He gathered all the generals to find a way to relieve the defenders of Mingshui County. It seemed clear to the generals that when the tunnels were dug to the foot of the city wall, the city would surely fall into the hands of Liu Hei Ta. General Luo Shi Xin offered to replace General Wang Jun Kuo to defend the City of Mingshui County. Li Shi Min agreed. Li Shi Min mounted up a small hill and waved a flag to send signals to Wang Jun Kuo to make a breakthrough. Wang Jun Kuo commanded his soldiers to fight very hard to make their breakthrough. At the same time, Luo Shi Xin and three hundred men fought their way into the city to replace Wang Jun Kuo to defend the city. Liu Hei Ta attacked the city day and night. It happened that it snowed heavily, and for eight days the Tang army reinforcements could not get close to the City of Mingshui County. On 25 February 622 the city of Mingshui County at last fell. Luo Shi Xin was captured. Liu Hei Ta admired his bravery and intended to spare him. But Luo Shi Xin would rather die than giv himself up. Then Liu Hei Ta killed him. Luo Shi Xin was only twenty years old when he died. When Li Shi Min learned that Luo Shi Xin had been killed, he was very sad. He bought back the dead body at a high price, and then held a grand funeral to bury Luo Shi Xin.

On 29 February the Tang army under Li Shi Min recovered the City of Mingshui County. In March, Li Yi's army and Li Shi Min's army joined forces on the south bank of the Mingshui River. The Tang army camped on the south to Mingshui River. A detachment was sent to camp on the north bank of the river. Food supplies were transported to Liu Hei Ta from Yizhou (now Yixian, Hebei Province), Beizhou (now Qinghe, Hebei Province), Cangzhou (now Yanshan, Hebei Province) and Yingzhou (now Hejian, Hebei Province) by water and by land. Cheng Ming Zhen, the governor of Yongning of the Tang Dynasty, commanded a thousand men to attack the transportation escorts and destroyed all the food supplies.

Li Shi Min's army and Liu Hei Ta's army confronted with each other for more than sixty days. On 23 March, Liu Hei Ta launched a surprise attack on Li Ji's camp. In return, Li Shi Min led an army in a sudden attack on the rear of Liu Hei Ta's army so as to relieve Li Ji's army. Liu Hei Ta turned back to fight against Li Shi Min. Liu Hei Ta's army encircled Li Shi Min and his men. Li Shi Min and his men fought to make a breakthrough. Many of the Tang soldiers were killed, but they could not break through. At this critical moment, Yuchi Jing De led some troops into the encirclement to rescue Li Shi Min. With Yuchi Jing De's help, Li Shi Min succeeded in breaking out.

Li Shi Min expected that when Liu Hei Ta's food supplies were exhausted, he would certainly launch a decisive battle. He sent some troops to build a dike across the upper reach of the Mingshui River to block the flow of water. Li Shi Min instructed the officer in charge of the dike, "When the battle with Liu Hei Ta is underway, break the dike."

On 26 March, Liu Hei Ta led twenty thousand men across the Mingshui River to the south bank and deployed his army in battle formation very close to Li Shi Min's camps. Li Shi Min personally commanded his cavalry in the attack on Liu Hei Ta's cavalry battalion and defeated it. Li Shi Min ordered his victorious cavalry to attack Liu Hei Ta's infantry. Liu Hei Ta commanded the men to fight with all their might. The battle started at noon and lasted till sunset. Liu Hei Ta saw that he was going to lose the battle, and he fled from the battlefield with Fan Yuan and about two hundred men. His soldiers did not know that he had run away and they went on fighting. The officer in charge of the dike in the upper reaches of the Mingshui River broke the dike, and the water swept down the river, in a wall ten feet deep. Many of Liu Hei Ta's defeated troops were trying to escape by crossing the river, but all of them were drowned. Liu Hei Ta's army was totally destroyed. Only Liu Hei Ta and Fan Yuan with the other two hundred men, including his younger brother Liu Shi Shan, and Wang Xiao Hu escaped into the area of the Turks.

Juanmaogua, the horse that carried Li Shi Min in the battle against Liu Hei Ta

When Xu Yuan Lang, King of Lu, learned that Liu Hei Ta had been defeated, he did not know what to do. Li Shi Min commanded his victorious army to march to the area of Lu (now the area of Shandong Province) to attack him. Incidentally, the Emperor of the Tang Dynasty summoned Li Shi Min to Chang'an. Li Shi Min handed over the leadership of the army to Li Yuan Ji, King of Qi, and went back to Chang'an. He reached it on 9 April. The Emperor went to Changleban (in the east of Chang'an) to welcome Li Shi Min. Li Shi Min gave the Emperor a detailed explanation of the favorable situation for defeating Xu Yuan Lang. Then the Emperor ordered Li Shi Min to go to Liyang (now Xunxian, Henan Province) to gather a great army and then march this army eastward to Jiyin (in the northwest of Caoxian, Shandong Province).

In July, Li Shi Min attacked Xu Yuan Lang and took more than ten cities. The victory of the Tang army under Li Shi Min shocked everyone in the area of Huai River and Sishui River (in the area of Jiangsu Province). Considering that most of the area between Huai River and Jishui River (now a section of the Yellow River in Shandong Province) had been brought to submission, Li Shi Min ordered Li Shen Tong, King of Huai'an, Ren Gui and Li Ji to lead an army to continue the war against Xu Yuan Lang. In July Li Shi Min led the main army to go back to Chang'an.

42. Du Fu Wei Submits to the Tang Dynasty

Du Fu Wei was the most powerful man in the area between the Huai River and the Yangtze River. When Li Shi Min attacked Wang Shi Chong in 621, he sent an envoy to Du Fu Wei to ask him to come over. Du Fu Wei agreed to submit to the Tang Dynasty. The Emperor of the Tang Dynasty sent an envoy to make Du Fu Wei Commander-in-chief of the Southeast Area and governor of the area between the Huai River and the Yangtze River. The Emperor also made him King of Wu. The Emperor granted Du Fu Wei the royal family name of Li. So Du Fu Wei became Li Fu Wei.

In November 621, Li Fu Wei sent General Wang Xiong Dan to attacked Li Zi Tong, Emperor of Wu. A battle was fought in Suzhou (now in Jiangsu Province). Li Zi Tong was defeated and retreated to Yuhang (now Hangzhou, Zhejiang Province). Another battle was fought outside the city of Yuhang. Li Zi Tong was defeated again. Li Zi Tong was at the end of his resources, and he surrendered. Li Fu Wei sent a party of soldiers to escort him to Chang'an. The Emperor of the Tang Dynasty released Li Zi Tong.

Wang Hua occupied the areas of Yi (now Yixian, in the southeast of Anhui Province) and Shi (now Shixian, in the southeast of Anhui Province) and declared himself king. Li Fu Wei sent General Wang Xiong Dan to attack Wang Hua.

Wang Hua held back Wang Xiong Dan's army at the entrance of Xin'andong, which was a narrow pass in Shi. Wang Hua's soldiers defending the narrow pass were well trained and he had confidence in them. Wang Xiong Dan ordered his strongest soldiers to hide themselves in the valley, while the older and weaker soldiers attacked Xin'andong. When the battle began, Wang Xiong Dan's soldiers pretended that they were defeated and retreated back to their camp. Wang Hua commanded his army to pursuit them, and the battle continued till sunset. Wang Hua led his army back to Xin'andong, only to find that it had been occupied by Wang Xiong Dan. Wang Hua had nowhere to go and had to surrender. From then on, Li Fu Wei occupied the vast area south to the Huai River and east to the Yangtze River and to the East China Sea.

In 622, Li Shi Min defeated Liu Hei Ta and attacked Xu Yuan Lang. Li fu Wei felt greatly threatened and realized that it was time to go to Chang'an. In July 622, Li Fu Wei arrived at Chang'an. The Emperor warmly welcomed him. The Emperor appointed Li Fu Wei Protector of the Crown Prince and the Governor of the Southeast Area. He was not to go back to that area but would stay in the capital. In the court, Li Fu Wei was in a rank even higher than Li Yuan Ji, King of Qi.

43. The Conflicts among the Brothers

It was Li Shi Min who first proposed to his father Li Yuan to rise up in arms against the Sui Dynasty and to march on Chang'an, the capital. So when Li Yuan rose up in Jinyang and started his march to Chang'an, he said to Li Shi Min, "If our cause is successful and I become an emperor, I will make you the crown prince." Li Shi Min knelt down and expressed his thanks to his father, while politely declining his offer. When Li Yuan conquered Chang'an and became the King of Tang, the generals and the staff urged Li Yuan to make Li Shi Min his heir apparent. When Li Yuan was going to declare his decision, Li Shi Min again declined the offer. So this matter was put aside. Who were the alternatives? Li Yuan's eldest son Li Jian Cheng was his father's successor by birth. He was a generous and straightforward man, but he was too much inclined to wine and beautiful girls. He liked hunting, too. Li Yuan's fourth son Li Yuan Ji, King of Qi, was a troublemaker. He had several hundred housemaids, whom he organized into armies to play fighting games: not mock battles, but real contests attacking each other with real swords and spears. Many of them were killed or wounded in these games. When he was in Jinyang, he shot at people in the streets with his bow, and took pleasure in watching people trying to dodge the arrows. Li Yuan did not like these two sons. Li Shi Min had been invaluable in establishing the Tang Dynasty. He overcame their most formidable enemies such as Xue Ren Gao,

Liu Wu Zhou, Dou Jian De, Wang Shi Chong and Liu Hei Ta. Li Shi Min had earned himself very high prestige and great power. Clearly, Li Yuan intended to let him replace Li Jian Cheng as the crown prince. Li Jian Cheng felt threatened. So he collaborated with Li Yuan Ji to get rid of Li Shi Min.

In his old age, Emperor Li Yuan had many beautiful young concubines. These young concubines gave birth to twenty princes for him. The Emperor made all of these princes kings. The beautiful young concubines tried in every way to establish good relationships with Li Yuan's three grown sons so as to consolidate their future position in the royal family. And Li Jian Cheng and Li Yuan Ji tried in every way to please them, too. They wanted the Emperor's young concubines to praise them in front of the Emperor so they could win favor. And there were rumors that Li Jiand Cheng and Li Yuan Ji had committed adultery with two of the concubines. But Li Shi Min did not do anything to please his father's concubines. He didn't consider that necessary, since he was a powerful man with no need to consolidate his position. So the concubines praised Li Jian Cheng and Li Yuan Ji in front of the Emperor, and said bad words about Li Shi Min.

Li Shi Min, King of Qin, was only second to his father, the Emperor of the Tang Dynasty, in power. He had many experienced generals and staff under him. He had a great army under his command. Why would he need to please his father's concubines? When he captured Luoyang, the Eastern capital of the Sui Dynasty, the Emperor of the Tang Dynasty sent several of his concubines to the Luoyang palaces to choose beautiful girls from the Sui Dynasty to serve as maids in the Tang palaces in Chang'an and to collect treasures from the royal store houses of the Sui Dynasty to be brought to Chang'an. The concubines took the opportunity to ask Li Shi Min for bribes, and asked him to provide official positions for their relatives. Li Shi Min said, "All the treasures have been counted and listed in the books and this inventory will be presented to the central government. As for official positions, they should be granted to those who are wise and competent." He refused to give anything to his father's concubines. So they hated Li Shi Min.

Li Shi Min granted Li Shen Tong, King of Huai'an, several hectares of land, because Li Shen Tong had rendered great military services for the Tang Dynasty. The Emperor had a favorite concubine named Zhang. Concubine Zhang's father had her ask the Emperor for the land already granted to Li Shen Tong. Then the Emperor ordered that the land be granted to Concubine Zhang's father. But Li Shen Tong refused to hand the land over to the concubine's father because the land had been granted to him by the order of Li Shi Min, King of Qin. Concubine Zhang said to the Emperor, "The land Your Majesty granted to my father has been taken by the King of Qin and he has granted it to Li Shen Tong." The Emperor was very angry. He summoned Li Shi Min and reproached him, "Is my imperial edict not as powerful as your order?" Several days later, the Emperor said to Pei Ji, the premier, "This boy has stayed away from me for a long time commanding an army fighting outside. He has been badly influenced by the intellectuals. He is not the son I knew in the old days."

Yin A Shu, father of Concubine Yin, was a local despot. One day Du Ru Hui, an official under Li Shi Min, rode past the gate of Yin A Shu's house. Suddenly, several servants dashed out from the gate and dragged Du Ru Hui from the horse and gave him a good beating. He was hurt, and one of his fingers was broken. Yin A Shu shouted at him, "What do you think you are. How dare you not unhorse when you passed the gate of my house!" Afterward, Yin A Shu was afraid that Li Shi Min would report that he had beaten Du Ru Hui to the Emperor. So Yin A Shu had his daughter tell the Emperor that an official under the King of Qin had bullied her father's family. The Emperor was incensed. He summoned Li Shi Min and reproached him, saying, "Your subordinates even dare to bully the family of my concubine. I can imagine how you treat ordinary people." Li Shi Min tried very hard to tell him the truth. But the Emperor would not listen to him.

The Emperor often held family banquets in the palace. At every banquet, the Emperor was very happy with all his young concubines around him. When Li Shi Min saw this happy scene, he thought of his own mother, Lady Dou. Lady Dou was the mother of Li Jian Cheng, Li Shi Min and Li Yuan Ji. But she died early and did not live to see her husband ascend the throne. When Li Shi Min thought of this, he was so sad that he shed tears. The Emperor didn't like to see Li Shi Min shedding tears during his happy moment. His concubines took the chance to say slanderous words against Li Shi Min. They said, "Now the whole country is at peace and is prosperous. Your Majesty is now old and you should enjoy your life. But the King of Qin sheds tears when Your Majesty feels happy with us. This shows that he hates us. When Your Majesty passes away, the King of Qin will not tolerate us and your young sons and will kill us all." Then they cried bitterly and said to the Emperor, "The Crown Prince is kind-hearted and dutiful. If Your Majesty trusts the safety of us and your young sons to the hands of the Crown Prince, we and your young sons may survive." These words made the Emperor sad. So he dismissed the idea of replacing the Crown Prince. The Emperor and his son Li Shi Min gradually drifted apart, and the Emperor was closer to Li Jian Cheng and Li Yuan Ji.

44. Li Jian Cheng Defeats Liu Hei Ta and the Death of Xu Yuan Lang

Liu Hei Ta, his younger brother Liu Shi Shan and Wang Xiao Hu came back from the area of the Turks in June 622 with the help of a Turkic army. In mid

June, Liu Hei Ta led the Turks to attack Dingzhou (now Dingzhou, Hebei Province). In September Liu Hei Ta took Yingzhou (now Hejian, Hebei Province). On 17 October 622 the Tang army under Li Dao Xuan, King of Huaiyang, fought a battle with Liu Hei Ta's army in Xiabo (now Xiabo Town of Shenzhou, Hebei Province). The Tang army was defeated. Li Dao Xuan was killed. When this shocking news reached Mingzhou (now Yongnian, Hebei Province), Li Yuàn, King of Lujiang and commander-in-chief of the Tang army in Mingzhou, gave up the city and ran away westward. Then the cities around that area all fell into the hands of Liu Hei Ta. In the next ten days, Liu Hei Ta recovered all the area originally occupied by him. On 27 October Liu Hei Ta entered Mingzhou, his former capital.

In October 622, the Emperor of the Tang Dynasty ordered Li Yuan Ji, King of Qi, to lead an army to pacify Liu Hei Ta. But Li Yuan Ji did not make much progress.

Wang Gui, the official in charge of the affairs of the palace of the Crown Prince, and Wei Zheng, the official in charge of the library of the Crown Prince's palace, said to Li Jian Cheng, the Crown Prince, "the King of Qin has made great contributions that cannot be surpassed by anybody. All the officials in the central government or in the local governments admire him and like to work under him. You are in the position of the Crown Prince only because you are the eldest son of the Emperor. You have not rendered great services that can convince other people of your ability. Now Liu Hei Ta has come back with only ten thousand men and insufficient food supplies. If you lead an army to attack him, you can defeat him easily. You'd better lead the expedition personally so that you may render military services to raise your reputation. You may take this opportunity to make friends with the powerful people in the local area to the east of the Xiaoshan Mountain. In this way you may secure yourself." Li Jian Cheng took their advice and asked the Emperor to let him lead an army to launch an expedition against Liu Hei Ta who had come back to the area north of the Yellow River. The Emperor readily agreed.

On 7 November 622 the Emperor issued his order that the Crown Prince would lead an army in an expedition against Liu Hei Ta. The Emperor appointed Li Jian Cheng marshal of the army sent by the central government. All the Tang armies in the areas to the east of the Xiaoshan Mountain (a mountain which is situated in the west part of Henan Province and the east part of Shaanxi Province, it was considered the demarcation between the western and eastern parts of China in ancient times) were put under his command. Li Jian Cheng had the absolute discretion to make decisions.

In December, Liu Hei Ta attacked Weizhou (now Daming, Hebei Province) but he could not take it. Li Jian Cheng and Li Yuan Ji arrived in Changle (now Nanle, in the northeast part of Henan Province) with a great army. Liu Hei Ta fielded an army to resist the Tang army. The confronting armies were deployed in battle array twice, but twice they were withdrawn to their respective camps. There was no battle. Wei Zheng suggested to the Crown Prince, "When Liu Hei Ta was defeated in March this year, nearly all of the generals under him were executed. Those who had run away were tracked down and put to death. All of their wives and children were thrown into jail. This is the reason why, when King of Qi first came and declared that the Emperor would pardon the rebels, nobody believed it and the order of pardon did not have any effect. Now we should release all the captives. We should say something nice before we send them back. Then in a short time, we may just sit here and wait for Liu Hei Ta's army to collapse." Li Jian Cheng accepted his advice and released all the captives.

Very soon, Liu Hei Ta's food supplies were exhausted, and the soldiers began to run away. Some of them even arrested their commander and came over to the Tang army. Liu Hei Ta was afraid that Li Jian Cheng's army would attack from the front and the army defending Weizhou would attack his rear. In that case, his army would be placed in a very dangerous position. So he retreated to Guantao (now in the southeast part of Hebei Province), on the east bank of Yongji Canal. There was no bridge across the canal, so a bridge had to be built before they could get across.

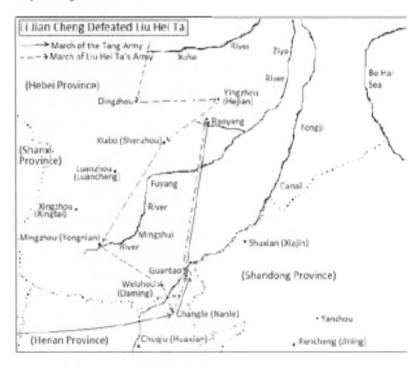

On 25 December, Li Jian Cheng and Li Yuan Ji arrived with a great army in pursuit of Liu Hei Ta. Liu Hei Ta ordered Wang Xiao Hu to deploy his army in battle formation along the bank of the canal to hold them off. He himself supervised the building of a bridge over the canal. As soon as the bridge was built, Liu Hei Ta crossed to the west bank and fled. His army soon disintegrated in flight. Many soldiers laid down their weapons and surrendered. The Tang army crossed the canal, using the bridge, in pursuit of Liu Hei Ta, but only a thousand Tang soldiers had crossed the bridge when it collapsed. So Liu Hei Ta escaped with several hundred men. Li Jian Cheng sent Liu Hong Ji to command the cavalry to pursue Li Hei Ta. Liu Hei Ta had to ride for his life without stopping to rest. He had only about a hundred men following him. They were all very tired and hungry. On 3 January 623 Liu Hei Ta reached Raoyang (now Raoyang, Hebei Province). Zhuge De Wei, the governor of Raoyang appointed by Liu Hei Ta, welcomed him by the gate of the city and invited him into the city. Liu Hei Ta refused to enter the city. Zhuge De Wei asked Liu Hei Ta, tears in his eyes, to go into the city again and again. At last Liu Hei Ta entered the city and took a rest in the market near the city gate. Zhuge De Wei brought food for him and his men. When they were eating, Zhuge De Wei sprang a surprise attack and arrested Liu Hei Ta and his followers. Zhuge De Wei presented the city of Raoyang to the Tang government and surrendered to the Tang army. He turned Liu Hei Ta over to Li Jian Cheng. Liu Hei Ta and his brother Liu Shi Shan were executed in Mingzhou. Before the execution, Liu Hei Ta looked up at the sky and said with a long sigh, "I would have been still leading a peaceful life, growing vegetables, if Gao Ya Xian had not come to induce me to rebel. It is Gao Ya Xian who has led me to my destruction."

Li Shi Min sent Li Shen Tong and Li Ji to attack Xu Yuan Lang in Caozhou (now Caoxian, Shandong Province). In February 623, Xu Yuan Lang gave up the city and ran away, but was killed by the people in a village.

45. Li Jian Cheng's Conspiracy to Take Power from His Father

Li Yuan Ji, King of Qi, once even offered to help kill Li Shi Min for Li Jian Cheng. He said to the Crown Prince, "I will kill him with my own hands for you." When Li Shi Min accompanied the Emperor on a visit to the house of Li Yuan Ji, Li Yuan Ji ordered Yuwen Bao, chief commander of the guards of his house, to hide in his bedroom to assassinate Li Shi Min. At that time, Li Jian Cheng was still a kindhearted man. He secretly told Li Yuan Ji to stop the action. Later, Li Yuan Ji said angrily to Li Jian Cheng, "I planned this for you, not for me."

As Li Shi Min's power grew, Li Jian Cheng felt increasingly uneasy. He decided that he should strengthen his own force. Without the Emperor's approval, he recruited brave warriors from the areas of the capital and all around China. These warriors were organized into teams of palace guards for the Crown Prince. He stationed these guards in the two Changlin Gates (the Crown Prince's palace gates), so this team of guards was called the Corps of Changlin. Li Jian Cheng secretly ordered Keda Zhi, the commander of his guards, to ask Li Yi, the commander-in-chief of the army stationed in Youzhou (now the area around Beijing), to send three hundred hand-picked cavalrymen to serve as guards of the Crown Prince. But all these actions were discovered and reported to the Emperor. The Emperor summoned Li Jian Cheng and reproached him. Keda Zhi was sent into exile in Suizhou (now Xichang, Sichuan Province).

Yang Wen Gan, commander-in-chief of the army stationed in Qingzhou (now Qingyang County, Gansu Province), was once a palace guard for the Crown Prince. He was a close friend of Li Jian Cheng. Li Jian Cheng secretly ordered him to recruit more warriors and send them to Chang'an, the capital. In June 624 the Emperor left Chang'an for Renzhi Palace, which was situated in Yijun (now in Shaanxi Province, which is one hundred and eighty kilometers north of Chang'an) to spend his summer vacation. He ordered Li Jian Cheng to stay in Chang'an to take care of state affairs. The Emperor ordered Li Shi Min and Li Yuan Ji to go with him. Li Jian Cheng urged Li Yuan Ji to kill Li Shi Min whenever he had a chance. After the Emperor had gone to Renzhi Palace, Li Jian Cheng sent General Erzhu Huan and Captain Qiao Gong Shan to deliver some armor to Yang Wen Gan and asked them to convey his order to Yang Wen Gan to attack Renzhi Palace. When Erzhu Huan and Qiao Gong Shan reached Binzhou (now Binxian, Shaanxi Province) on their way to Qingzhou, they sent an urgent report to the Emperor that Li Jian Cheng had ordered Yang Wen Gan to mount an armed rebellion and that Li Jian Cheng himself would rise up in the capital. At the same time, a man named Du Feng Ju also went to Renzhi Palace to lodge an accusation against Li Jian Cheng. When the Emperor heard all this, he was furious. He had Li Jian Cheng summoned to Renzhi Palace. Li Jian Cheng was petrified. He did not have the courage to go to see the Emperor. Xu Shi Mo, an official in charge of the general affairs of the Crown Prince's palace, urged Li Jian Cheng to occupy the capital and rebel against his own father. But Zhao Hong Zhi, the general secretary of the the Crown Prince's palace, suggested that Li Jian Cheng should go to Renzhi Palace without any guards to beg his father to pardon him. Li Jian Cheng took his advice and went to Renzhi Palace.

When he was thirty kilometers away from Renzhi Palace, Li Jian Cheng left all his subordinates behind and went forward to see his father with no more than several guards. When he appeared before his father, he knelt down and bowed to the ground, striking his head on the floor, to beg his father to pardon him. He hit his head so hard on the ground that he fainted away. The Emperor was still outraged. He ordered that Li Jian Cheng be kept in house custody that night and be provided with bad food. The Emperor sent Yuwen Ying to Qingzhou to summon Yang Wen Gan to Renzhi Palace. When Yuwen Ying reached Qingzhou, he told Yang Wen Gan everything that had happened in Renzhi Palace. Then Yang Wen Gan rose in armed rebellion. The Emperor sent an army to put it down.

On 26 June, the Emperor summoned Li Shi Min to discuss the military situation. Li Shi Min said, "Yang Wen Gan is just a clown who dares to defy the central government. I expect that he will be killed by one of his generals. If not, we can just send a general with an army to take care of him." The Emperor said, "No, Yang Wen Gan served under Li Jian Cheng for quite a long time and his rebellion mainly has to do with Li Jian Cheng. I think many people will respond to his call. You should lead an army to put a stop to this. When you come back, I will make you crown prince. I do not want to kill my own son. I will make him King of Shu in the southwest. He will only have a small army. In the future, if he submits to your rule, you should preserve his life. If he does not submit to your rule, you can bring him to submission easily."

As soon as Li Shi Min left with an army to quell Yang Wen Gan's rebellion, Li Yuan Ji and the Emperor's concubines spoke in defense of Li Jian Cheng, and some officials in the central government, such as Feng De Yi, tried to rescue Li Jian Cheng. Then the attitude of the Emperor towards Li Jian Cheng changed abruptly. He released Li Jian Cheng and let him go back to Chang'an, the capital, and take charge of the state affairs. He did not investigate Li Jian Cheng's conspiracy any more.

Yang Wen Gan took Ningzhou (now Ningxian, Gansu Province), then took Baijiabao (now Qingyang County, Gansu Province). When Li Shi Min, King of Qin, reached Ningzhou, Yang Wen Gan's army collapsed. On 5 July, Yang Wen Gan was killed by one of his subordinates. His head was cut off and sent to Chang'an. Yuwen Ying was arrested and executed.

46. The Controversy of Moving the Capital to another City

The Eastern Turkic Khanate was a strong khanate. The soldiers of this khanate were all cavalrymen. The Turkish army could move very quickly. The Turks often invaded the border areas of the Tang Dynasty. In August 622, the Turks attacked and took Dazhen Pass (in the southeast of Zhangjiachuan County, Gansu Province). The Emperor of the Tang Dynasty did not have enough forces to drive them out, so he sent Zheng Yuan Chou, the minister in charge of ceremonial sacrifices to the gods and ancestors, to negotiate with Jiali Khan (Ashina Duobi) of the Eastern Turkic Khanate. At that time, the Eastern Turks had more than three hundred thousand cavalrymen. There had been a peace treaty between the Tang Dynasty and the Turks. But the Turks broke the treaty and invaded the Tang territory. Zhang Yuan Chou on behalf of the Emperor of the Tang Dynasty promised quantities of gold, silver and all kinds of treasures every year as tribute to Jiali Khan of the Eastern Turkic Khanate so that the Turks retreated and stopped invasion.

But still, the Turks never stopped invading. Their army invaded Guanzhong and threatened Chang'an, the capital. Someone suggested to the Emperor, "The reason why the Eastern Turks have repeatedly attacked the area of Guanzhong is that there are many beautiful women, and gold, silver and silk in Chang'an. If we burn the capital to the ground and turn it into ruins, and move the capital elsewhere, then the Eastern Turks will stop their incursions." The Emperor agreed, and sent Yuwen Shi Ji to Fancheng (now Xiangfan City, Hubei Province) to find a place to build a new capital. Li Jian Cheng, Li Yuan Ji and Pei Ji all agreed with the suggestion. Xiao Yu knew that it was not a good idea, but he did not say anything.

Only Li Shi Min said to the Emperor, "The alien nations have always been a threat to the Chinese people and have caused many disasters. But Your Majesty is a great and powerful emperor. Your Majesty, like a great dragon, has arisen from among the common people and has pacified all China and restored peace and order to China. Your Majesty has an army of a million men, which is invincible. Why should we move the capital elsewhere, just because alien nations have invaded the border areas? If we do this, we will become a laughing stock and we will be ashamed. In the Han Dynasty, Huo Qu Bing was only a general, but he was determined to drive away the Huns and he lived up to his words and drove the Huns away. I am the King of Qin. I have a rank much higher than that of Huo Qu Bing. I pledge to Your Majesty, in several years time, I will capture Jiali Khan and bring him to Your Majesty. You will still have time to move the capital later, if I fail to accomplish this." The Emperor said, "Good!" Li Jian Cheng retorted, "During the Han Dynasty, Fan Kuai, the brother-in-law of Emperor Gaozu, once boasted that he could defeat the Huns with an army of a hundred thousand men. But later he felt less cocky and stopped saying that. What the King of Qin has said is somewhat like that." Li Shi Min said, "Now the situation is different and our strategies are different. Fan Kuai was just a buffoon. There is no comparison. I am sure we will conquer the area to the north of the desert in less than ten years. This is a promise." Encouraged by Li Shi Min, the Emperor decided not to move the capital to another place.

47. Li Shi Min Uses His Wits to Repulse the Eastern Turks

In August 624 Jiali Khan (Ashina Duobi) and his nephew Tuli Khan (Ashina Shibobi), of the Eastern Turks, mobilized all the soldiers of the whole nation to launch a large-scale invasion of the Tang Dynasty from Yuanzhou (now Guyuan, Ningxia Huizu Autonomous Region). The Emperor of the Tang Dynasty sent Li Shi Min and Li Yuan Ji with an army to march to the north to resist the army of the Eastern Turks. At that time, it rained hard continuously and the roads and bridges were all damaged by floods. Food supplies could not be transported to the camps of the army. The soldiers were tired. The weapons were damaged. Li Shi Min's army encountered the Eastern Turks in Binzhou (now Binxian, Shaanxi Province) suddenly. A battle was unavoidable.

On 12 August Jiali Khan and Tuli Khan with an army of ten thousand cavalry-men suddenly appeared to the west of the city of Binzhou. They deployed their army in battle formations. Each Khan stood at the head of his battle formation. The officers and men of the Tang army were afraid. Li Shi Min said to Li Yuan Ji, "Now the cavalrymen of the enemy have given great pressure on us. We must not show to the enemy that we are cowards. We have to fight the battle. Will you attack the enemy formations with me?" Li Yuan Ji said, "The enemy army is so powerful. Why should we take our enemy lightly and go out to fight with such a strong enemy? You will regret when we are defeated." Li Shi Min said, "If you do not dare to go out of the camps with me to fight, I will go alone. You may stay here to watch the battle." Then Li Shi Min with a hundred cavalrymen rode to the enemy formation. Li Shi Min shouted to Jiali Khan, "The Tang government and you have reached a friendly agreement and you have promised not to invade our territory any more. But now you have gone back on your own promise and have invaded very far into our territory. I am the King of Qin. If you want to fight a duel with me, I will be very glad to fight with you. If you want to attack me with all your men, I will resist your attack with these one hundred cavalrymen." Jiali Khan did not expect that Li Shi Min would come personally to his battle formation so closely. He was not certain what trick Li Shi Min was playing. So he just smiled and did not respond to Li Shi Min's words. Then Li Shi Min got even closer and rode to Tuli Khan's battle formation and shouted to Tuli Khan, "In the past, we held a ceremony in which we burned incense and took an oath. You swore to me that you would share weal and woe with me and we would help each other. Now you have gone so far as to lead an army to attack me. You have forgotten all the warranties you made in that ceremony." Tuli Khan kept silent and did not make any response. Then Li Shi Min urged his horse forward and intended to cross a brook between the two confronting armies. Jiali Khan had seen Li Shi Min talking with Tuli Khan for some time and he had overheard just a few words, something about promises made and swearing an oath. This certainly aroused Jiali Khan's suspicions. He suspected that there was some secret deal between Tuli Khan and Li Shi Min. He also suspected that there was a great Tang army waiting to ambush his army. So he sent an envoy to say to Li Shi Min, "Your Excellency need not cross the brook. I have come all the way here just to restate the agreement between us." Then the cavalry of the Eastern Turks turned back to their camps.

After that, it rained even harder. Li Shi Min said to the generals under him, "Most of the Eastern Turks are good archers. They depend very much on the bows to win battles. But now it has been raining for days and it is very humid. The cords of their bows are damp and cannot shoot. We live in houses and cook food with fire so all our weapons have been kept in dry places. We must seize this chance to defeat the Turks." That night, covered by the darkness, the Tang army moved very close to the main camps of the Eastern Turks in the rain. By the time the Turks saw the Tang army, they were shocked. Li Shi Min sent an envoy to Tuli Khan who analyzed the situation for him. Tuli Khan accepted Li Shi Min's advice. So in the military strategy meeting held by Jiali Khan, Tuli Khan was against the decision to fight the Tang army. So Jiali Khan decided to find a peaceful solution with Li Shi Min. He sent Tuli Khan to the camps of the Tang army to sue for peace. Li Shi Min promised to make peace with the Eastern Turks. Tuli Khan took this chance to establish a good relationship with Li Shi Min.

48. The Incident at Xuanwu Gate

Li Jian Cheng stepped up his plan to kill Li Shi Min. One evening, Li Jian Cheng invited Li Shi Min to dinner, and put some poison in Li Shi Min's liquor. After Li Shi Min drank the liquor, he suddenly felt a great pain in his heart and spat out a lot of blood. Li Shen Tong, King of Huai'an, helped Li Shi Min back to Li Shi Min's house, the Western Palace. When the Emperor got the news, he hurried to Li Shi Min's house to see him. He said to Li Jian Cheng, "The King of Qin has no capacity for liquor. From now on, you should not ask the King of Qin to drink with you any more." Then he went into Li Shi Min's bedroom and said to him, "You were the first one to put forward the great strategy to march to Chang'an. Then you conquered the most powerful warlords in China. You have made great contributions to the state. I intended to make you my successor and crown prince. But you declined the offer. Li Jian Cheng is my eldest son. So he naturally became my successor and then crown prince. He has been in this position for quite a long time. I am not hardhearted enough to deprive him of his rights to succeed to the throne. It seems that you three brothers hate each other very much. If all of you stay in the capital, there will be conflicts sooner or later. I will send you back to Luoyang as the head of the special government to rule over the territory east to the Xiaoshan Mountain. You may have all the flags and ceremonies as an emperor." Li Shi Min said, with tears in his eyes, that he would not go because he could not tear himself from his father, the Emperor. The Emperor said, "All of China is one family. The western capital Chang'an and the eastern capital Luoyang are not far from each other. When I miss you, I can go to the eastern capital to visit you. You should not feel so sad to leave me."

When Li Shi Min was about to set out for Luoyang, Li Jian Cheng and Li Yuan Ji discussed the matter secretly. They came to this conclusion: "If the King of Qin goes to Luoyang, he will have the vast territory and many cities under his control. And he will have military forces under his command. Then it will be very difficult to bring him to submission. If he is made to stay in the capital, then he will not be a powerful man. Then it will be easy for us to kill him."

Li Jian Cheng and Li Yuan Ji asked some of the officials to present a secret memorandum to the Emperor. The memorandum read, "When the generals and officials under the King of Qin got the news that the King of Qin was going to the Eastern Capital, they all jumped for joy. It seems that once they leave Chang'an, they will never return." Then they sent some officials to analyze the consequence of sending Li Shi Min to Luoyang for the Emperor. At last, the Emperor changed his mind and withdrew his order to send Li Shi Min to the Eastern Capital.

Li Jian Cheng, Li Yuan Ji and the concubines of the Emperor all worked very hard to slander Li Shi Min in front of the Emperor. The Emperor believed them and was going to punish him by depriving him of his rights as a king. Chen Shu Da said to the Emperor, "The King of Qin has made great contributions to the empire. He should not be deprived of his rank as a king. He is a staunch man with moral integrity. If he is punished, he will not be able to tolerate the blow. In that case, something that is irreparable might happen to him. An then it will be too late for Your Majesty to feel regrets." Then the Emperor dismissed his intention to deprive Li Shi Min of his rights as a king.

The officials under Li Shi Min were all worried. They did not know what to do. Fang Xuan Ling, who was in charge of examination of officials in the Office of the King of Qin, said to Zhangsun Wu Ji, who was in charge of legal department of the Office of the King of Qin, "Now the hatred between the King of Qin and the Crown Prince and King of Qi has become serious. Once conflicts break out, all the officials of the Office of the King of Qin will be killed. China will be in chaos again. We'd better persuade the King of Qin to act now so as to save the empire from falling at this critical moment." Zhangsun Wu Ji said, "I have this idea in my mind for quite a long time but I have not told anybody about it. Since we share the same view, I should report our idea to the King of Qin."

So Zhangsun Wu Ji went to see Li Shi Min, King of Qin. The King of Qin summoned Fang Xuan Ling to discuss the matter. Fang Xuan Ling said, "Your Excellency has made such great contributions to the realm that no one can surpass you. You have every right to succeed to the throne. Now the situation is critical. Conflict is inevitable. This is the opportunity that Heaven has granted to Your Excellency. Your Excellency should not hesitate to seize this opportunity." Then the King of Qin asked Zhangsun Wu Ji, Fang Xuan Ling and Du Ru Hui (who was the military secretary of the Office of the King of Qin) secretly to make preparations.

Portrait of Zhangsun Wu Ji

Portrait of Fang Xuan Ling

Li Shi Min was powerful because he had many brave generals under his command. Li Jian Cheng and Li Yuan Ji tried to seduce them to betray Li Shi Min and come to their side. The Crown Prince secretly gave a cart load of gold and silver to Yuchi Jing De. Then he wrote a letter to Yuchi Jing De to ask him to come to his service. The letter read, "I know that you are a virtuous man. I hope I can be a friend of yours." Yuchi Jing De replied, "I was born in a very poor family and grew up in very difficult circumstances. By the end of the Sui Dynasty, when the whole realm was in chaos, I joined the rebel army and served in that army for a very long time. I committed grave crimes against the Tang Dynasty. It was the King of Qin who saved me from destruction and let me start a new life. Now I am a general in the office of His Excellency. I will repay his kindness by serving His Excellency heart and soul. I would even die for him. I cannot accept such valuable gifts since I have not rendered any service for Your Highness. If I had any secret dealings with Your Highness, I would be unfaithful to the King of Qin. I think that Your Highness would agree that any person who betrays his master to gain a fortune is despicable." When Li Jian Cheng got the reply, he was furious and made up his mind to destroy Yuchi Jing De.

When Yuchi Jing De told Li Shi Min what had happened, Li Shi Min said, "I know you are a very devoted and resolute man. No matter how much gold is put in front of you, you will not be moved. If they give you any gifts next time, you may just accept them. Then you may know the conspiracy they are plotting. Isn't that a marvelous idea? Otherwise, you will be in great trouble." Not long later, Li Yuan Ji sent an assassin to Yuchi Jing De's house to find a chance to kill him. Yuchi Jing De was informed. He ordered his guards to open wide the gates and doors of his house. He lay on his bed with the door wide open. The assassin entered the court of the house several times and saw Yuchi Jing De lying on his bed, but he did not dare to go in the bedroom. At last he left.

Portrait of Du Ru Hui

Li Yuan Ji decided to frame Yuchi Jing De. He accused Yuchi Jing De of treason in front of the Emperor. The Emperor gave the order to throw Yuchi Jing De into jail. The authority investigated Yuchi Jing De's case and found him guilty. He was sentenced to death. Li Shi Min did his best to rescue Yuchi Jing De. At last, Yuchi Jing De was released.

Li Yuan Ji also framed Cheng Zhi Jie, the commander-in-chief of the cavalry of the Office of the King of Qin. The Emperor appointed Cheng Zhi Jie governor of Kangzhou (now Chengxian, Gansu province). Cheng Zhi Jie said to Li Shi Min, "If the arms and legs of Your Excellency are all cut off, how long will the body survive? I will stay in this office at the risk of death penalty. I hope Your Excellency will make up your mind soon." Li Jian Cheng and Li Yuan Ji tried to buy Duan Zhi Xuan, the commander-in-chief of the second army of the Office of the King of Qin, with gold and silver. Duan Zhi Xuan also refused to take the gifts. Then Li Yuan Ji said to Li Jian Cheng, "The wisest and most resourceful strategy planners in the Office of the King of Qin are Fang Xuan Ling and Du Ru Hui. We should try to get them out of the Office of the King of Qin." So they presented false accusation against them to the Emperor. Soon the Emperor ordered the two strategists out of the Office of the King of Qin and they were not allowed to go back without the permission of the Emperor.

At that time, only Zhangsun Wu Ji, Gao Shi Lian, the general secretary of the command of the garrison of the capital, Hou Jun Ji, a general of the guards, and Yuchi Jing De remained in the Office of the King of Qin. They urged Li Shi Min to take action to kill Li Jian Chang and Li Yuan Ji. Li Shi Min still hesitated and could not make up his mind. Then Li Shi Min asked the opinion of Li Ji, the commander-in-chief of the Lingzhou (now Lingwu, Ningxia Huizu Autonomous Region) command, but Li Ji did not give any reply. Then Li Shi Min asked the opinion of Li Jing, commander-in-chief of the regiments. Li Jing did not give any reply either. So Li Shi Min respected them very much.

Portrait of Yuchi Jing De

It happened that General Ashina Yushe of the Eastern Turkic Khanate with several hundred thousand cavalry marched southward to invade the border of the Tang Dynasty. They laid siege to Wucheng (now Dingbian, Shaanxi Province). Li Jian Cheng, the Crown Prince, recommended Li Yuan Ji to replace Li Shi Min to lead an army to march northward to meet the army of the Eastern Turkic Khanate. The Emperor agreed to his recommendation and ordered Li Yuan Ji to lead General Li Yi and General Zhang Ji with an army to reinforce Wucheng. Li Yuan Ji asked the Emperor to transfer Yuchi Jing De, Cheng Zhi Jie, Duan Zhi Xuan and Qin Shu Bao to his army. He also asked the Emperor to put the picked troops of Li Shi Min's army under his command. Li Yuan Ji went to see the Emperor and asked the Emperor to kill Li

Shi Min. The Emperor said, "The King of Qin has made great contributions in pacifying the whole realm. He has not committed any crime. On what grounds shall we put him to death?" Li Yuan Ji said, "The King of Qin often goes against Your Majesty's orders. When he took the Eastern Capital, he stayed there for quite a long time and would not come back to Chang'an. He distributed money and fine fabric to his subordinates so as to make them devoted to him. Does this indicate he plans a rebellion? If Your Majesty decides to put him to death, we can find a lot of reasons." But the Emperor would not listen to him.

Li Jian Cheng said to Li Yuan Ji, "Now you have got all the experienced soldiers and fierce generals of the Office of the King of Qin. You have now several hundred thousand men under your command. I will hold a banquet by the side of Kunming Lake to see you off. The King of Qin will also attend. I will order several warriors to kill the King of Qin in the banquet. Then I will report to the Emperor that the King of Qin died suddenly. The Emperor will believe what I report to him. Then I will ask the Emperor to hand over the power to me. When I get the throne and become emperor, I will make you successor to the throne. You may kill any of those generals who were originally of the Office of the King of Qin but now under your command." Wang Zhi, the general secretary of the office of the Crown Prince, overheard their conversation, and he secretly reported what Li Jian Cheng had said to Li Shi Min.

Li Shi Min passed it on to Zhangsun Wu Ji and Yuchi Jing De. Zhangsun Wu Ji urged Li Shi Min to take action immediately. Li Shi Min gave a deep sigh and said, "The Crown Prince and the King of Qi and I are brothers. It is a crime if I kill them. I hope they will take action first. In that case, I will be justified to retaliate and lead an army against them. Isn't that better?" Yuchi Jing De said, "Everybody is afraid of death. It is human nature. All of us are doing our best to protect Your Excellency at the risk of our own lives. I think it is Heaven's will that we should do so. Now, disaster is about to fall upon us. But Your Excellency still hesitates and delays in taking action. Even if Your Excellency thinks lightly of your own life, Your Excellency should think of the interest of the whole empire and your royal family. If Your Excellency does not take our advice, I will take off and hide myself in the forests and mountains. I do not want to be bound and be killed like a pig." Zhangsun Wu Ji said, "If Your Excellency does not take Yuchi Jing De's advice, the opportunity will slip from the fingers of Your Excellency and Your Excellency will not have a second chance. Yuchi Jing De will certainly run away, and then I will also have to run away. I will not be able to serve Your Excellency anymore." Still, Li Shi Min said, "My idea is not totally wrong. You should further think it over." Yuchi Jing De said, "Your Excellency has been hesitating over such an important matter. This shows that Your Excellency is not wise. Your Excellency cannot take resolute action in front of such a crisis. This shows that Your

Excellency is not brave. The eight hundred brave warriors Your Excellency has maintained have now entered the palace of Your Excellency. They are all now put on their armor and got their weapons ready. The ball is rolling. Your Excellency cannot stop it."

Li Shi Min gathered all the generals and staff in the Office of the King of Qin to discuss the matter. They were all of the same opinion: "The King of Qi is a fierce and malicious man. He will certainly not be satisfied in serving his brother Li Jian Cheng all his life. We hear that one of the generals under him said to the King of Qi, 'When the two characters 'Yuan Ji' of the name of Your Excellency are put together, they will form the character of 'Tang'. Your Excellency will become the emperor of the Tang Dynasty.' Li Yuan Ji said with joy, 'If we get rid of the King of Qin, it will be easy to take care of the Crown Prince.' Now their conspiracy to kill Your Excellency is still going on, but King of Qi is now planning to take over the power from the Crown Prince. King of Qi is a troublemaker. If they succeed in their conspiracy, the fight between them will begin. Then China will be in great chaos again. Your Excellency is a wise and competent person. It is easy for Your Excellency to capture these two men. Your Excellency should not think too much of reputation and virtuousness. Your Excellency should put the interest of the whole empire in the first place." Li Shi Min still hesitated. Then one of the staff asked Li Shi Min, "What kind of man does Your Excellency think Shun was?" "He was the greatest ruler in Chinese history. He was the most virtuous man," Li Shi Min replied. The man continued, "Shun's father once tried to kill Shun by ordering him to dig the dirt from the bottom of a well, then dumping more soil down into the well to bury him alive. But Shun dug a tunnel to escape. If he had not done so, he would have been buried at the bottom of the well. His father asked him to repair the roof of the barn. When he was on the top of the roof, his father set fire on the barn intending to burn him to death. With the help of his straw hat, he jumped down from the roof and escaped. If he had not done so, he would have been burned to ashes. If he had died, he would not have become the wisest ruler of China. As the saying goes, if your father is going to beat you with a small rod, you may just let him beat you; but if your father is going to beat you with a big rod, you will have to run away because he might beat you to death. The most important thing is to stay alive." Then Li Shi Min ordered to have a tortoise shell burned so as to tell whether their action would be successful or not. At that time, Zhang Gong Jin, one of his staff, came into the room from outside. He took up the tortoise shell on the table and threw it to the floor and said, "The purpose of divination is to help us make decisions. We do not need to make any decision. If the result of the divination tells us that it would be unlucky for us to take action, shall we stop our action?" Then Li Shi Min became resolute to take action.

Li Shi Min sent Zhangsun Wu Ji to summon Fang Xuan Ling and Du Ru Hui to his office. Fang Xuan Ling said, "The Emperor has issued an order that we are prohibited to accept orders from the King of Qin. If we go to see the King of Qin without the permission from the Emperor, we will surely be put to death. So we cannot go to see His Excellency." Zhangsun Wu Ji came back and told Li Shi Min what Fang Xuan Ling had said. Li Shi Min was very angry; he said to Yuchi Jing De, "Fang Xuan Ling and Du Ru Hui have really betrayed me!" He untied his sword and handed it over to Yuchi Jing De. He said, "Go to see if they will come or not. If they will not come, you may cut off their heads with this sword." Yuchi Jing De and Zhangsun Wu Ji hurried to see Fang Xuan Ling and Du Ru Hui. When Yuchi Jing De saw the two, he said to them, "The King of Qin has made up his mind. You'd better go to see the King of Qin and help him make a plan. It is not safe for the four of us to walk together in the streets. Let's go separately." He asked them to disguise themselves as Taoist priests. Fang Xuan Ling, Du Ru Hui and Zhangsun Wu Ji walked together. Yuchi Jing De took another road. That night, they made a detailed plan for their action.

On 3 June 626, the Taibai Star (Venus) appeared in the sky in daytime. Fu Yi, the head of the national observatory, reported to the Emperor, "The Taibai Star appeared in the sky over the Qin area. This is the sign that the King of Qin will become emperor." Incidentally, Li Shi Min went to the palace to see the Emperor. The Emperor showed the report to him. Li Shi Min took advantage of the situation and accused Li Jian Chang and Li Yuan Ji of adultery with the Emperor's young concubines. Li Shi Min said, "I have not done anything that is harmful to my brothers. But they now intend to kill me. They are actually seeking revenge on me for Wang Shi Chong and Dou Jian De. If I were killed by the Crown Prince and King of Qi, I would not be able to see Your Majesty any more. And I would be ashamed to meet Wang Shi Chong and Dou Jian De in hell." The Emperor was surprised to hear all this. He said, "I will summon them to the court tomorrow morning and investigate this case personally. You'd better come to the court early tomorrow morning."

On the morning of 4 June, Li Shi Min led an army to lay ambush at the Xuanwu Gate (the gate in the wall of the palace of the Emperor) with Zhangsun Wu Ji, Yuchi Jing De, Fang Xuan Ling, Du Ru Hui, Yuwen Shi Ji, Gao Shi Lian, Hou Jun Ji, Cheng Zhi Jie, Qin Shu Bao, Duan Zhi Xuan, Qutu Tong, Zhang Shi Gui and others. One of the Emperor's concubines got all the information of Li Shi Min's report and she sent somebody to pass the information to Li Jian Cheng. He immediately sent for Li Yuan Ji to discuss the situation. Li Yuan Ji said, "We should mobilize all the army under our control to prepare for war. We may tell the Emperor that we are ill and cannot go to the court. At the same time we will sit quietly to see how the situation develops." Li Jian Cheng said, "All my guards are ready for battle. They are on the alert. You and I may go to the court to see what has happened." And they both went. They rode directly to Xuanwu Gate at the palace of the Emperor. At this time, the Emperor had summoned Pei Ji, Xiao Yu, Chen Shu Da and others to the court and they were ready to hear the case.

As Li Jian Cheng and Li Yuan Ji rode to Lin Hu Hall, near the Xuanwu Gate, they sensed that danger was lying ahead. They turned their horses immediately and rode towards the palace of the Crown Prince. Li Shi Min rode quickly after them, shouting, "Why don't you go to the court?" Li Yuan Ji turned and drew his bow three times. He was so nervous that he could not draw his bow fully, so all his arrows fell to the ground half way. Li Shi Min drew his bow and aimed at Li Jian Chen and shot at him. Li Jian Cheng was killed right away. Yuchi Jing De followed Li Shi Min with seventy men and rode after Li Yuan Ji. He ordered his men to shoot at Li Yuan Ji. Li Yuan Ji fell from his horse. But at this moment Li Shi Min's horse got spooked and rode right into the woods. Li Shi Min was struck by a branch of a tree and fell to the ground. He fell to the ground so heavily that he could not get up immediately. Li Yuan Ji rose to his feet and ran at Li Shi Min. He got hold of Li Shi Min's bow and tried to strangle Li Shi Min with the cord of the bow. Yuchi Jing De quickly rode up, and Li Yuan Ji tried to run away on foot. Yuchi Jing De caught up with him and shot an arrow at him. Li Yuan Ji was killed. Yuchi Jing De got off his horse and cut the heads of the Crown Prince and Li Yuan Ji off their dead bodies. Feng Li, the commander-in-chief of the guards of the palace of the Crown Prince, got the news that the Crown Prince had been killed. He and the deputy commander-in-chief Xue Wan Che and Xie Shu Fang led two thousand picked troops of the guards of the palace of the Crown Prince and of the King of Qi to attack Xuanwu Gate fiercely. Zhang Gong Jin shut the gate and defended the gate bravely. The battle went on for quite a long time. Then Xue Wan Che ordered his men to attack the palace of the King of Qin. The situation was tense. The soldiers of the Office of the King of Qin were very worried. At that time Yuchi Jing De arrived and showed the heads of the Crown Prince and Li Yuan Ji to the troops of the Crown Prince, who lost heart and ran away. Xue Wan Che rode to hide in Zhongnan Shan Mountain. Feng Li and Xie Shu Fang also ran away to hide themselves in the wilds.

The Emperor waited in the court for quite a long time, but Li Jian Cheng and Li Yuan Ji did not come. At that time two thousand of the Crown Prince's best troops were attacking Xuanwu Gate. Stray arrows dropped into the halls of the palace. Li Shi Min sent Yuchi Jing De into the Emperor's palace to protect him. Yuchi Jing De went into the palace with his hamlet and armor on and with a spear in his hand. He walked straight to the Emperor. The Emperor was shocked to see that Yuchi Jing De was fully armed. He asked, "Who has rebelled today? Why have you come here?" Yuchi Jing De replied, "The Crown Prince and King of

Qi staged an armed rebellion. The King of Qin has suppressed the rebellion and killed the Crown Prince and King of Qi. The King of Qin was afraid that Your Majesty would be frightened. So he has sent me here to protect Your Majesty." The Emperor said to Pei Ji, "I did not expect this. What shall I do?" Xiao Yu and Chen Shu Da said, "Li Jian Cheng and Li Yuan Ji did not participate in planning our uprising. They were not much help in the establishment of the Tang Dynasty. They were jealous of the King of Qin who has made such great contributions to the Tang Dynasty. So they conspired to kill the King of Qin. Now that the King of Qin has suppressed their rebellion, and the people of the whole nation have confidence in him. Your Majesty had better make him the crown prince and pass the power to him. Then the whole nation will be stable." The Emperor said, "You are right. That is just what I was thinking to do."

At that time, the army of the King of Qin and the army of the Crown Prince and King of Qi were fighting. Yuchi Jing De asked the Emperor to issue an order to stop the fighting and the order that all the armies should be put under the command of the King of Qin. The Emperor issued these two orders as Yuchi Jing De had said.

The incident at Xuanwu Gate

Yuwen Shi Ji, the general secretary of the Office of the King of Qin, went out of the palace to declare the orders of the Emperor. The fighting stopped. The Emperor sent Pei Ji to the palace of the Crown Prince to explain to the officers and men what had happened and to disband the army of the Crown Prince. Then the Emperor summoned Li Shi Min to his palace and comforted him. Touching his head gently, the Emperor said to Li Shi Min, "These days I nearly made the mistake of believing what Li Jian Cheng and Li Yuan Ji said, and doing something harmful to you." Li Shi Min put his head on his father's chest and wept like a child.

All the sons of Li Jian Cheng and Li Yuan Ji were killed.

The generals under Li Shi Min proposed to kill all of the trusted followers of Li Jian Cheng and Li Yuan Ji as well. But Yuchi Jing De strongly opposed the idea. He said, "Li Jian Cheng and Li Yuan Ji were the arch-criminals. Now they have been killed. If we punish their subordinates, it will not help the stability of the empire." So the followers of Li Jian Cheng and Li Yuan Ji were spared.

On the same day, the Emperor issued an imperial order which read, "The arch-criminals are Li Jian Cheng and Li Yuan Ji. All their followers are spared. From now on, all government affairs should be reported to the King of Qin, who will make the decisions."

On June 5, Feng Li and Xie Shu Fang came out to surrender. But Xue Wan Che was still in hiding. Only after Li Shi Min had sent several persons to explain the policy to him did Xue Wan Che come out to surrender. Li Shi Min said, "Feng Li and Xue Wan Che are devoted to their masters. They are devoted and righteous men." He set Feng Li and Xue Wan Che free.

On June 7, the Emperor formally made Li Shi Min Crown Prince. He issued another imperial order which read, "From now on, all military and state affairs should be handled by the Crown Prince before they are reported to me."

On June 12, the Emperor put Yuwen Shi Ji in charge of the general affairs of the palace of the Crown Prince; Zhangsun Wu Ji and Du Ru Hui in charge of the political affairs; Gao Shi Lian and Fang Xuan Ling were put in charge of the affairs of the palace of the Crown Prince; Yuchi Jing De became commander-in-chief of the guards of left wing of the palace of the Crown Prince; Cheng Zhi Jie became commander-in-chief of the guards of the right wing of the palace of the Crown Prince. The Emperor granted all the treasures in the palace of the former King of Qi to Yuchi Jing De.

Wei Zheng, the official in charge of the library of the palace of the former Crown Prince, had often urged the former Crown Prince Li Jian Cheng to kill Li Shi Min. After Li Shi Min killed Li Jian Cheng, he summoned Wei Zheng to his office. He asked Wei Zheng, "Why did you drive a wedge between us brothers?" Wei Zheng replied calmly, "If the former Crown Prince had taken my advice, he would not have been killed. Since I worked for him, I had to do my best to maintain his best interest." Li Shi Min had long admired Wei Zheng's talent. When he heard what Wei Zheng had said, he smiled. Then he appointed Wei Zheng general secretary of the palace of the Crown Prince. Li Shi Min also appointed General Xue Wan Che, the former vice commander-in-chief of guards of the palace of the former Crown Prince, as deputy commander-in-chief of the guards of Li Shi Min's palace.

CHAPTER THREE. THE REIGN OF EMPEROR LI SHI MIN

49. Li Shi Min Becomes Emperor of the Tang Dynasty

On 8 August 626, Li Yuan, the Emperor of the Tang Dynasty, issued an imperial order to the effect that he would pass the throne to Li Shi Min. Li Shi Min refused to accept the offer, but Li Yuan insisted on passing the throne to him.

On 9 August, Li Shi Min ascended the throne in Xiande Hall of the palace for the Crown Prince and became the second emperor of the Tang Dynasty. He respected his father as Father Emperor. On 21 August, Li Shi Min, the Emperor, made his wife Lady Zhangsun Empress. Empress Zhangsun was a virtuous woman. She had tried her best to mend the bad relations between Li Shi Min and his two brothers. After she became Empress, she practiced thrift. She led a very simple life. Li Shi Min respected her very much. On 8 October 626 Li Shi Min made his eldest son Li Cheng Qian the Crown Prince. At that time Li Cheng Qian was eight years old.

50. Emperor Li Shi Min Meets Jiali Khan of the Eastern Turkic Khanate at the Bridge over the Weishui River

In July 626, Jiali Khan commanded a great army of a hundred thousand cavalrymen to attack Wugong (now Wugong, Shaanxi Province). On 24 August, the Eastern Turks attacked Gaoling (now Gaoling, Shaanxi Province). On 26 August, Yuchi Jing De, the commander-in-chief of the army group of Jingzhou (now Jingchuan, Gansu Province) fought a battle with the Eastern Turks in Jingyang (now Jingyang, Shaanxi Province) and defeated the Eastern Turks. But on

28 August, Jiali Khan of the Eastern Turkic Khanate moved his main force to the northern end of the bridge over the Weishui River, threatening Chang'an, the capital of the Tang Dynasty. He sent Zhishi Sili, one of his generals, as an envoy to Chang'an to see Li Shi Min, the Emperor of the Tang Dynasty. He had a mission to collect information and spy on the situation in Chang'an. When Zhishi Sili saw the Emperor of the Tang Dynasty, he said to him, "Jiali Khan and Tuli Khan have arrived with a million men today." Li Shi Min reproached him, "I and your khan have made a peace settlement. We have presented him with an abundance of gold and silver and other precious goods. Now your khan has breached the treaty between the Tang Dynasty and Eastern Turks by leading an army to invade into our territory. You have done great harm to us. We have done nothing wrong to your khan. You have gone so far as to come to me to boast the strength of your khan. Now I will order your head to be chopped off before I fight your khan." Zhishi Sili was frightened and begged the Emperor to spare his life. The two premiers, Xiao Yu and Feng De Yi, suggested that Zhishi Sili be sent back. The Emperor said angrily, "If I send him back, they will think that I am afraid of them. That will encourage them to harm us more." So they put Zhishi Sili in jail.

Li Shi Min led Gao Shi Lian, Fang Xuan Ling and General Zhou Fan with six cavalrymen to ride out of Xuanwu Gate. They rode directly to the southern bank of Weishui Rive to talk to Jiali Khan across the water. Li Shi Min accused Jiali Khan of breaching their agreement. When the officers and men of the army of the Eastern Turks saw Li Shi Min, they couldn't help but dismount and bow to him in awe. Not long later, the great army of the Tang Dynasty arrived with flags streaming in the air and the armor of the Tang army shining under the sun. Jiali Khan found that Zhishi Sili had not come back and the Emperor of the Tang Dynasty had come alone. Now that the great army of the Tang Dynasty had arrived, Jiali Khan was worried. Li Shi Min, the Emperor of the Tang Dynasty, ordered his army to move back from the bridge and to deploy in battle formation. He himself would stay alone on the bank to talk to Jiali Khan of the Eastern Turkic Khanate. Xiao Yu thought that it would be unsafe for the Emperor to stay alone to talk to Jiali Khan, so he stopped the Emperor's horse and asked him not to go. But the Emperor said, "I have thought about it for a long time. The reason why Jiali Khan has come to a place so close to our capital with all his army is that he thinks that there has been an internal conflict in our empire and that I would not dare to fight with them because I have only recently ascended the throne. If I shut the gates of the capital and stay inside, that will show to them that I am afraid of them. Then Jiali Khan will set his soldiers to loot the areas around the capital. Then we will not be able to control the situation. I came alone without any army with me only to show to the Turks that I take them lightly. Then my great army came to make them believe that we will meet them in battle. Jiali Khan did not expect all this.

Now he is at a total loss as to what he should do. The Turks have penetrated deep into our territory. The soldiers are quite scared to be so deep in enemy territory. If we fight with them, we will surely win. If we make a peace settlement with them, the settlement will surely last. This step is critical to overcome the Turks. You just look on and see the result." That day, Jiali Khan sent an envoy to ask the Emperor to make peace with them. The Emperor gave permission. After that, the Emperor rode back to his palace. On the second day, the Emperor rode out of the capital to the bank of the Weishui River. The Emperor of the Tang Dynasty and Jiali Khan of the Eastern Turkic Khanate met at the bridge. They held a ceremony of peace making. They had a white horse killed and swore to keep their promise. After that, the army of the Eastern Turks withdrew.

Xiao Yu asked the Emperor, "Before we made peace with the Turks, the generals asked Your Majesty to let them fight. But Your Majesty did not give permission. We were all puzzled. But very soon, the Turks withdrew. Will Your Majesty tell us why?" Li Shi Min said, "As I have observed, although there were many Turkish soldiers, they were not disciplined. What the Khan and his courtiers wanted was money and goods. When they asked for a peace settlement, Jiali Khan stayed alone on the northern bank while all his high-ranking officers and nobles came to see me. If I gave a banquet and made them all drunk in the banquet, I could easily have captured all of them. Then I might attack the Turks' army. It would be easily defeated. I have ordered Zhangsun Wu Ji and Li Jing to lay ambush in Binzhou. If the Turks were defeated and withdrew back to the north, our army under Zhangsun Wu Ji and Li Jing would attack them in the front and I would attack them from the rear. Then we might easily destroy the Turks' army. But I did not want to destroy the Eastern Turks by means of war, because I have just ascended the throne. The state is not yet stable. The people are still living in dire poverty. They need peace to recover from the civil war. When war breaks out between China and the Turks, the people will suffer. And if the Turks are defeated, they will hate us all the more. They will become more united and prepare themselves for war against us. Then the war will be endless. Then we will not be able to achieve our purpose. So I did not use the military power. Instead, I promised them peace and gave them silk and other valuables. The Turks will become more conceited and arrogant. They will not be always in the alert. We may wait till there are disagreements and conflicts between the Khan and his nobles. Then we will seize the chance to destroy the Eastern Turkic Khanate once and for all." Xiao Yu and the others were all convinced.

In September, Jiali Khan of the Eastern Turkic Khanate presented three thousand horses and ten thousand sheep to the Emperor of the Tang Dynasty, but the Emperor of the Tang Dynasty did not accept them. He ordered Jiali Khan to let all the people they had captured come back to China.

51. Li Shi Min Trains His Army in His Palace

On 22 September 626 Li Shi Min led the officers and men of his guards into the front courtyard of Xiande Hall of the palace to practice arrow shooting. He said to them, "Since ancient times, China and the Turks each had their times of prosperity and decline. Xuan Yuan, the great emperor of the ancient times, was a great warrior. He drove the Turks back to the north. King Xuan of the Zhou Dynasty defeated the Turks in the area of Taiyuan. But the emperors of the Han Dynasty, the Jin Dynasty and the Sui Dynasty did not train their soldiers well. When the Turks came, they could not withstand their invasion and many Chinese people were killed by the Turks. Now, I don't spend money on building of palaces. I let the peasants enjoy their life. Soldiers should be well trained in shooting arrows and riding horses. We should be always in the alert against the Turks' invasion. When the time comes, you will be invincible. When there is war, I will be your commander to fight against the invaders. I hope the Chinese people may have a peaceful life."

Everyday, several hundred officers and men practiced shooting in the courtyard in front of the hall. The Emperor personally presided over the examination of their training. He gave awards to those who passed the exam. Some of the courtiers warned the Emperor, "In accordance with the laws, those who bring weapons into the place where the emperor lives should be hanged. Now the ordinary soldiers are pulling bows and shooting arrows in the courtyard of the palace and Your Majesty is among them. In case one of those soldiers is lunatic and harms Your Majesty, the security of the state will be endangered." But Li Shi Min would not accept their warning. He said, "The emperor should consider the whole state as one family. The people all over China are the children of the emperor. The emperor should care for every one of them. Why should I be suspicious of my guards?" The soldiers knew that the Emperor cared about them very much and had great expectation of them. So they practiced very hard. In several years' time, they all were highly trained experts.

52. Li Shi Min Grants Rewards to the Officials and Generals Who Made Great Contributions

In September 626 Li Shi Min made Zhangsun Wu Ji Duke of the State of Qi, Fang Xuan Ling Duke of the State of Xing, Yuchi Jing De Duke of the State of Wu, Du Ru Hui Duke of the State of Cai, and Hou Jun Ji Duke of the State of Lu. In October, Li Shi Min granted the benefit of the tax on peasant households to the ministers and generals in accordance with their contributions: Pei Ji had one thousand five hundred peasant households; Zhangsun Wu Ji, Wang Jun Kuo, Yuchi Jing De, Fang Xuan Ling and Du Ru Hui each had one thousand three hundred; Zhangsun Shun De, Chai Shao, Li Yi, Li Xiao Gong (King of Zhao Prefecture) each had one thousand two hundred; Hou Jun Ji, Zhang Gong Jin and Liu Shi Li each had one thousand; Li Ji and Liu Hong Ji each had nine hundred; Gao Shi Lian, Yuwen Shi Ji, Qin Shu Bao and Cheng Zhi Jie each had seven hundred; An Xing Gui, An Xiu Ren, Qutu Tong, Xiao Yu, Feng De Yi and Liu Yi Jie each had six hundred; Li Shen Tong (King of Huai'an) had five hundred; Qian Jiu Long, Fan Shi Xing, Gongsun Wu Da, Li Meng Chang, Duan Zhi Xuan, Pang Qing Yun, Zhang Liang, Li Jing, Du Yan and Yuan Zhong Wen each had four hundred.

A ceremony was held to declare the decision. Li Shi Min ordered Chen Shu Da to read out his imperial decision. Then Li Shi Min said to all of the officials and generals present, "My consideration of your contributions might not all be proper. You may air your opinions." Then the generals began to argue. Li Shen Tong, King of Huai'an, who was the uncle of Li Shi Min, said, "I first rose in Guanzhong to respond to your uprising in Taiyuan. Now Fang Xuan Ling and Du Ru Hui are just civil officials. But they rank higher than me. I am not convinced this is right." Li Shi Min said, "It's true that you first rose in Guanzhong to respond to our uprising. But you rose in Guanzhong also for self protection. When the area to the east of Xiaoshan Mountain was in chaos, you were authorized to pacify that area. But when Dou Jian De marched to the south, all the army under your command was destroyed by Dou Jian De. When Liu Hei Ta rebelled, you were defeated by Liu Hei Ta. Fang Xuan Ling and others made strategic plans in the command tent and contributed greatly to stabilizing the Tang Dynasty. Now I grant rewards to you according to your contributions. There is no doubt that they made greater contributions and should rank above you. You are my uncle, my closest relative. I will give you any valuables I have. But I cannot grant you the same benefits that I grant to those who have made greater contributions than you." At these words, all the generals were won over.

When Li Yuan had ascended the throne of the Tang Dynasty, he listed all the family members of his father, grandfather and great grandfather. There were over thirty of them. Li Yuan made all of them kings. When Li Shi Min ascended the throne, he found that it was a great burden to the people. He said to his ministers, "Since the Han Dynasty, only the sons and brothers of the emperors were made kings. As for distant kinfolk, apart from those who contributed enormously, like Liu Ze and Liu Jia, they were not made kings. Now all the distant kinfolk have been made kings. It is a great burden for the people to provide for so many kings." So for kings who were members of the imperial clan but had not established great contributions, Li Shi Min ordered a reduction in rank to that of duke, at county level.

53. Li Shi Min's Ways of Government

Li Shi Min decided to call his reign "Zhenguan." Zhen means "correct," Guan means "observe." The two words put together (Zhenguan) means "observe correctly" or "observe from the correct point of view." The first year of his reign was 627, so it was the first year of Zhenguan.

After Li Shi Min ascended the throne, he was determined to make China a prosperous and powerful empire. He not only encouraged his ministers to make proposals, but also encouraged them to point out his mistakes. Li Shi Min sent envoys to several places to oversee the conscription of new soldiers. Feng De Yi, one of the premiers, presented a memorandum to the Emperor. It read, "The conscription age is eighteen years old. But some young men of sixteen and seventeen are quite tall and strong. They can be conscripted into the army." Li Shi Min agreed with his suggestion and issued an imperial order to conscript those young men who were not yet eighteen years old but were tall and strong enough into the army. Wei Zheng was strongly against this order and refused to sign onto it. Li Shi Min was angry. He summoned Wei Zheng and Wang Gui to the palace and scolded them. Li Shi Min said, "If the young men under eighteen are really short and small, they should not be conscripted into the army. Those young men under eighteen who are tall and strong enough can be conscripted into the army. There is nothing wrong in conscripting them into the army. Why are you so stubborn as to refuse to sign on my imperial order?" Wei Zheng said sternly, "If we drain the fish pond, we can catch all the fish in the pond. But there will be no fish in the pond next year. If we burn the woods to hunt the wild animals, we can hunt down all the wild game in the woods. But there will not be any wild game in the woods next year. If we conscript all the young men under eighteen into the army, who will till the land and pay taxes and who will serve as conscript labor? In recent years, our soldiers could not fight well in battles. This is not because there are too few soldiers in the army. It is because the soldiers are treated unfairly, so they do not fight resolutely. If we conscript more young men into the army and let them do other things rather than fighting, it would not improve the situation. If we just conscript the smart and strong young men who are eighteen years old into the army and treat them fairly, they will fight bravely. The decisive factor in battles is the quality of the army, not the quantity of the army."

And he went on. "Your Majesty often says, 'As the Emperor of the empire, I will treat my people with faith and honesty. And I require my ministers and my people to root out dishonest behavior.' But since Your Majesty ascended the throne, Your Majesty has broken Your Majesty's promises in at least three important matters. How can Your Majesty gain faith from the people?" The Emperor was greatly surprised and asked, "In what matters have I broken my promises?" Wei Zheng said, "When Your Majesty had just ascended the throne, Your Majesty issued an order which read, 'All the debts and taxes owed by the people to the government and the government properties owed by the people to the government need not be repaid.' Then Your Majesty ordered the government department in charge of the matter to list the items of government properties which are not required to be returned to the government. Your Majesty became the Emperor from the King of Qin. The Office of the King of Qin is surely a government organization. But the properties of the Office of the King of Qin are not included in the list. If the properties of the Office of the King of Qin do not belong to the government, then to whom do these properties belong? The second thing: Your Majesty issued an order to exempt the people in Guanzhong from paying tax for two years and the people outside Guanzhong to be exempted from doing conscript labor for one year. All the people were very happy about that. But later Your Majesty issued another order which read, 'This year, most of the able bodied men have served conscript labor. If the exemption of conscript labor starts from this year, most people cannot enjoy this favor. If the taxes have been collected, then the taxes should be delivered to the government treasury. All the exemptions will start next year.' Then all the taxes which had been collected and had just been returned to the people according to the former imperial order were collected again in accordance with the second order. This caused great confusion among the people. All the taxes collected in kind have been provided as army supplies; the exemption of conscript labor will start next year. Who will believe the promises made by Your Majesty again? Your Majesty relies on the local officials such as the governors of the prefectures and governors of counties to govern the whole realm. They are responsible for collecting taxes and other state affairs. Now Your Majesty is going to conscript young men under eighteen into the army. Your Majesty suspects that your officials will deceive Your Majesty by not conscripting those who are tall and strong enough but not yet eighteen into the army. Your majesty sent out special envoys to keep an eye on them. This is against the principle of governing the realm with faith."

The Emperor was glad when he heard the bold criticism. He said, "I thought you were very stubborn and I thought you did not understand politics very much. Just now, your comments on important matters have touched the core of the matters. If a government does not have credibility, then the people will not be able to follow the laws. Then there will be no peace in China. I admit I have made a mistake." Then the Emperor issued an order not to conscript those young men who were tall and strong enough but not yet eighteen years old. He granted a jar made of gold to Wei Zheng for his bold and good advice.

Li Shi Min upheld the principle of putting the interest of the people first. Li Shi Min once said to his ministers, "I as the Emperor must put the interest of the people first. If I damage the interest of the people for my own interest, it would be like cutting the flesh off my thigh to feed my stomach. I will feel full in my stomach. But my whole body would be greatly damaged. In order to stabilize the whole realm, I must restrain myself. If I act correctly, I will be able to bring all the disorder under control. My point is: the thing which harmed previous emperors was not from outside, but all the greedy desires of the emperors themselves. These greedy desires brought great disasters to the realm and the emperors. In some cases, dynasties were destroyed and emperors were killed. Greedy emperors not only harm the governance of the realm, but also harm greatly the interest of the people. Then the people will rebel and the realm will be in great chaos. I always bear this in mind. I will not indulge myself in doing whatever I like to do." So Li Shi Min was very careful in every decision he made.

In the year when Li Shi Min ascended the throne, there were natural calamities of droughts and unseasonable frosts. Grain production was greatly affected. The price of food was very high. At the same time, the Turks often invaded the border areas of the Tang Dynasty. But the Emperor insisted on working for the interest of the people and practicing wise governance and showing grace to the people. At that time, in the areas of the capital, to the east of the Yellow River, to the south of the Yellow River, and in the east part of Long (now Gansu Province), crop failure was especially grave. A bolt of silk could only be exchanged for a decaliter of grain. The people were hungry. Many people had to sell their children to get clothes and food. The Emperor ordered the local governments to relieve the people in calamity stricken areas and exempt them from taxes that year. The Emperor issued an order to the local officials to take money from the official treasury to buy back the children and return them to their parents. Some people had to leave their home place and go to other places for food. But they did not have any complaints. In 629 there was a good harvest in the area of Guanzhong; all the people who had left Guanzhong for food came back to Guanzhong, and there was peace and order in the whole realm.

Dai Zhou, a high ranking official in the ministry of war, was a faithful, honest and proper, upright and fair man. The Emperor appointed him deputy head of the Supreme Court. At that time many people applied for official positions. In order to get a position, some applicants made up false personal records. The Emperor hated these behaviors and issued an imperial order that those who had made up false personal records should confess their wrong doings; otherwise, if they were found out, they would be put to death. Indeed, some of the applicants were found to have really made up personal records. The Emperor ordered to put them to death. But Dai Zhou only sentenced them to be sent into exile according to law. The Emperor said to Dai Zhou angrily, "You have sentenced the cases in accordance with the laws, but by doing so you have caused me to lose credibility." Dai Zhou said, "The order by Your Majesty was issued when Your Majesty was in a rage at a certain time. Laws have been promulgated in the whole realm and should have public credibility. But later Your Majesty found out that it was improper to put them to death and the cases should be judged in accordance with Law. This shows that Your Majesty has suppressed your anger and preserved the public credibility of the laws." The Emperor said gladly, "You can judge cases in accordance with laws. I won't worry about that anymore." Dai Zhou insisted on sentencing cases according to the laws, even against the will of the Emperor. Since Dai Zhou was in charge of legal affairs, there was no miscarriage of justice in the whole realm.

In December 632 the Emperor heard cases personally. When he saw that some criminals were sentenced to death, he had pity on them. He ordered the convicts be allowed to go home and come back in autumn the next year to be executed. He also ordered all the criminals who had been sentenced to death to be allowed to go home and come back to Chang'an at an appointed time to accept their death penalty. Three hundred and ninety death penalty convicts in the whole realm were allowed to go home. Next year, at the appointed time, all the convicts came back to Chang'an to accept their death penalty. None of them ran away. The Emperor issued an order to set all of them free.

54. The Tiele Tribes to the North of the Eastern Turkic Khanate and the Western Turkic Khanate

In the vast areas to the north of Hanhai Desert (now the Gobi Desert, which lies in the southern area of Mongolia and the northern area of Inner Mongolia Autonomous Region of China), there was a big horde of Tiele (Chile) which consisted of many tribes. In the area to the southeast of Jinshan Mountains (now the Altay Mountains, between Xinjiang Uygur Autonomous Region of China and Mongolia), there was the Tribe of Xueyantuo (Syr-Tardush). To the north of the Tribe of Xueyantuo in the south area to the Suolingshui River (Selenge River in Mongolia), there was the Tribe of Uigur. To the north of the Tribe of Uigur along the upper reaches of the Jianhe River (now the Yenisei River, in Siberian Russia) and to the south of Tanman Mountain (the Sayan Mountains in Siberia) there was the Tribe of Dubo (Tuvas). To the northeast of the Tribe of Dubo along the area of Xiaohai Lake (now Lake Baikal, Siberia), there was the Tribe of Guligan (Kurykan). In the area to the east of Xueyantuo and along the Tongluoshui River (Tuul River in Mongolia), there was the Tribe of Duolange. In the areas to the east of the Suolingshui River (Selenge River in Mongolia), there were other tribes: the Tongluo, Pugu, Bayegu, Xijie, Adie, and the Baixi. In the area south of the Tribe of Duolange were the Qibi. The lifestyle and social customs of these tribes were almost the same as those of the Turks.

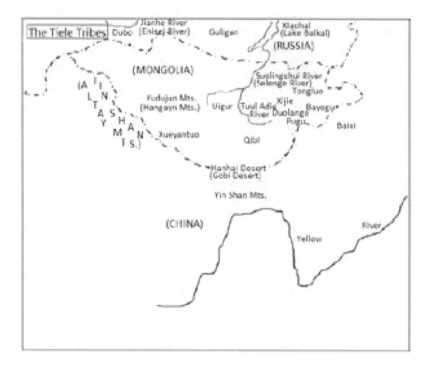

When the Western Turkic Khanate under the rule of Heshana Khan (on the throne from 604 to 610) was strong, the tribes of Tiele submitted themselves to the Western Turkic Khanate. But Heshana Khan levied heavy taxes on the Tiele, which caused great resentment. Heshana Khan was angry and killed more than a hundred chiefs of the tribes. Then the Tiele tribes betrayed Heshana Khan. They elected Qibi Geleng, the chief of the Tribe of Qibi, as Yiwuzhenmohe Khan. He established his headquarters north of Tanhan Mountain (now Bogda Mountain, north of the Tian Shan Mountains, Xinjiang Uygur Autonomous Region of China). And they elected Yishi Bo, the chief of the Tribe of Xueyantuo, as Yete Junior Khan. The Tribe of Xueyantuo moved north of Yanmoshan Mountain (a branch of the Altay Mountains between Xinjiang Uygur Autonomous Region of China and Mongolia) and stayed there. In 610 Ashina Shekuei became Shekuei Khan of the Western Turkic Khanate. He was a capable ruler, and the Western Turkic Khanate became strong again. Then Qibi Geleng of the Tribe of Qibi and Yishi Bo of the Tribe of Xueyantuo cancelled their titles as khan and junior khan, and the Tiele tribes submitted themselves to the Western Turkic Khanate again.

Six of the sub tribes of the Uigur people who remained in the Yudujun Mountains (Hangayn Mountains in Mongolia) submitted themselves to Shibi Khan of the Eastern Turkic Khanate.

Under the rule of Tongyehu Khan (619–628), the Western Turkic Khanate once again became weak, and Yishi Yinan, the grandson of Yishi Bo, the chief of the Tribe of Xueyantuo, led seventy thousand families of the Tribe of Xuyantuo to submit to the authority of Jiali Khan of the Eastern Turkic Khanate.

55. The Decline of the Eastern Turkic Khanate

Originally the people of the Eastern Turkic Khanate were honest and simple folk. Their laws were simple and clear. But later Jiali Khan placed his trust in Zhao De Yan, from China, and gave him great power. Zhao De Yan used the power conferred on him to change the customs of the people of the Eastern Turkic Khanate. He issued many complicated laws and policies. The people of the Eastern Turkic Khanate were in great confusion as to how to follow such laws and policies, which led to dissension turmoil.

Seeing that the Eastern Turkic Khanate had begun to decline, the Tribe of Xueyantuo, the Tribe of Uigur and the Tribe of Bayegu turned against Jiali Khan of the Eastern Turkic Khanate one after another in 627. Jiali Khan was very angry, and in December 627 he sent Yugu Shad (General Ashina Yugu), his elder brother's son, to command a hundred thousand cavalrymen to attack these tribes. Yaoluoge Pusa, the chief of the Tribe of Uigur, commanded five thousand cavalrymen in resisting the attack. A battle was fought in Malieshan Mountain (in the area to the north of Gobi Desert in Mongolia). The cavalrymen of the Tribe of Uigur under Yaoluoge Pusa fought very bravely and defeated the strong Eastern Turkic cavalrymen under Yugu Shad. Yugu Shad ran away with his men. Yaoluoge Pusa chased them to Tianshan Mountain (now Hangayn Mountains, Mongolia) and captured many Turkic cavalrymen. The Tribe of Uigur became very strong. The Tribe of Xueyantuo under Yishi Yinan also attacked the Eastern Turkic Khanate and defeated the Eastern Turkic cavalry under the command of four generals of the Eastern Turkic Khanate. Jiali Khan of the Eastern Turkic Khanate lost control of these tribes and the people of the Eastern Turkic Khanate left Jiali Khan. The Eastern Turkic Khanate became weaker and weaker. Incidentally, there was heavy snow that year. The snow on the ground was as thick as three feet or more. Horses and sheep froze and starved to death, and the people of the Eastern Turkic Khanate had nothing to eat. Jiali Khan was afraid that the army of the Tang Dynasty would take advantage of this natural disaster and decide to attack. So Jiali Khan commanded a great army to the area of Shuozhou (now the area of Shuozhou, Shanxi Province), under the pretext of making a hunting trip, to make preparation to resist the attack by the Tang army.

At that time, Zheng Yuan Shu, an envoy sent by the Emperor of the Tang Dynasty to the Eastern Turkic Khanate, came back from his mission. He reported to the Emperor, "The rise and decline of the tribes in the north can be predicted by the number of their horses and sheep. Now the people of the Eastern Turkic Khanate are starving. The cows, horses and sheep of the Eastern Turkic Khanate are thin and weak. This signals the fall of the Eastern Turkic Khanate. They must collapse within three years." The Emperor agreed with his calculation. Many ministers and generals suggested attacking the Eastern Turkic Khanate. But the Emperor said, "We have just made a peace agreement with Jiali Khan. If we now break the peace agreement, it will be an act of unfaithfulness. If we take advantage of their natural disaster to attack them, it will not be a benevolent act on my part. If we make use of their unfavorable situation and win victory, we will go against the ethics of war. Even if all the tribes of the Eastern Turks betray Jiali Khan and all their cattle die, I will not start an attack on the Eastern Turkic Khanate. I will not attack the Eastern Turkic Khanate until Jiali Khan has taken action against us."

The Emperor of the Tang Dynasty had sent Li Dao Li, King of Gaoping, on a mission to the Western Turkic Khanate. In December 627 Tong Yehu Khan (Ashina Tong) of the Western Turkic Khanate sent him back, with Zhenzhu Tong Irkin (the chief of a sub tribe), to the court of the Tang Dynasty to see the Emperor. Zhenzhu Tong Irkin presented the Emperor with a set of reins decorated with gold and five thousand good horses. Zhenzhu Tong Irkin had come to escort the princess of the royal clan of the Emperor of the Tang Dynasty to the Western Turkic Khanate to marry Tong Yehu Khan.

But Jiali Khan of the Eastern Turkic Khanate did not wish to see the Western Turkic Khanate establish good relations with the Tang Dynasty. So he sent an army to attack the Tang border areas, and he sent an envoy to threaten Tong Yehu Khan of the Western Turkic Khanate, saying, "If you want to marry the princess of the Tang Dynasty, you should be aware that she will have to be escorted through my territory." Tong Yehu Khan was worried and at last gave up the idea of marrying the princess of the Tang Dynasty.

Tuli Khan (Ashina Shibobi) established his headquarters in the area north of Youzhou (now the area to the north of Beijing) to rule over the area of the eastern part of the Eastern Turkic Khanate. Then the Tribe of Xi (in the north part of Hebei Province) and the Tribe of Xi (in the west part of Liaoning Province) broke away and submitted themselves to the Tang Dynasty. Jiali Khan blamed Tuli Khan for letting these tribes to break away from the Eastern Turkic Khanate. When Yugu Shad was defeated by Yaoluoge Pusa, the chief of the Tribe of

Uigur, Jiali khan ordered Tuli Khan to carry out an expedition against the Uigur and the Xuyantuo. But in April 618 Tuli Khan was defeated and he slunk back, alone. Jiali Khan was in a rage and held Tuli Khan in custody for more than ten days. Tuli Khan was severely beaten. Now, Tuli Khan hated Jiali Khan, and he secretly made up his mind to betray him.

After Tuli Khan was released and went back to his headquarters in Youzhou (now north of Beijing), Jiali Khan ordered Tuli Khan to send him some soldiers, but Tuli Khan refused to do so. Instead, Tuli Khan sent a letter to the Emperor of the Tang Dynasty requesting to an audience with him in Chang'an. When the Emperor got the letter, he said to the officials around him, "In the past when the Turks were strong, there were a million soldiers in the army of the Eastern Turkic Khanate. With this great army, the Turks invaded China many times. And because of this the rulers of the Eastern Turkic Khanate became very proud and they lost the support of the people. Now Tuli Khan is requesting an audience with me. If he were not at the end of his resources, he would not do that. When I read this letter, I am happy on the one hand, and I am worried on the other. I am happy because now that the Eastern Turkic Khanate has become weak, there will be peace in the border areas. But If I make a mistake like those made by the rulers of the Eastern Turkic Khanate, I will follow their fate. This is a real concern. You must try your best to point out my errors and help me to overcome my mistakes."

In April 628 Jiali Khan sent a great army to attack Tuli Khan. On 21 April 628 Tuli Khan sent an envoy to Chang'an asking the Emperor to rescue him. The Emperor discussed this matter with his ministers and generals. The Emperor said, "I and Tuli Khan are sworn brothers. Now he is in great danger. I will have to save him. But I have made a peace agreement with Jiali Khan. What shall I do?" Du Ru Hui, the minister of war, said, "The people of the Northern Tribes are not trustworthy. They will break the peace agreement anyway. If we do not conquer the Eastern Turks now, when they are in chaos, we will regret it later. As the ancient teaching goes, you must seize the chance to conquer your enemy while there is chaos in the enemy state." Then the Emperor ordered General Zhou Fan to station his army in the area of Taiyuan (now the area of Taiyuan, Shanxi Province) to prepare to attack the Eastern Turkic Khanate. Many officials suggested to the Emperor that the Emperor should send people to repair the Great Wall to hold back the Eastern Turks. The Emperor said, "The areas of the Turks are very cold. There is frost in midsummer. There are often natural disasters in those areas. But Jiali Khan does not do any virtuous deeds to save the people. This shows that he goes against the will of Heaven. The Northern Tribes migrate frequently. This shows they do not make best use of their land. The burial custom of the Northern Tribes was to burn the dead. But now they bury their dead people under the ground and make graves. This shows that they do not respect the tradition handed down from their ancestors. Now Jiali Khan attacks his nephew Tuli Khan. This shows that Jiali Khan does not treasure the relationship with his close relatives. Now if Jiali Khan has committed these four grave errors, I can predict that the Eastern Turkic Khanate will fall very soon. I will destroy Jiali Khan for you. So it is not necessary to repair the Great Wall to resist the Eastern Turks."

As Jiali Khan became weak, the tribes to the north of his Khanate betrayed him and turned to the Khanate of Xueyantuo. The chiefs of the tribes elected Yishi Yinan as khan, but Yishi Yinan did not dare to take up the position. The Emperor of the Tang Dynasty went ahead with his plans to attack the Eastern Turkic Khanate. In December 628 the Emperor sent General Qiao Shi Wang to Xueyantuo with an imperial appointment order to make Yishi Yinan Zhenzhu-piga Khan. And the Emperor granted him drums and flags. Yishi Yinan was very glad. He sent envoys to Chang'an to pay tribute to the Emperor. He established his headquarters in Yudujun Mountain (Hangayn Mountains in Mongolia). The Tribes of the Uigurs, the Bayegu, the Tongluo, the Pugu and the Xi submitted themselves to Yishi Yinan.

In the area between Huangshui River (now Xar Moron River in the southeast of Inner Mongolia Autonomous Region of China) and Huanglong (now Chaoy-ang, Liaoning Province), there was the Tribe of Khitan, which was composed of eight sub tribes. The family name of the Chief of Khitan was Dahe. The Tribe of Khitan had an army of forty-three thousand men. At first the Tribe of Khitan submitted to the Eastern Turkic Khanate. Then in April 628, Dahe Mohui, the Chief of the Tribe of Khitan, led his people to submit to the Tang Dynasty. Jiali Khan of the Eastern Turkic Khanate sent an envoy to the Emperor of the Tang Dynasty requesting an exchange: the Emperor of the Tang Dynasty should hand over the people of the Tribe of Khitan to the Eastern Turkic Khanate and in re-turn Jiali Khan would hand over Liang Shi Du to the Tang Dynasty. The Emperor said to the envoy, "The people of Khitan and the people of the Turks are two different races. Now the Tribe of Khitan has come to submit to me. On what ground does Jiali Khan demand that I turn the Tribe of Khitan over to him? Liang Shi Du, on the other hand, is Chinese. He has occupied my land and robbed my people. But he is protected by the Eastern Turks. Every time I sent army against him, the Turks came to his rescue. Now Liang Shi Du is like a fish in my cooker. I will catch him some day. And even if I cannot catch him, I will not hand over the people who have submitted to me in exchange for this man."

The Emperor of the Tang Dynasty knew that the Eastern Turkic Khanate was declining and would not be ablt to protect Liang Shi Du anymore. He wrote a letter to Liang Shi Du demanding him to surrender, but Liang Shi Du refused.

Then the Emperor sent General Liu Min and General Liu Lan Cheng of the army under Xiazhou command (in the area around Uxin Qi, Inner Mongolia Autonomous Region) to attack Liang Shi Du. They sent cavalrymen to ruin the crops in the areas under his control. When they captured officials or officers under Liang Shi Du, they turned them into spies and sent them back to the court of Liang to sow discord among Liang Shi Du and his ministers and generals. The State of Liang became weaker and weaker. His ministers and generals surrendered to the Tang Dynasty one after another. Li Zheng Bao and Xin Liao Er, important generals under Liang Shi Du, secretly planned to capture Liang Shi Du and bring him to surrender to the Tang Dynasty. But their plan was discovered by Liang Shi Du. So Li Zheng Bao and Xin Liao Er had to run away to the Tang Dynasty. From then on, Liang Shi Du was suspicious of his ministers and generals.

General Liu Min knew that it was the right time to defeat Liang Shi Du, so he wrote to the Emperor requesting consent to attack the State of Liang. Then the Emperor sent General Chai Shao and General Xue Wan Jun to lead a great army to attack the State of Liang. The Emperor sent General Liu Min and Liu Lan Cheng to lead their army east to the city of Shuofang (now a city to the north of Uxin Qi, Inner Mongolia Autonomous Region) to threaten the capital of the State of Liang. Liang Shi Du asked the Eastern Turks to rescue him. Liang Shi Du with the Eastern Turks came out of the city of Shuofang. General Liu Lan Cheng ordered his soldiers to conceal their flags and stop beating drums. He ordered all the soldiers to stay inside the fence of their camps and not to go out to fight. At night, Liang Shi Du began to withdraw. Now, General Liu Lan Cheng commanded his army to pursue Liang Shi Du's army and defeated it. Liang Shi Du retreated into the city of Shuofang and a great army of the Eastern Turks came to rescue him. The Tang Army under General Chai Shao met the Eastern Turks twenty kilometers away from the city of Shuofang. The Tang army fought bravely and defeated the Eastern Turks. Then the Tang army marched forward to lay siege to the city of Shuofang. The Eastern Turks did not dare to rescue Liang Shi Du anymore. Liang Shi Du ran out of food. On 26 April Liang Luo Ren, Liang Shi Du's cousin, killed him and opened the city gates to surrender to the Tang army. The Emperor of the Tang Dynasty renamed the area of Shuofang to Xiazhou.

56. The Destruction of the Eastern Turkic Khanate

In August 629 Yishi Yinan, the chief of the Tribe of Xueyantuo, sent his younger brother Tong Tegin to Chang'an to have an audience with the Emperor of the Tang Dynasty and to present rich tribute. The Emperor of the Tang Dynasty granted him a precious sword and a precious whip. The Emperor said, "If anyone under you has committed a serious crime, you may kill him with this sword. If anyone under you has committed a minor crime, you may lash him with this whip." Yishi Yinan was very appreciative of these gifts from the Emperor of the Tang Dynasty. When Jiali Khan heard about this, he saw that it was not good news. He sent envoys to see the Emperor of the Tang Dynasty expressing his intention to submit to the Emperor of the Tang Dynasty.

Zhang Gong Jin, the commander-in-chief of the army of Daizhou Command (Daizhou: now an area around Daixian, Shanxi Province) wrote a memorandum to the Emperor of the Tang Dynasty. The memorandum read, "Jiali Khan has always been doing what he wants to do at his own will. He is extremely vicious. He has killed many upright people and he has been close to the wicket people. He has become a fatuous and self-indulgent ruler. This is the first reason that he can be defeated. The Tribes of Tongluo, Pugu, Uigur and Xueyantuo have elected their own rulers and have prepared to attack the Eastern Turkic Khanate. Now all these tribes originally subordinated to Jiali Khan have turned against him. This is the second reason that he can be defeated. Tuli Khan attacked the Tribe of Xueyantuo and the Tribe of Uigur but was defeated. He was badly punished by Jiali Khan. When Yugu Shad attacked the Tribe of Uigur, he was defeated and ran away. This shows that Jiali Khan's generals and men can be easily defeated. This is the third reason that Jiali Khan can be defeated. There is frost in the area of the north very early. Food supply in the north is short. This is the fourth reason that Jiali Khan can be defeated. Jiali Khan distrusts his own people but trusted the people of other races. But the people of other races would easily betray him. When they face a great army sent by Your Majesty, they will surely turn against Jiali Khan. This is the fifth reason that he can be defeated. Now many people from the central part of China have settled down in the area in the north. Most of them have come together to occupy mountains and forests for self defense. When our army marches out of the Great Wall, they will come out to assist our army. This is the sixth reason that Jiali Khan can be defeated." The Emperor fully agreed with his opinion.

The Emperor decided to send armies to attack the Eastern Turkic Khanate because Jiali Khan of the Eastern Turkic Khanate had gone against the peace treaty by sending army to rescue Liang Shi Du when the Tang armies were attacking Liang Shi Du. In August 629 the Emperor of the Tang Dynasty appointed Li Jing (the minister of war) as the commander-in-chief of a great army to carry out an expedition against the Eastern Turkic Khanate. Zhang Gong Jin was appointed deputy commander-in-chief of this great army.

In November 629 the Emperor of the Tang Dynasty appointed Li Ji as the commander-in-chief of the army of the Tongmo Route, Li Jing as the commander-in-chief of the army of the Dingxiang Route, Chai Shao as the commander-in-chief of the army of the Jinhe Route, Xue Wan Jun as the Commander-in-chief of the army of the Changwu Route. The total number of the soldiers on these routes was over a hundred thousand. All these armies were under the command of Li Jing, the minister of war. The armies of these routes marched to attack the Eastern Turkic Khanate from different directions.

Li Dao Zong, King of Rencheng, attacked the Eastern Turks in Lingzhou (now Lingwu, Ningxia Huizu Autonomous Region) and defeated them.

In December 629 Tuli Khan, Yushe Shad and Yinnai Tegin of the Eastern Turkic Khanate commanded the armies under them to come to submit to the Tang Dynasty. Tuli Khan came to Chang'an to have an audience with the Emperor of the Tang Dynasty. The Emperor said to the ministers and generals around him, "In the past Father Emperor submitted to the Turks for the interest of the people. When I think of this, I always felt painful in my heart. Now the chiefs of the Turks have come to submit to the Tang Dynasty. This helps to wipe out the past humiliation. I now feel greatly relieved."

Seeing that the Eastern Turkic Khanate was going to collapse, many minority nationality tribes submitted to the Tang Dynasty. The chief of the Tribe of Mohe which lived in the area of the lower reach of Heilongjiang River (now in Heilongjiang Province) sent envoys to Chang'an to have an audience with the Emperor of the Tang Dynasty. The Emperor was very glad. He said, "Now the Tribe of Mohe has come to submit to the Tang Dynasty from afar. This is because the Eastern Turks have submitted to the Tang Dynasty. There is an ancient saying which goes 'There is no best way to conquer the northern tribes'. Now I have made China a strong empire and the northern tribes have come to submit to me. This is the best way to bring the tribes to submission."

In January 630 Li Jing commanded his great army of Dingxiang Route to march to the Eastern Turkic Khanate from Mayi (now Shuozhou, Shanxi Province). He himself led three thousand valiant cavalrymen to ride very quickly to Eyangling Mountain which was situated to the south of Dingxiang (now Horinger, Inner Mongolia Autonomous Region) to threaten the city of Dingxiang. Jiali Khan did not expect that the Tang army had come so suddenly. He said in great surprise, "All the Tang armies must have come. Otherwise Li Jing would not have come with such a small isolated army." Jiali Khan was frightened. Li Jing sent spies to sow discords among Jiali Khan and his subordinates. Kangsumi, the chief of a sub tribe of the Eastern Turks, came to surrender to Li Jing, bringing with him Empress Xiao, the wife of Emperor Yang Guang of the Sui Dynasty, and Yang Zheng Dao, the grandson of Emperor Yang Guang. Li Jing sent a party of soldiers to escort Empress Xiao and Yang Zheng Dao back to Chang'an. Then Li Jing commanded his army to start a surprise attack on the city of Dingxiang and took it. Jiali Khan escaped to Tieshan Mountain which was situated to the north of Yin Shan Mountains (now Yin Shan Mountains, Inner Mongolia

Autonomous Region). When the Emperor of the Tang Dynasty knew that Li Jing had defeated Jiali Khan in Dingxiang, He made Li Jing Duke of the State of Dai. He said to the courtiers around him, "In the Han Dynasty, General Li Ling was ordered to attack the Huns with five thousand men. But he was defeated and was captured by the Huns. Even so his deeds were recorded in the book of history. Now Li Jing has penetrated deep with only three thousand light cavalrymen into the headquarters of the Eastern Turks and has recovered the city of Dingxiang. His powerful combat strength has struck terror into the hearts of the Turks. This is unprecedented in history. This victory is enough to revenge the battle beside Weishui River."

At the same time, Li Ji commanded his army of the Tongmo Route to march from Yunzhong (now Datong, Shanxi Province) to Baidao (now Hohhot, Inner Mongolia Autonomous Region). A battle was fought in Baidao. The Tang army won a great victory over the Turks.

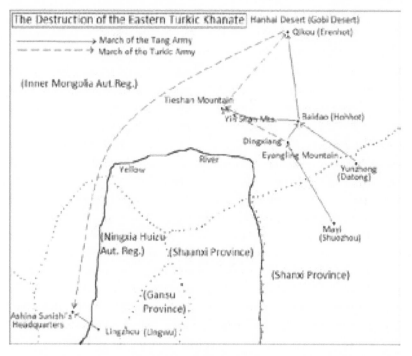

When Jiali Khan was defeated in Dingxiang, he retreated to Tieshan Mountain (to the north of Yin Shan Mountains, Inner Mongolia) with about forty thousand men. Li Jing commanded his army to march into Yin Shan Mountains (now Yin Shan Mountains, Inner Mongolia). A battle was fought and the Turks were defeated again. Jiali Khan was afraid. So he sent Zhishi Sili as his envoy to Chang'an. The Emperor received him. Zhishi Sili on behalf of Jiali Khan apologized for his offence against the Tang Dynasty and promised that the Eastern

Turkic Khanate would submit to the Tang Dynasty and Jiali Khan himself would come to Chang'an to subordinate himself to the Emperor of the Tang Dynasty. The Emperor sent Tang Jian, the minister in charge of minority nationality affairs, to Jiali Khan to confirm that he accepted his submission and to console Jiali Khan. Jiali Khan showed subservience outwardly, but actually he was waiting for spring to come when the grass in the grasslands would become green and his horses would become strong again. Then he could cross Hanhai Desert (now the Gobi Desert, between the border of Mongolia and Inner Mongolia Autonomous Region of China) and escape to the north.

Portrait of Li Jing

Li Jing led his army to Baidao to join forces with Li Ji. Li Jing and Li Ji discussed the next step they should take. Li Ji said, "Although Jiali Khan has been defeated, he still has a great army. If he crosses the desert, goes to the north and unites with the tribes of Tiele, it would be very difficult for us to bring him to submission because it is very far away and the way to the north is very difficult. Now, while Tang Jian is in Jiali Khan's court to convey the Emperor's intention to accept his submission, Jiali Khan's vigilance must be relaxed. If we launch a surprise attack, we will defeat him easily." Li Jing said happily, "Very good idea. This is the same stratagem used by General Han Xin to defeat the State of Qi when Li Yi Ji succeeded in persuading the King of the State of Qi to surrender to Liu Bang, King of the State of Han." So they made their plans to attack Jiali Khan when his guard was down. Then Li Jing told their decision to Zhang Gong Jin, the deputy commander-in-chief. Zhang Gong Jin said, "The Emperor has accepted Jiali Khan's surrender and his envoy is now in Jiali Khan's court. We should not start a surprise attack on him." Li Jing said, "This is a rare chance for military action. We must not miss it. The life of Tang Jian is not important." Li Jing commanded his army to start marching at night. Li Ji commanded his army to march to Qikou (now within the area of Erenhot, Inner Mongolia), which was the entrance to the Hanhai Desert, to prevent Jiali Khan from getting away across the desert. When the Tang army under Li Jing reached Yin Shan Mountains, they saw a thousand tents in which the Turks were sleeping. The Tang soldiers captured all these Turks and brought them to march forward.

When Jiali Khan saw that the envoy sent by the Emperor of the Tang Dynasty had come, indeed, all his worries were removed and he was at ease. He did not expect that the Tang army would attack at such a time. Li Jing sent General Su Ding Fang with two hundred cavalrymen as vanguards to ride ahead of the main force. That day there was a heavy fog. The cavalrymen rode forward in the protection of the heavy fog. When the fog lifted, the Tang army was only two thousand meters away from the camp of the Eastern Turks. They could see the command tent of Jiali Khan with a big flag with a wolf's head emblem flying high. General Su Ding Fang and his two hundred cavalrymen rode forward to the command tent, killing more than a hundred Turks on the way. When Jiali Khan saw the Tang army, he was shocked and rode away with ten thousand men. His wife Princess Yicheng was killed in the confusion. His son Dieluoshi was captured. Tang Jian, the envoy sent by the Emperor of the Tang Dynasty, came back to the Tang army. When the main force under Li Jing came to join in the battle, more than ten thousand Turkic soldiers were killed. More than three hundred thousand Turkic people, men and women, were captured. And the Tang army also got more than three hundred thousand horses and cattle.

Portrait of Li Ji

Jiali Khan with his ten thousand men rode to Qikou, intending to cross the desert to the north, only to find that the great Tang army under the command of Li Ji was already lined up in battle formation, waiting for them. Jiali Khan had to try his luck, so he commanded his men to attack the Tang army. It very soon became clear that they could not prevail, so he turned back and rode away with several followers. The chief of a big sub tribe of the Eastern Turks came to surrender the whole sub tribe to the Tang army. Jiali Khan fled to southwest, intending to go to the Tuyuhun Khanate (in the area of Gansu Province and Qinghai Province). After this victory, a vast area from Yin Shan Mountains (now Yin Shan Mountains, Inner Mongolia) in the south, and north to the boundary of Hanhai Desert (Gobi Desert), was added to the territory of the Tang Dynasty.

In March the chiefs of the minority tribes around China gathered together before the gate of the palace in Chang'an. They all asked the Emperor of the Tang Dynasty to take up the title of "Heavenly Khan." He said, "I am already the Emperor of the Tang Dynasty. If I take up the title of Heavenly Khan, I will have to manage the affairs of the tribes." All the chiefs of the tribes and the ministers of the Tang Dynasty knelt down to beg the Emperor of the Tang Dynasty to take up the title of Heavenly Khan. From then on, the Emperor styled himself "Heavenly Khan" when he issued imperial edicts to the chiefs of the tribes.

The Emperor of the Tang Dynasty appointed Tuli Khan (Ashina Shibobi) Grand General of the Right Army of the Guards and made him King of Beiping Prefecture.

At that time, Jiali Khan's nephew Ashina Sunishi commanded a sub tribe of fifty thousand households of the Eastern Turks in the southwest. Ashina Sunishi established his headquarters in the area northwest to Lingzhou (now Lingwu, Ningxia Huizu Autonomous Region). With the power of Jiali Khan declining and many people betraying him, Ashina Sunishi was still devoted to Jiali Khan. When Jiali Khan was defeated in Qikou, he fled to the southwest and found refuge in the sub tribe under the command of Ashina Sunishi. Jiali Khan intended to go further southwest to the Tuyuhun Khanate. Li Dao Zong, King of Rencheng, was the commander-in-chief of the army of the Datong Route. When he learned that Jiali Khan had come to the area of Lingzhou, he commanded his army to march forward to threaten the headquarters of Ashina Sunishi, demanding that he arrest Jiali Khan. When Jiali Khan got the wind of this, he rode away with several followers at night and went into hiding in the mountains. Under great pressure from the Tang army under Li Dao Zong, Ashina Sunishi had to race after Jiali Khan and caught him in the mountains. On March 15, Zhang Bao Xiang, the deputy commander-in-chief of the army of the Datong Route, started a surprise attack on the headquarters of Ashina Sunishi and captured Jiali Khan. Ashina Sunishi surrendered to the Tang Dynasty with the sub tribe of the Eastern Turks under him. From then on, there was no enemy in the area south of the Desert.

Jiali Khan was escorted to Chang'an. On April 3, a grand ceremony of presenting the captives was held. The Emperor of the Tang Dynasty ascended the Shuntian Tower (the tower in the middle gate of the city wall of Chang'an) to accept Jiali Khan's surrender. Jiali Khan was brought before the Emperor, and he knelt down with great shame. The Emperor of the Tang Dynasty scolded Jiali

Khan, saying, "You relied on the prosperous situation developed by your father and brother and invaded China at your own will. This at last led to your own destruction. This is your first crime. You made peace treaties with me several times and then broke the agreements. This is your second crime. You are a warmonger. You have caused the deaths of many of Turkic soldiers and Chinese soldiers. This is your third crime. You ordered your soldiers to destroy the crops in my territory and loot my people. This is your fourth crime. I forgave you for your offences and intended to preserve your khanate. But you delayed and would not come on time. This is your fifth crime. But since our peace treaty made by the bridge over the Weishui River, you have not carried out a massive invasion into the territory of the Tang Dynasty. This is the reason why I have decided to spare you." At these words, Jiali Khan wept, and said that he regretted the crimes he had committed. He expressed his thanks to the Emperor of the Tang Dynasty, and then left. The Emperor of the Tang Dynasty ordered that Jiali Khan and his family members be allowed to live in the guest house for distinguished visitors and he provided very good food for them.

When the Father Emperor heard the news that Jiali Khan had been captured, he was very glad. He said, "Emperor Gaozu of the Han Dynasty was surrounded by the Huns in Baideng. He had no chance for revenge. Now my son has destroyed the Eastern Turkic Khanate. I have entrusted the power to rule over China to the right person. I need not worry anymore." Then the Father Emperor summoned the Emperor and the high ranking officials and the kings and their queens to Lingyange Palace, where the Father Emperor held a grand banquet to entertain them. When everyone was warm with wine, the Father Emperor played the Chinese lute. The Emperor got up and danced to the music. The high ranking officials went up to the Father Emperor and proposed toasts to the health of the Father Emperor. The banquet went on happily until midnight.

Since the Eastern Turkic Khanate had been totally destroyed, some of the sub tribes of the Eastern Turks went to the north to submit to the Tribe of Xueyantuo and some went to the Western Regions (the area including Xinjiang Uygur Autonomous Region of China and parts of Central Asia). More than a hundred thousand Eastern Turks surrendered to the Tang Dynasty. The Emperor of the Tang Dynasty ordered the ministers to discuss what to do with the Eastern Turks who had surrendered. Most of the ministers held this view: the northern tribes had always caused great trouble to China, since ancient times; now that they had been defeated, they should all be moved to the area south of the Yellow River; their tribes should be divided and settle down in different counties in the area of Yan (now in the southwest part of Shandong Province) and the area of Yu (now Henan Province); the men of the Eastern Turks should be taught how to grow crops and the women should be taught how to weave cloth so that the nomadic people would become peasants; the area originally inhabited by the Eastern Turks would become uninhabited so the troubles caused by the Turks could be removed forever.

Wen Yan Bo, Duke of the State of Yu, once took part in the battle in Taigu against the Eastern Turks but was captured by the Turks. Jiali Khan knew that Wen Yan Bo was a favorite minister of Emperor Li Yuan of the Tang Dynasty and demanded him to tell the important information about the garrison of the Tang army. But Wen Yan Bo kept silent and never told anything to Jiali Khan. Kiali Khan was very angry and kept him in the coldest place in Yin Shan Mountains. It was after the demand of Emperor Li Shi Min that Jiali Khan released Wen Yan Bo and sent him back to Chang'an. In the discussion about what to do with the Eastern Turks who had surrendered, Wen Yan Bo said, "When Emperor Guangwu of the Later Han Dynasty defeated the Huns, he placed the Huns who had surrendered in Wuyuansai (now Wuyuan, Inner Mongolia Autonomous Region). The Tribes of the Huns were kept intact. The Huns became a buffer for the Han Dynasty; the Huns did not leave their homeland and they kept their lifestyle and traditions. In this way the Huns were comforted. Now if the Eastern Turks were placed in the areas of Yan and Yu, it will be against the nature and living habits of the Eastern Turks. This is not the right way to provide for the benefit of the people of the Eastern Turks. I hope Your Majesty will adopt the policy favored by Emperor Guangwu. In this way an area that was originaly sparsely inhabited will became a populated area. By doing so, Your Majesty will show to the Turks that Your Majesty equally cares for the benefit of the Eastern Turks."

The Emperor of the Tang Dynasty at last adopted Wen Yan Bo's proposal. He let the Eastern Turks go back to the places where they had originally lived. In the original area of the Eastern Turkic Khanate from Youzhou (now the area to the north of Beijing) in the east to Lingzhou (now Lingwu, Ningxia Huizu Autonomous Region) in the west, ten army commands were established. In Dingxiang, a General Command was established to tend and control the Turks in the east part; in Lingzhou, a General Command was established to tend and control the Turks in the west part.

The Emperor of the Tang Dynasty appointed Tuli Khan Commander-in-chief of the Command of Shunzhou (now an area in the west of Chengde, Hebei Province) and allowed him command the sub tribe of the Eastern Turks under him to go back to the area of Shunzhou. Before Tuli Khan went back to Shunzhou, the Emperor of the Tang Dynasty summoned him to the court and said to him, "In the past your grandfather Ashina Rangan was defeated by Ashina Yongyulü and lost his power. He went to Emperor Wen of the Sui Dynasty for help. Emperor Wen made him Qimin Khan. With the help of Emperor Wen of the Sui Dynasty, Qimin Khan got back the power to control the Eastern Turkic Khanate and the

Eastern Turkic Khanate became strong and prosperous again. The Eastern Turks never repaid the kindness of Emperor Wen of the Sui Dynasty. When your father Shibi Khan was in power, he invaded the border area of China many times. Now it is Heaven's will to bring disasters to the Eastern Turks. You came to submit to me — at the end of your resources. The reason why I will not make you khan is that I am afraid the history of your grandfather will be repeated. I must find another way to handle our relationship with the Eastern Turks. I hope that there will be peace in the border areas of China and I hope that your tribe will last forever. So I have only appointed you commander-in-chief of Shunzhou. You must rule over that area in accordance with the laws of China. You must discipline your subordinates. You must not invade the borders of China. If you go against the laws of China, you will be punished severely."

Tuli Khan commanded his sub tribe to go back to the area of Shunzhou. In 631 the Emperor of the Tang Dynasty summoned him to Chang'an. Tuli Khan died of illness in Bingzhou (now the area around Taiyuan, Shanxi Province) on his way back to Chang'an, at the age of twenty-nine. The Emperor of the Tang Dynasty was very sad and held a grand ceremony to mourn for the death of Tuli Khan.

Jiali Khan stayed in Chang'an. He was given palaces and lands. But he was not used to living in houses. He set up a big tent in the courtyard of his palace and he and his family members lived in it as if they were still living in the grasslands. He fell into a depression. Jiali Khan often shed tears and sang sad songs. The Emperor had pity on him. He appointed Jiali Khan Governor of Guozhou (now Lingbao, in the west part of Henan Province) because there were mountains and many wild animals so that Jiali Khan might often go hunting there. But Jiali Khan declined the Emperor's offer. Then the Emperor granted him the title of the Grand General of the Right Army of the Guards and granted him more houses and lands. The Emperor said to Jiali Khan, "In the past, Qimin Khan lost his power to control the Eastern Turkic Khanate and came to Emperor Wen of the Sui Dynasty for help. Emperor Wen gave him a lot of food and cloth and sent a great army to help Qimin Khan get back the power. But when the Eastern Turkic Khanate revitalized and your brother Shibi Khan succeeded your father to the throne, Shibi Khan turned against the Sui Dynasty. He went so far as to surround Emperor Yang Guang of the Sui Dynasty in Yanmen. Now the Eastern Turkic Khanate has been destroyed. The reason leading to the destruction of the Eastern Turkic Khanate is that the Eastern Turks repaid the kindness shown to them with ingratitude." Jiali Khan died in 634. The Emperor of the Tang Dynasty ordered the former officials under Jiali Khan to hold a funeral ceremony. Jiali Khan's dead body was burned into ashes in accordance with the funeral tradition of the Turks. Then Jiali Khan's ashes were buried in a place east of Bashui

River (which flows through the east to Chang'an and then into Weihe River in Shaanxi Province).

57. The Expedition against the Tuyuhun Khanate

The Tuyuhun Khanate was situated in an area west of Tao He River (now Tao He River in Gansu Province), east of Bailan (now the area of Dulan and Barun, Qinghai Province), north of Gansong (now Songpan, Sichuan Province) and south of Qinghai Hu Lake (now Qinghai Hu Lake, Qinghai Province). It had an area of more than two hundred thousand square kilometers. The Tribe of Tuyuhun were a nomadic people. Although they had built cities, they did not live in houses in the cities. They lived in tents. They had the meat of the cattle they raised and cheese made from the milk of their cattle for food. They got a fine breed of horses from Persia (now Iran). They raised these fine horses along the area of Qinghai Hu Lake. This kind of horses could cover a distance of five hundred kilometers in a day. So they named these horses "Qinghai Horses."

During the reign of Emperor Yang Guang of the Sui Dynasty, Murong Fuyun, the khan of the Tuyuhun Khanate, led a great army to invade the territory of the Sui Dynasty in March 609. The army of the Sui Dynasty defeated the army under Murong Fuyun, who narrowly escaped. Murong Fuyun sent his eldest son Murong Shun to the Sui Dynasty as a hostage. Murong Fuyun himself found refuge in the Tribe of Dang Xiang who lived in the area to the west of Chishui (now in the east of Guide, Qinghai Province). But by the end of the Sui Dynasty, Murong Fuyun recovered the area of the Tuyuhun Khanate and became strong again. Since his eldest son Murong Shun was still in Chang'an, he made his second son the crown prince. When Li Yuan ascended the throne of the Tang Dynasty, he sent an envoy to Murong Fuyun to make peace with him and ask him to attack the area of Liangzhou (now Wuwei, Gansu Province) which was still occupied by the army of Li Gui. He promised to let Murong Shun go back to the Tuyuhun Khanate if Murong Fuyun completed his task. Murong Fuyun was very glad and commanded an army to attack the area of Liangzhou and completed his task. He handed Liangzhou over to the army of the Tang Dynasty and retreated. Emperor Li Yuan let Murong Shun go back to the Tuyuhun Khanate. After Murong Shun had come back to the Tuyuhun Khanate, he was made King of Daning. He was always unhappy because he had lost the chance to be the crown prince. During the reign of Emperor Li Shi Min of the Tang Dynasty, Murong Fuyun led his army to invade the territory of the Tang Dynasty. Murong Fuyun sent an envoy to Chang'an to have an audience with the Emperor of the Tang Dynasty. Even before the envoy had left Chang'an, Murong Fuyun commanded a great army to invade the area of Shanzhou (now the area of Ledu, Xining and Huangzhong,

Qinghai Province) and looted the people of that area and then left. The Emperor of the Tang Dynasty was very angry. He sent an envoy to blame Murong Fuyun and summon him to Chang'an. But Murong Fuyun refused to go in the excuse that he had been ill. Murong Fuyun sent an army to invade Lanzhou (now Lanzhou, Gansu Province) and Kuozhou (now Guide, Qinghai Province). Li Yun Ying, the governor of Shanzhou, wrote a memorandum to the Emperor of the Tang Dynasty. It read, "Now Qinghai horses, those wonderful horses, are grazing in the area around Qinghai Hu Lake. If a group of light cavalrymen is sent to attack that area, we can get a lot of good horses." The Emperor took his advice and in June 634, he sent General Duan Zhi Xuan to carry out the task. But when the Tang army was fifteen kilometers away from Qinghai Hu Lake, Duan Zhi Xuan would not advance anymore and ordered the soldiers to pitch camp. So the army of Tuyuhun collected all the horses grazing in the area around Qinghai Hu Lake and drove them away. Li Jun Xian, the second commander of the Tang army, selected some elite troops and rode quickly from a side road and caught up with some of the Tuyuhun soldiers in Xuanshui Town, which was situated just to the south of Qinghai Hu Lake. The Tuyuhun army was defeated. The Tang army captured more than twenty thousand cows and sheep.

At that time Murong Fuyun was already old. The power was in the hands of Tianzhu King, the premier of the Tuyuhun Khanate. The Emperor of the Tang Dynasty sent Zhao De Kai to persuade Murong Fuyun to stop invading the Tang Dynasty. But Murong Fuyun and Tianzhu King detained Zhao De Kai. The Emperor sent more than ten envoys to Murong Fuyun, demanding that he release Zhao De Kai, but Murong Fuyun refused to do so.

In November 634, the army of Tuyuhun invaded Liangzhou (now Wuwei, Gansu Province). In December the Emperor issued an imperial order to carry out an expedition against the Tuyuhun Khanate. By this time, Li Jing was already very old. The Emperor said to his ministers and generals, "It would be best if Li Jing could take up the position of commander-in-chief of this army." When Li Jing heard this, he went to see Fang Xuan Ling. He said, "Although I am old, I can still command this expedition." Fang Xuan Ling conveyed what Li Jing had said to the Emperor. The Emperor was very happy. He appointed Li Jing as the commander-in-chief of the army of the Xihai Route to head the whole expedition army; He appointed Hou Jun Ji as commander-in-chief of the army of the Jishi Route, and Li Dao Zong, King of Rencheng, as the commander-in-chief of the army of the Shanshan Route. Hou Jun Ji and Li Dao Zong were the deputies of Li Jing. The Emperor appointed Li Da Liang as commander-in-chief of the army of Qiemo Route, Li Dao Yan as commander-in-chief of the army of the Chishui Route, Gao Zeng Sheng as the commander-in-chief of the army of the Yanze Route. The Emperor also ordered the army of the Turks and the army of the Tribe of Qibi to take part in the expedition. The army of the Tribe of Qibi was commanded by General Qibi Heli.

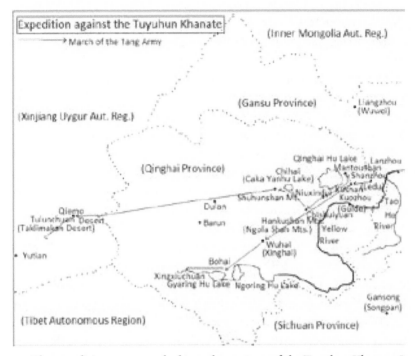

The expedition army marched into the territory of the Tuyuhun Khanate. In April 635 the Tang army under Li Dao Zong defeated Murong Fuyun in Kushan Mountain (a mountain situated to the southeast of Qinghai Hu Lake and south of Huangyuan, Qinghai Province). More than four hundred Tuyuhun soldiers were killed or captured. Murong Fuyun escaped to the west with his main force. He ordered his soldiers to burn all the grass in that area so that the Tang army horses would have nothing to eat. Seeing that all the grass had been burned away, Li Dao Zong said to Li Jing, "Bohai Lake is a remote place and very few people have been there. Murong Fuyun has escaped to the west and we do not know where he is now. The grass has been burned away, and our horses are hungry. It would be better for us to go back to Shanzhou. When the horses are strong again, we may attack Murong Fuyun again." Hou Jun Ji was strongly again this suggestion. He said, "I don't think so. Last year Duan Zhi Xuan defeated Murong Fuyun. But as soon as he turned back to Shanzhou, Murong Fuyun had already commanded his army to the city of Shanzhou. This was because the Tuyuhun Khanate was preserved intact and the army of Tuyuhun still obeyed Murong Fuyun's orders. Now Murong Fuyun has been defeated. He ran away in a great hurry. He did not send out scouts to research the situation. Murong Fuyun has lost contact with his ministers and generals. We may make use of Murong Fuyun's difficult situation to complete our task. Although Bohai is far away from here, we still can manage to get there." Li Jing found that argument compelling, and agreed.

Then Li Jing divided the whole army into two routes: Li Jing, Li Da Liang, Xue Wan Jun and his brother Xue Wan Che commanded an army to take the northern route; Hou Jun Ji and Li Dao Zong commanded an army to take the south route.

The Tang army of the north route marched northward. They met the Tuyuhun army in Mantoushan Mountain (now Riyue Shan Mountain, Qinghai Province). General Xue Gu Er under Li Jing commanded the light cavalrymen to attack the Tuyuhun army. In the battle, the Tang soldiers killed a king of Tuyuhun and five hundred Tuyuhun soldiers. The Tang army moved westward. They met the Tuyuhun army in Niuxindui (situated on the southern bank of Qinghai Hu Lake, Qinghai Province). The Tang army defeated the Tuyuhun army. The Tang army marched southward to Chishuiyuan (to the southeast of Xinghai, Qinghai Province). General Xue Wan Jun and his brother Xue Wan Che commanded some troops to march ahead of the main force. Suddenly an army of Tuyuhun appeared and surrounded the troops under Xue Wan Jun. Xue Wan Jun and Xue Wan Che fought bravely. Xue Wan Jun and Xue Wan Che both were hit by the spears of the enemies and fell from their horses. They had to fight on foot. Six out of ten soldiers of the Tang army were killed. When General Qibi Heli got the news, he commanded several hundred cavalrymen to ride forward to the battlefield. He broke into the encirclement, fought very bravely and killed many Tuyuhun soldiers. He saved Xue Wan Jun and Xue Wan Che and the Tang Troops, a great success. In this battle, Murong Xiaojun, King of Nanchang of the Tuyuhun Khanate, was captured. The Tang army got tens of thousands of cattle. Li Jing commanded the Tang army of the north route to Chihai (now Caka Yanhu Lake, Qinghai Province) where the Tang army met the Tribe of Tianzhu. A battle was fought. The Tang army defeated the Tribe of Tianzhu and captured two hundred thousand cows and sheep. Li Da Liang marched his army to Shuhunshan Mountain (to the west of Caka Yanhu Lake) and met an army of Tuyuhun. After a battle, the Tang army under Li Da Liang captured a king of the Tuyuhun Khanate and fifty thousand cattle. Li Jing commanded his victorious army to march further west to Qiemo (now Qiemo, Xinjiang Uygur Autonomous Region). At that time Murong Fuyun with his army was by the side of Tulunchuan Desert (now Taklimakan Desert, Xinjiang Uygur Autonomous Region) intending to go through the desert to Yutian Kingdom (in the area of Yutian and Hotan, Xinjiang Uygur Autonomous Region). Murong Shun, Murong Fuyun's eldest son, killed Tianzhu King and led the people of Tuyuhun to surrender to the Tang army. Seeing that the situation was very unfavorable to him, Murong Fuyun commanded his main force to go into the desert. General Qibi Heli wanted to lead some light cavalrymen to start a surprise attack on Murong Fuyun. Xue Wan Jun was strongly against Qibi Heli's suggestion because last time he and his brother were surrounded by the army of Tuyuhun when he commanded a small force to go ahead of the main force. Qibi Heli said, "Now our enemies do not have a city wall to protect themselves. They just live in the open air. If we don't take this chance to start a surprise attack while they have gathered together, they might scatter and go in all directions and cannot be found. If we lose this chance, it would be difficult for us to destroy Murong Fuyun." General Qibi Heli selected a thousand cavalrymen and rode directly into the desert. Xue Wan Jun had to lead the main force after him. There was no water in the desert. The soldiers had to cut the skin of their horses with their swords and drink the blood from the horses' wounds. Several days later, they caught up with Murong Fuyun and his men. Qibi Heli commanded his cavalrymen to start a surprise attack on the camp of the Tuyuhun army. He saw the command tent of Murong Fuyun and rode to it. Murong Fuyun escaped with a hundred cavalrymen. In that battle, the cavalrymen under Qibi Heli killed several thousand Tuyuhun soldiers and captured Murong Fuyun's wife and childred. They also captured two hundred thousand cattle. Murong Fuyun saw that there was no hope for him, so he killed himself.

Under the command of Hou Jun Ji and Li Dao Zong, the Tang army of the south route marched southward. They crossed Hankushan Mountain (now Ngola Shan Mountain, Qinghai Province). It was a very difficult journey. The place was desolate and uninhabited. They marched for a thousand kilometers in this wilderness. It was extremely cold. Although it was summer, there was frost. Then they passed Poluozhengu Valley. There was no water in that area. The soldiers had to put ice into their mouths and fed the horses with snow. After they passed Poluozhengu Valley, they reached Wuhai (now Kuhai Lake, to the southwest of Xinghai, Qinghai Province) where they met with a Tuyuhun army. In that battle the Tang soldiers killed many Tuyuhun soldiers and captured a king of the Tuyuhun Khanate. After a month's march the Tang army at last reached Bohai (now Ngoring Hu Lake and Gyaring Hu Lake, Qinghai Province) and then reached Xingxiuchuan (now Xingxiu Hai and Yoigilanglêb Qu, Qinghai Province) which was the farthest source of the Yellow River. After they had completed their task, the Tang army of the south route marched to Dafeichuan (now Qoijê which is situated to the south of Qinghai Hu Lake, Qinghai Province) and joined forces with the Tang army of the north route under Li Jing.

Li Jing sent an envoy back to Chang'an to report their victory. The Emperor ordered Li Jing to make Murong Shun King of Xiping Prefecture, and the Emperor granted Murong Shun the title of Quhulügandou Khan. The Emperor was afraid that the people of Tuyuhun would not submit to the rule of Murong Shun, so he ordered Li Da Liang to lead a strong army to support Murong Shun.

58. Li Yuan, the Father Emperor, Passes Away

In May 635 the Father Emperor fell seriously ill. He issued an imperial order telling the Emperor that the Emperor should resume attending to the state affairs as soon as possible after his funeral and that the mausoleum of the Father Emperor should be constructed on the basis of money saving. On 6 May 635 the Father Emperor died in Gongchui Hall of Da'an Palace at the age of seventy. After discussion it was decided that the posthumous title of the Father Emperor should be "Emperor Dawu" (Mighty Warrior) and his temple title should be "Gaozu," indicating that of all the ancestors of the Tang Dynasty, he had made the greatest contributions. On 27 October 635 the Father Emperor was buried in Xianling Mausoleum (which is situated in Sanyuan, Shaanxi Province).

59. Empress Zhangsun Passes Away

Empress Zhangsun had married Li Shi Min when she was thirteen years old. She gave birth to three sons and one daughter. The three sons were: Li Cheng Qian who was the Crown Prince, Li Tai who was made King of Pu, and Li Zhi who was made King of Jin. A wise and educated lady, she never interfered in state affairs. The Emperor sought to discuss with her the rewards he should make to the ministers and generals who had performed great services and the punishment of those who had committed crimes. Empress Zhangsun replied, "A hen never crows at dawn because this is the duty of a rooster. I am a woman and I should not make any comments on state affairs." She did a great job in the management of Li Shi Min's imperial harem. She strictly observed female virtues. She wrote thirty volumes of "Principles for Women." On 21 June 636 Empress Zhangsun passed away in Lizheng Hall of Taiji Palace. When she died, the Emperor was extremely sad. She was buried in Zhaoling Mausoleum.

60. Wu Shi Yue's Daughter Becomes One of Emperor Li Shi Min's Concubines

When Li Yuan rose in Taiyuan and led an army to march to Chang'an, Wu Shi Yue took part in the march as an officer in charge of military supplies. When Li Yuan became Emperor of the Tang Dynasty, Wu Shi Yue was made Duke of Taiyuan Prefecture. After Li Shi Min ascended the throne of the Tang Dynasty, Wu Shi Yue was promoted to the minister of works, and was made Duke of the State of Ying. Wu Shi Yue had a daughter. She was so pretty that the Emperor heard about her. In November 638 the Emperor summoned her to his imperial harem and she became one of his concubines. At that time she was fourteen years old. She was given the Title of Cairen Wu. Cairen was the title of a concubine of the fifth rank of all the concubines (the Emperor had more than eighty concubines who were divided into eight ranks).

61. The Reinstatement of the Eastern Turkic Khanate

After the destruction of the Eastern Turkic Khanate, many Turks stayed in the areas south of the Yellow River. Tuli Khan's younger brother Ashina Jieshilü followed Ashina Shibobi (Tuli Khan) to the court of the Tang Dynasty. The Emperor of the Tang Dynasty appointed him general. But Ashina Jieshilü was a man without virtue. Ashina Shibobi often criticized him, so Ashina Jieshilü hated his brother and accused him falsely of conspiring to rebel. The Emperor resented his mean behavior, so he did not grant him any promotion. Now, Ashina Jieshilü hated the Emperor, and he conspired to assassinate him. He secretly gathered about forty officers formerly under his command to carry out his scheme. In April 639 the Emperor was staying in Jiucheng Palace (in Linyou, Shaanxi Province, which is one hundred and sixty kilometers northwest to Chang'an). As a rule, Li Zhi, King of Jin, would come out of the palace gate at about four o'clock to arrange the guards of the palace. At night, on April 11, Ashina Jieshilü and his men hid themselves behind the palace wall, waiting for Li Zhi to come out so they could seize him and kill him. Incidentally, there was a great wind that night. Li Zhi did not come out of the palace gate, and having gone this far, Ashina Jieshilü was afraid that their action would be found out. So he decided to storm the palace gate. They broke four defensive lines. Many of the royal guards were killed. But General Sun Wu Kai commanded his men to counter attack. Ashina Jieshilü had to escape. But he was captured and executed.

After this incident, the ministers said to the Emperor that it was not a good idea to let the Turks stay in the areas south of the Yellow River. So the Emperor decided to reinstate the Eastern Turkic Khanate and let all the tribes of the Turks go back to their homeland. In June 639 he granted Ashina Simo, King of Huaihua Prefecture, the title of Yiminishuqilibi Khan. The Emperor ordered him to take all the Turks and cross the Yellow River and go back to the areas of the original Eastern Turkic Khanate. But the Turks were afraid of the Tribe of Xueyantuo, so they would not go beyond of the Great Wall. The Emperor sent Guo Si Ben, the minister of agriculture, to Yishi Yinan, Zhenzhupiga Khan of the Xueyantuo Khanate, with a letter bearing the seal of the Emperor. The letter read, "Jiali Khan of the Eastern Turkic Khanate thought that he was very powerful. So he invaded the territory of the Tang Dynasty frequently and numerous Chinese people were killed by his army. I sent an army to defeat him. The tribes of the Turks submitted to the Tang Dynasty. I forgave all the wrongs they had done and encouraged them to do good deeds. I granted them high ranking positions as I granted positions to my own officials and generals. I treated the people of the Turks as my own people. I defeated the Eastern Turkic Khanate only for the purpose of punishing Jiali Khan for all the harm he had done to the Chinese people. I did not intend to hold the land of the Eastern Turkic Khanate forever. After Jiali Khan was overthrown, I intended to reinstate the Eastern Turkic Khanate by having another khan rule over this khanate. This is the reason why I let the tribes of the Turks stay in the areas south of the Yellow River and let the horses, cattle and sheep of the Turks graze in the grasslands in the areas south of the Yellow River. Now the population of the Eastern Turks has greatly increased and the number of the horses, cattle and sheep has greatly grown. Now it is time for me to fulfill my promise to reinstate the Eastern Turkic Khanate. I have made Ashina Simo khan of the Eastern Turkic Khanate. He is going to take his people across the Yellow River and back to their homeland. I made you khan of the Xueyantuo Khanate before I made Ashina Simo khan of the Eastern Turkic Khanate. You are considered as the great khan because I made you khan long ago. Ashina Simo is considered as the junior khan because he was made khan later than you. You live in the area north of the desert. The Turks will live in the area south of the desert. Each of you will stay in your own territory and should not invade each other. If any one of you invades the territory of the other, I will send an army to punish the invader." Yishi Yinan respectfully accepted the imperial order and promised to do as the Emperor ordered him to do.

The Emperor gave a farewell banquet in Qizheng Hall of the palace. In the banquet, the Emperor asked Ashina Simo to come to him. The Emperor said, "When a person sees that the trees and grass are growing prosperously, he feels very happy in his heart. I have provided for your people, and your people have become prosperous. I feel very happy. Now you are leaving. I am reluctant to let you go. But the tombs of your father and mother are in the north. Now you are going back to your homeland. I have held this banquet to see you off." Ashina Simo said with tears in his eyes, "I will never forget the kindness of Your Majesty to reinstate the Eastern Turkic Khanate. I hope the people of the Eastern Turks will serve the Tang Dynasty generation after generation so as to repay the grace Your Majesty has shown to the people of the Eastern Turks."

The Emperor ordered to have a platform built by the bank of the Yellow River. Then a grand ceremony was held on that platform to make Ashina Simo Yiminishuqilibi Khan of the Eastern Turkic Khanate. The Emperor granted Ashina Simo drums and flags for the Honor Guard of a khan. The Emperor also made General Ashina Zhong Left Virtuous King, and Ashina Nishu Right Virtuous King, and appointed them premiers of the Eastern Turkic Khanate to assist Ashina Simo. In July 639 Ashina Simo brought the people of the Eastern Turks, a hundred thousand in all, forty thousand soldiers, with ninety thousand horses, back to the original lands of the Eastern Turks. He established his headquarters in Dingxiang (now Horinger, Inner Mongolia Autonomous Region).

62. The Conquest of the Kingdom of Gaochang

The Kingdom of Gaochang was situated in the northwest, more than two thousand kilometers away from Chang'an. Formerly the place of Gaochang was called Cheshi. In the Former Han Dynasty (206 BC–9 AD), Emperor Xuan of the Han Dynasty (91 BC–49 BC) sent troops with their wives and children to Cheshi to garrison that place and reclaim wasteland for cultivating food grains. They built fortresses to defend that place. The Han army established their headquarters in Gaochang City. The Kingdom of Gaochang had twenty-one cities. Its capital was Gaochang City (now Gaochang City Site, southeast to Turpan, Xinjiang Uygur Autonomous Region). The important cities of the Kingdom of Gaochang were the city of Tiandi (now Lüqün, southwest to Shanshan, Xinjiang Uygur Autonomous Region) and the city of Jiaohe (now a place to the northwest of Turpan, Xinjiang Uygur Autonomous Region). It had an area of about a hundred thousand square kilometers. Its location was of critical importance. The businessmen and envoys of the countries in the Western Region had to pass the Kingdom of Gaochang before they could reach China. The land of the Kingdom of Gaochang was rich. Wheat and rice could grow twice a year in the Kingdom of Gaochang. Cotton grew in this kingdom. The people of this kingdom used cotton to weave cloth. This kingdom had an army of over ten thousand men.

During the period of the Sui Dynasty, the king of the Kingdom of Gaochang was Qu Bo Ya. He went to the court of the Sui Dynasty during the reign of Emperor Yang Guang. Emperor Yang Guang granted him the highest honorable position, appointed him governor of Cheshi (the area around Turpan, Xinjiang Uygur Autonomous Region) and made him Duke of the State of Bian. The family of Yuwen was a close relative of Emperor Yang Guang. Emperor Yang Guang granted the title of Princess Huarong to a girl of this family and married her to Qu Bo Ya. In 619 (which was the second year of the reign of Emperor Li Yuan of the Tang Dynasty) Qu Bo Ya died. Qu Bo Ya's son Qu Wen Tai succeeded his father and became king of the Kingdom of Gaochang. He sent an envoy to the court of the Tang Dynasty to report the death of his father to Emperor Li Yuan of the Tang Dynasty. Emperor Li Yuan sent Zhu Hui Biao, governor of Hezhou, to Gaochang City to mourn for the death of Qu Bo Ya. In 624 Qu Wen Tai presented to Emperor Li Yuam two lovely little dogs, one male and one female. They were just six inches tall and a foot long. They could guide a horse by holding the reins in their mouths. They could present acrobatic shows by holding burning candles in their mouths. When Li Shi Min ascended the throne of the Tang Dynasty in 625,

Qu Wen Tai presented the Emperor with the furs of black foxes. In 630 Qu Wen Tai went to Chang'an to have an audience with the Emperor. When he left, the Emperor granted many gifts. Queen Yuwen wanted to be a relative of the royal family of the Tang Dynasty. So the Emperor granted her the royal family name of Li and granted her the title of Princess Changle.

But later Qu Wen Tai became hostile to the Tang Dynasty. He blocked the way to the Tang Dynasty. He detained the businessmen and envoys of the countries in the Western Regions and did not allow them to go to China. To the east of the Kingdom of Gaochang, there was the Kingdom of Yiwu (in the area of Hami, in the northeast part of Xinjiang Uygur Autonomous Region). At first this kingdom submitted to the Western Turkic Khanate. But during the reign of Emperor Li Shi Min of the Tang Dynasty, the Kingdom of Yiwu submitted to the Tang Dynasty. Then Qu Wen Tai colluded with Shaboluoyehu Khan of the Western Turkic Khanate and attacked the Kingdom of Yiwu. The Emperor of the Tang Dynasty sent an envoy with a letter written by the Emperor to Qu Wen Tai to reproach him. The Emperor asked Qu Wen Tai to send Guanjun Ashina, Qu Wen Tai's chief minister, to the court of the Tang Dynasty to discuss this matter. But Qu Wen Tai refused to send Guanjun Ashina. Instead he sent Qu Yong, a low ranking official, to Chang'an to apologize for their attacking of the Kingdom of Yiwu. By the end of the Sui Dynasty, there was great chaos in China. Many people of China ran to the Eastern Turkic Khanate. After Jiali Khan of the Eastern Turkic Khanate was captured by the Tang army, the Chinese people who had gone to the Eastern Turkic Khanate went to the Kingdom of Gaochang. The Emperor of the Tang Dynasty ordered Qu Wen Tai to send them back to China, but Qu Wen Tai refused to do so. Instead, he detained all these people and hid all of them in the area of the Kingdom of Gaochang. Not long later, Qu Wen Tai colluded with Yipi Shad (General Yipi) of the Western Turkic Khanate to attack the Kingdom of Yanqi (in the area of Yanqi Hui Autonomous County, Xinjiang Uygur Autonomous Region), a kingdom to the southwest of the Kingdom of Gaochang, and occupied three cities of the Kingdom of Yanqi. The army of the Kingdom of Gaochang captured all the people of these three cities and then left. The king of the Kingdom of Yanqi lodged a complaint to the Emperor of the Tang Dynasty. The Emperor of the Tang Dynasty sent Li Dao Yu, the minister in charge of foreign relations, to the Kingdom of Gaochang to investigate into this matter. In 639 the Emperor of the Tang Dynasty said to the envoy sent by Qu Wen Tai, "Your king has not paid any tributes to me for several years. He ignores the etiquette which should be shown by a vassal state to its suzerain. At the beginning of this year, all the kings of the vassal states of the Tang Dynasty came to have an audience with me. But Qu Wen Tai did not come. He is now fortifying his cities to prepare to resist my expedition army. Last time I sent an envoy to him. Qu Wen Tai said to my envoy, 'The eagles fly in the sky. Pheasants fly in the bushes. Cats walk in the halls and the rats hide themselves in their holes. Each of them stays in the place it belongs to. Isn't that marvelous?' All the envoys sent by the states of the Western Region were detained by Qu Wen Tai. He sent an envoy to Yishi Yinan, Khan of the Xueyantuo Khanate, and said to him, 'You are the khan of a big khanate. You are an equal to the Emperor of the Tang Dynasty. Why should you kneel down in front of the envoy sent by the Emperor of the Tang Dynasty?' He is impolite to his suzerain. He sows discord among the friendly states. If I do not punish him, how can I encourage the kings of the other states to do good deeds? Next year, I will send an expedition army to punish your king." Yishi Yinan, Khan of the Xuyantuo Khanate, sent an envoy to the Emperor with a letter offering to send officers as guides to show the way for the Tang army to attack the Kingdom of Gaochang. The Emperor accepted Yishi Yinan's offer. The Emperor of the Tang Dynasty sent Tang Jian, the minister in charge of the civil affairs, to the Xueyantuo Khanate to coordinate the attack of the Kingdom of Gaochang. The Emperor still hoped that Qu Wen Tai would realize his wrong doings and reform himself. So the Emperor sent an envoy to Qu Wen Tai with a letter written by him, showing the consequence if he continued to be hostile to the Tang Dynasty and summoning him to the court of the Tang Dynasty. But Qu Wen Tai refused to go in the excuse that he was ill.

In November 639 the Emperor appointed Hou Jun Ji as commander-in-chief of the army of Jiaohe Route, Xue Wan Jun as deputy commander-in-chief of this army. When Qu Wen Tai got the information that the army of the Tang Dynasty would march to attack the Kingdom of Gaochang, he said to his ministers and generals, "The Tang Dynasty is more than three thousand five hundred kilometers away from here. There is a desert of one thousand kilometers wide. In the desert, there is neither water nor grass. In winter the wind is piercingly cold. In summer the wind is like burning fire. If anyone is caught by the wind, he will be killed. How can a great army pass this desert? Last time when I went to Chang'an, I could see that the areas of Qin and Long were bleak and desolate. Now the Emperor of the Tang Dynasty has sent an army to attack me. If there are many soldiers in this army, they cannot get enough food supply. If there are fewer than thirty thousand men in the Tang army, I can cope with them. I will wait at ease for the fatigued Tang army. If they are halted in front of my strong city walls, their food supply will be consumed in twenty days and will have to retreat. Then I will attack them when they are retreating. Then I will surely defeat the Tang army" So he did not care about the Tang army. But in August 640 news suddenly came that the Tang army had crossed the desert (now Kumtag Desert) and was approaching the capital. Qu Wen Tai was so scared that he fell seriously ill and then died. His son Qu Zhi Sheng succeeded his father to the throne of the Kingdom of Gaochang. At that time the Tang army had reached Liugu (now a place to the northwest of Turpan) which was just one hundred kilometers away from Jiaohe. A scout reported to Hou Jun Ji that the funeral of Qu Wen Tai would be held in Gaochang City the next day; all the important figures of the Kingdom of Gaochang would gather there to attend the funeral of Qu Wen Tai. The generals under Hou Jun Ji suggested that they should attack Gaochang City while the funeral was going on. By doing so, all the important people of the Kingdom of Gaochang would be captured in one battle. Hou Jun Ji said, "No, we cannot do that. The Emperor has sent us to punish Qu Wen Tai because Qu Wen Tai was proud and ungracious. He did not observe the ethics he should have observed. If we start a surprise attack while they are holding a funeral ceremony, this will not be a righteous act for a punitive army." So Hou Jun Ji gave up the chance to attack Gaochang City. He commanded his army to march to the City of Tiandi. When Hou Jun Ji reached the City of Tiandi, he sent an envoy to the city demanding the defenders to surrender. But the general defending Tiandi bluntly refused. The next morning, the Tang army started an attack. By noon that day the city was taken by the Tang army. The Tang army captured seven thousand people of Gaochang. Then Hou Jun Ji sent General Xin Liao Er to lead an army as the vanguard of the main force to march to Gaochang City at night of the same day. When the Tang army under Xin Liao Er reached Gaochang City, the army of Gaochang came out to fight against the Tang army. The army of Gaochang was defeated and retreated into the city.

Not long later the main force of the Tang army arrived at the foot of the city wall of Gaochang City. Qu Zhi Sheng sent a letter to Hou Jun Ji which read, "The one who offended the Emperor was my father, the late king. He has been punished by Heaven. He is already dead. I have succeeded to the throne for just a few days. I hope you will have pity on me." Hou Jun Ji sent a reply letter to Qu Zhi Sheng. It read, "If you realize your crimes and repent, you should bind your hands with a rope and come to the gate of my camps to surrender." Qu Zhi Sheng hesitated and would not come out of the city. Hou Jun Ji ordered his soldiers to fill the ditch around the city wall with bags of sand and then the Tang troops crossed the ditch to attack Gaochang City. When Hou Jun Ji was appointed commander-in-chief of the expedition army, he recruited many carpenters who could make city attacking devices. When the Tang army reached Gaochang City, Hou Jun Ji ordered the carpenters to fell trees to make city attacking devices. The Tang soldiers launched big stones with the stone launchers. The stones rain down the city. The Gaochang soldiers had to hide themselves in houses. Then the Tang soldiers built a movable watch tower of thirty meters tall with wheels on it. At the top of the tower, a soldier could see the inside of the city and direct the targets to the soldiers who operated the stone launchers. This caused great casualties to the Gaochang army.

At the beginning when Qu Wen Tai learned that the Emperor was sending an army to attack the Kingdom of Gaochang, he sent an envoy to the Western Turkic Khanate asking Shaboluoyehu Khan of the Western Turkic Khanate to rescue him when the Tang army came. Shaboluoyehu Khan agreed and sent a general to lead an army to station in the City of Futu (now Jimsar, Xinjiang Uygur Autonomous Region) which was about one hundred and eighty kilometers away from Gaochang City. When the Tang army came, the general of the Western Turkic army surrendered to the Tang army with the City of Futu. Qu Zhi Sheng saw that he could not get help from anywhere. So he opened the city gate of Gaochang City and surrendered to the Tang army. Then Hou Jun Ji sent his army to attack other places of the Kingdom of Gaochang. The Tang army took three prefectures, five counties and twenty-two cities in all. They captured thirty thousand people of Gaochang and four thousand horses.

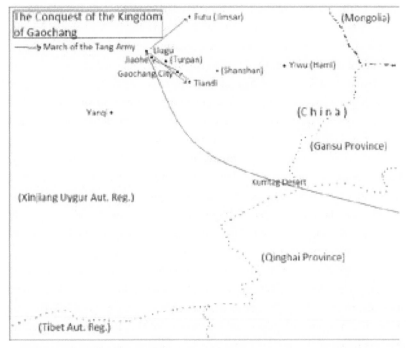

After conquering the Kingdom of Gaochang, Hou Jun Ji sent an envoy back to Chang'an to report the great victory to the Emperor and then commanded his triumphant army to return to Chang'an bringing Qu Zhi Sheng, all the ministers and generals and nobles of the Kingdom of Gaochang with them. The Emperor decided to include the Kingdom of Gaochang into the territory of the Tang Dynasty and turn the lands of the Kingdom of Gaochang into prefectures and counties. In September 640 the Emperor turned the Kingdom of Gaochang into Xizhou and turned the area of the City of Futu into Tingzhou. The Emperor established Anxi (meaning pacifying the west) Military Command in the City of Jiaohe and ordered troops to garrison there.

63. Princess Wencheng Is Married to Songtsen Gampo, King of Tubo (Tibet)

Tubo (Tibet) was situated about four thousand kilometers southwest to Chang'an. It was a very cold place. Rice could not grow in that area. Hulless barley, wheat and buckwheat grew in that area. The people of Tubo raised yaks, pigs, dogs, sheep and horses. Tubo was rich in gold, silver, copper and tin. The people of Tubo were brave. They would rather die on the battlefield than die of illness. The capital of Tubo (Tibet) was Luoxie (now a place to the north of Lhasa, Tibet Autonomous Region).

In 634 Songtsen Gampo, King of Tubo, sent an envoy to Chang'an to pay tribute to the Emperor of the Tang Dynasty. The Emperor sent Feng De Xia as his envoy to pay a visit to Songtsen Gampo. When Feng De Xia reached Luoxie, Songtsen Gampo received him with great pleasure. Songtsen Gampo heard that the khan of the Turks and the khan of Tuyuhun had married princesses of the Tang Dynasty. In August 638 he sent an envoy to go to Chang'an with Feng De Xia with quantities of gold to ask the Emperor to marry a princess to him. But the Emperor turned down this request. The envoy went back to Luoxie and said to Songtsen Gampo, "When I first arrived to Chang'an, I was treated very well. The Emperor of the Tang Dynasty promised to marry a princess to Your Majesty. But the khan of Tuyuhun came and said something against Your Majesty in front of the Emperor. Then the Emperor of the Tang Dynasty refused to marry a princess to Your Majesty." Songtsen Gampo was very angry and raised a great army to attack Tuyuhun. The khan of Tuyuhun could not resist the attack and he had to escape to the area north of Qinghai (now Qinghai Hu Lake, Qinghai Province). The army of Tubo occupied the territory of Tuyuhun and captured all the people and cattle. Then Songtsen Gampo commanded two hundred thousand men to be stationed to the west of Songzhou (now Songpan, Sichuan Province). He sent envoys to Chang'an with gifts of gold, claiming that they had come to escort the princess to Tubo. But not long later Songtsen Gampo commanded his army to attack Songzhou. Han Wei, the commander of the Tang army in Songzhou, came out of the city to fight against the Tubo army but was defeated. In August 638 the Emperor of the Tang Dynasty appointed Hou Jun Ji as the commander-in-chief of the army of the Dangmi Route, General Zhishi Sili as the commander-in-chief of the army of the Bailan Route, General Niu Jin Da as the commander-in-chief of the army of the Kuoshui Route, General Liu Jian as the commander-in-chief of the army of the Taohe Route. They commanded fifty thousand cavalry and infantry to fight against the army of Tubo. General Niu Jin Da commanded the Tang army under him to march ahead as vanguards. On September 6, seeing that Tubo troops were not prepared, General Niu Jin Da launched a surprise attack on their camps at night. More than one thousand Tubo soldiers were killed. Songtsen Gampo was shocked. So he led his army to retreat. He sent envoys to Chang'an to apologize to the Emperor for his offence, and again he asked the Emperor to marry a princess to him. The Emperor of the Tang Dynasty promised to marry a princess to him. Songtsen Gampo sent Lu Dongzan, the premier of Tubo, to Chang'an with five thousand ounces of gold and many other treasures to present to the Emperor as betrothal gifts.

In January 641 the Emperor of the Tang Dynasty granted the title of Princess Wencheng to a girl of the royal clan and married her to Songtsen Gampo. He appointed Li Dao Zong, King of Jiangxia Prefecture, to preside over the wedding ceremony and to escort Princess Wencheng to Tubo. Songtsen Gampo commanded an army to Bohai (now the area around Ngoring Hu Lake and Gyaring Hu Lake, Qinghai Province) to wait for Princess Wencheng. On January 15, Princess Wencheng started her long journey to Tubo (Tibet). The party started from Chang'an and went westward: they crossed Long Shan Mountain (which is situated in the southeast of Gansu Province and west of Shaanxi Province), then reached Tianshui (now Tianshui, Gansu Province); they went west to Linxia (now Linxia, Gansu Province); they reached Shancheng (now Xining, Qinghai Province); they went west to Mantou Shan Mountain (now Riyue Shan Mountain which is situated to the east of Qinghai Hu Lake, Qinghai Province); then the party turned south and went past Qabqa and Hainan; then they reached Bohai where Songtsen Gampo was waiting for Princess Wencheng.

When Li Dao Zong arrived, Songtsen Gampo strictly held the ritual of father-in-law and son-in-law. Then Songtsen Gampo and Princess Wencheng and the party crossed Bayan Har Shan Mountain; they crossed Tongtian He River and reached Yushu (now Yushu which is situated in the southeast of Qinghai Provinc); then they reached Zadoi; they went past Tanggula Shan Mountain (which lies on the border of Qinghai province and Tibet Autonomous Region) and entered into the area of Tubo (Tibet); they went past Nyainrong and Nagqu (both in the area of Tibet); at last they reached Luoxie, the capital of Tubo (Tibet). Songtsen Gampo said to his relatives, "No one in all the generations of my father and grandfather ever married a princess of the great countries. Now I am very fortunate to marry a princess of the Tang Dynasty. I have decided to build a palace for the princess so as to show the honor I now enjoy to the generations to come." A grand palace was built on the Marpo Ri Hill in Lhasa for Princess

Wencheng of the Tang Dynasty. This palace still exists today, which is the famous Potala Palace in Lhasa, Tibet Autonomous Region.

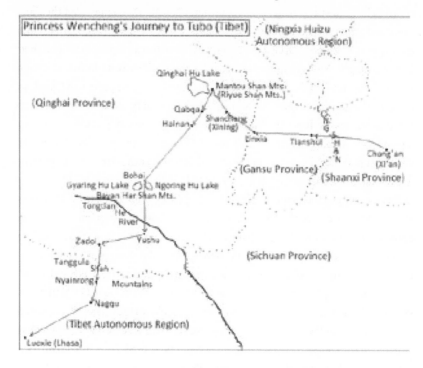

64. The Defeat of the Xueyantuo Khanate

Yishi Yinan, Zhenzhupiga Khan of the Xueyantuo Khanate, had always
wanted to attack the newly reinstated Eastern Turkic Khanate. In November
641, Yishi Yinan got news that the Emperor of the Tang Dynasty had decided to
go to Tai Shan Mountain (now in Shandong Province) to hold a grand ceremony
offering sacrifices to Heaven in February 642. Yishi Yinan said to his ministers
and generals, "The Emperor of the Tang Dynasty is going east to Tai Shan Mountain. All the generals and ministers and his army will follow him to Tai Shan
Mountain. There will be very few Tang troops in the border areas. If I attack
Ashina Simo at that time, I can easily defeat him." Then he ordered his son Dadu
Shad to raise a great army of two hundred thousand men from the Xueyantuo
Khanate, the Tribe of Tongluo, the Tribe of Pugu, the Tribe of Uigur, the Tribe
of Mohe and the Tribe of Xi. Dadu Shad commanded this great army to cross the
Hanhai Desert (Gobi Desert) to Baidaochuan which was a place to the north of
Baidao (now Hohhot, Inner Mogolia Autonomous Region). Dadu Shad stationed
his army there threatening to attack Dingxiang (now Horinger, Inner Mongolia)

where the headquarters of Ashina Simo, the khan of the Eastern Turkic Khanate, was located.

Ashina Simo led the people and the army of the Eastern Turkic Khanate to retreat to the area within the Great Wall and sent an envoy to ask the Emperor of the Tang Dynasty for help. The Emperor ordered Zhang Jian, the commander-in-chief of the Tang army in Yingzhou (now Chaoyang, Liaoning Province), to command an army of cavalrymen to attack the eastern border area of the Xueyantuo Khanate. Then the Emperor appointed Li Ji as commander-in-chief of the Tang army of Shuozhou Route to command sixty thousand infantry and one thousand two hundred cavalry to march to the Eastern Turkic Khanate from Shuozhou (now Shuozhou, Shanxi Province). He appointed General Li Da Liang as the commander-in-chief of the Tang army of Lingzhou Route to command forty thousand infantry and five thousand cavalry to attack the Xueyantuo army from Lingzhou (now Lingwu, Ningxia Huizu Autonomous Region). He appointed General Zhang Shi Gui as commander-in-chief of the Tang army of Qingzhou Route to command ten thousand seven hundred soldiers to march from Yunzhong (now Datong, Shanxi Province). He appointed General Li Xi Yu as commander-in-chief of the Tang army of Liangzhou Route to command an army to march from Liangzhou (now Wuwei, Gansu Province) to the west of the Xueyantuo Khanate. The generals went to say farewell to the Emperor. The Emperor said to them, "Yishi Yinan thinks that his khanate is very strong. He has sent his army to cross the vast desert to the south. The Xueyantuo army has travelled more than a thousand kilometers. Their horses are very tired now. The most important thing in commanding an army is to advance as quickly as possible when the situation is favorable and to retreat as quickly as possible when the situation is unfavorable. Now the army of Xueyantuo has not been able to attack the Eastern Turkic Khanate by surprise when the Eastern Turkic Khanate was not prepared. Now Ashina Simo has led his people into the area within the Great Wall. In this situation, Dadu Shad has not retreated quickly. I have ordered Ashina Simo to burn away all the grass in that area. The Xueyantuo army will run out of the food supply for the army and for the horses very soon. They cannot get food from the fields. Just now the scouts have come to report to me that the skin of the trees in that area has been eaten by the horses of the Xueyantuo army. You should cooperate with the army of the Eastern Turkic Khanate. You don't need to fight quick battles. You may wait till the Xueyantuo army retreats. Then you will pounce upon your enemy. Then you will surely win."

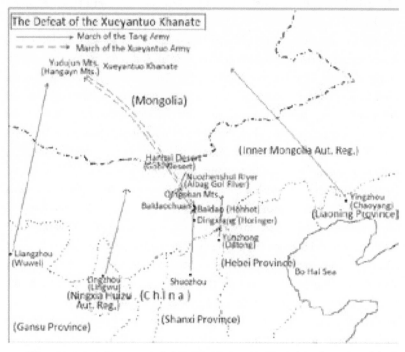

Then the generals commanded their army to march to their designated destination. Seeing that the Tang army was coming, Dadu Shad commanded his army to retreat. In December 641 Li Ji and his army went past Baidaochuan (now in the north of Hohhot, Inner Mongolia Autonomous Region) and came into Qingshan Mountain (now Daqing Shan Mountain, situated to the north of Hohhot, Inner Mongolia Autonomous Region), where they saw the retreating Xueyantuo army. Dadu Shad continued to retreat to the north. Li Ji commanded six thousand cavalrymen to pursue the Xueyantuo army. More than ten days later Li Ji's army caught up with the Xueyantuo army by Nuozhenshui River (now Aibag Gol River, in the north part of Inner Mongolia Autonomous Region). Dadu Shad knew that he could not break away from the pursuing Tang army. So he arranged his army into a battle formation which lasted for five kilometers. In the past Yishi Yinan developed a tactic of fighting battles on foot. He broke his army into many groups each of which consisted of five soldiers. When the army reached the battlefield, all the soldiers came down from their horses. One soldier of the group of five took care of the five horses, and the other four soldiers carried their weapons to go ahead to fight with the enemies on foot. When they defeated the enemies, the soldier taking care of the five horses should bring the horses to the four soldiers fighting in front and the whole army would pursue the enemies on horseback. Yishi Yinan put this tactic in the battles against the armies of the Western Turkic Khanate under Shaboluo and General Ashina She'er, and won resounding victories. This time Dadu Shad also adopted this tactic. Li Ji ordered the Eastern Turkic army to attack the battle formation but was defeated by the Xueyantuo army. The Xueyantuo soldiers ran after the Turkic solders. Then Li Ji ordered the Tang army to march forward. Dadu Shad ordered his soldiers to shoot. Many horses of the Tang army were killed by arrows. Li Ji ordered all the soldiers to dismount from their horses and ordered them to charge the enemy with long spears. The Xueyantuo army's battle formation was broken. Xue Wan Che, the deputy commander-in-chief, ordered several thousand cavalry to attack the Xueyantuo soldiers taking care of the horses. The Xueyangtuo soldiers lost their horses and did not know what to do. In this battle, three thousand Xueyantuo soldiers were killed, and fifty thousand were captured. Dadu Shad and some soldiers escaped. But when the escaped soldiers of the Xueyantuo Khanate reached the north of the desert, they were caught by a snow storm. Eight out of ten Xueyantuo soldiers died in the bitter cold.

Yishi Yinan sent an envoy to the Emperor begging to make peace with the Eastern Turks. The Emperor received the envoy before the envoy went back to the Xueyantuo Khanate. The Emperor said, "I made an agreement with your khan before. It was specified that the demarcation for the Xueyantuo Khanate and the Eastern Turkic Khanate was the desert. If anyone invaded the other, I would punish the invader. Now your khan thought that the Xueyantuo Khanate was strong and sent an army to cross the desert to invade the territory of the Eastern Turkic Khanate. Now General Li Ji just commanded several thousand cavalry and defeated your army of tens of thousands. Go back and tell your khan to think carefully before he takes any action."

65. The Close Relationship between the Emperor and His Ministers and Generals

Wei Zheng gave the Emperor much good advice. He would remonstrate with the Emperor even when the Emperor was in a rage. In 637 Wei Zheng presented a memorandum to the Emperor which read, "It is said that if a person wants a tree to grow tall and broad, he must let the root of the tree grow strong and firm in the soil; if a person wants a river to flow far and wide, he must dredge the source of the river to make it deep; an emperor who wants to stabilize his empire must perform many good deeds for the people so as to show his grace to his people. If the source of a river is not deep, how can he expect the river to flow far and wide? If the root of a tree is not strong and firm, how can he expect the tree to grow tall and broad? If an emperor does not perform many good deeds for the people, how can he expect stability and peace in his empire? Even a stupid man like me knows that it won't do. So a wise man can understand this much better. An emperor sitting on the throne holds the supreme power and he has the responsibility to administer the vast realm. He is sitting in the most sacred position. He should do his best to ensure that the well being of his people will last forever. If he does not prepare for danger in times of peace, if he does not get rid of his extravagance and practice thrift, if he does not perform good deeds for the people, if he cannot control his greedy desires, that would be like hoping for the tree to grow while cutting off its roots, and hoping the river will flow far and wide while blocking its source.

"The emperors of all the dynasties in history all accepted the great responsibilities Heaven had placed on them. They were virtuous while in hard times; but when they succeeded in obtaining the power to rule over the realm, they were not as virtuous as before. Many of them began well, but very few of them ended well. Does that mean that it is easy to win the power to rule over the realm but difficult to preserve it? When he was fighting for the power to rule over the realm, he had great ability; but he did not have sufficient ability to preserve it. Why? Because in hard times, the emperor treated his subordinates sincerely; but when he had achieved his goal, he became very proud of himself and looked down upon others. When the emperor treated others with sincerity, even the tribes in the remote north and the people in the barbarian south would unite as one and gathered around the emperor. If the emperor assumed an arrogant air, his closest relatives became strangers. If the emperor rules the people by severe laws and harsh punishments, the people will do their best to avoid punishment, but they would not cherish the slightest appreciation of the emperor. Outwardly they are obedient, but inwardly they are not. Whether the enmity of the people is very strong is not the most important thing. The most important thing is whether the people are for the emperor or against the emperor. The people are like the water of a river. The water of a river may carry the boat on it and allow the boat to sail on it. But the water of a river may also overturn the boat. A ruler must be very careful about that. It would be most dangerous to harness galloping horses drawing a carriage with rotten ropes.

"If an emperor ruling over the people sees something good and desires to obtain it, he should think that he has already had enough so as to control his desires; if he wants to carry out great construction projects, he must think that the projects should be stopped so as to let the people have a rest; when he is afraid that he is in danger sitting in the highest position and holding the supreme power, he should think that he should cultivate himself to be modest; if he is afraid that he is too proud of himself, he should think that the streams all flow into big rivers and the seas because the rivers and the seas are located in a lower position; when he enjoys hunting trips and tours for pleasure, he should think that he must limit these trips to three times in a year; if he worries that he has become slack, he should think that he must have a good beginning and a good ending in doing anything; if he worries that he has been ill-informed, he should think that he must be modest so as to accept the opinions of his subordinates; if he worries that wicket ministers might say slanderous words against upright courtiers in front of him, he must think that he should rectify himself and keep away the wicked ministers; when he wants to grant rewards to somebody, he must make sure that he is not acting out of a sudden impulse without careful consideration; if he is going to punish somebody, he must make sure that he has not given in to sudden anger.

Portrait of Wei Zheng

"The above ten points for deliberation may help Your Majesty to develop the virtues of Your Majesty. If your Majesty can choose the capable persons and put them to the proper positions and follow the good advices, then the wise and capable men will provide their good stratagems and the brave men will fight with all their might for Your Majesty; benevolent men will give their graces to the people and devoted persons will be loyal to Your Majesty. All the ministers and generals will do their best for Your Majesty. Then there is harmony between Your Majesty and the ministers and generals. In this case Your Majesty may enjoy the pleasures in the trips. Then Your Majesty may live as long as the immortals. Your Majesty may govern the whole realm by doing nothing that goes against nature. Why should Your Majesty labor yourself so hard to do the jobs of the subordinates of Your Majesty and give up the best practice of governing the realm by doing nothing that goes against nature?" After the Emperor had read this memorandum, he heartily accepted the advices and personally wrote an imperial letter to praise this memorandum.

In January 643 Wei Zheng fell ill. The Emperor sent envoys to visit Wei Zheng and gave medicine to him. He sent General Li An Yan to stay at Wei Zheng's home so that if Wei Zheng's illness became serious, General Li An Yan would immediately report it to the Emperor. Wei Zheng's house was very simple. The bed room was very small. At that time a hall in the palace was under construction. The Emperor ordered the construction of that hall to be stopped and all the materials moved in order to construct a big bed room at Wei Zheng's house. The big bed room was constructed within five days. When Wei Zheng became seriously ill, the Emperor personally went to his home to visit him. The Emperor touched Wei Zheng gently and shed tears. The Emperor asked Wei Zheng what he wanted, Wei Zheng said, "I don't worry about anything about myself. I only worry about the survival of the Dynasty." Several days later the Emperor dreamed of Wei Zheng at night as if Wei Zheng was still alive. In the morning it was reported to the Emperor that Wei Zheng had died that night at the age of sixty-four. The Emperor went to Wei Zheng's home and cried bitterly. The Emperor granted Wei Zheng the funeral ceremony of the official of the first rank and allowed him to be buried in the area of Zhaoling Mausoleum which was under construction for the Emperor. When the dead body of Wei Zheng was about to be carried on a carriage to his tomb, Wei Zheng's wife asked somebody to convey her words to the Emperor, "Wei Zheng has been very frugal all his life. Now he is buried with the ceremony of an official of the first rank and the ceremony is very grand. I am afraid that this is not what Wei Zheng would have wanted." But the Emperor insisted on holding this grand ceremony. He ordered all the generals and officials to accompany the carriage carrying Wei Zheng's remains to the outskirts of Chang'an. The Emperor himself stood at the tower in the West Garden for the royal family to see Wei Zheng off. The Emperor wrote the characters to be carved on the tablet for the tomb of Wei Zheng. In the later days, the Emperor missed Wei Zheng very much. He said, "People use copper to make mirrors so as to make sure that they have put on his clothes and hat properly. People use history as a mirror so as to know the rise and fall of the dynasties. A person can be used as a mirror. With his advice, I could act properly. Now that Wei Zheng is dead, I have lost a mirror."

General Yuchi Jing De had made great contributions to the Tang Dynasty. So he was proud of himself. One day in September 634 the Emperor held a grand banquet in Qinshan Palace. Yuchi Jing De was invited to present in that banquet. He was assigned to sit on a seat in a very honorable position. But he found that a person was sitting on a seat in a more honorable position. He was very angry and shouted at the man, "What great contributions have you established that you are sitting in a position more honorable than mine?" Li Dao Zong, King of Rencheng, who was sitting on a seat less honorable to Yuchi Jing De's, stood up and tried to persuade Yuchi Jing De to stop that. Yuchi Jing De was so angry that he hit Li Dao Zong very hard by the eye and almost made him blind. The Emperor was very unhappy and dismissed the banquet. He said to Yuchi Jing De, "I once read the history book of the Han Dynasty. From the history book, I found that Emperor Gaozu of the Han Dynasty had had many of the persons who had contributed greatly in the establishment of the Han Dynasty killed. I felt unhappy about what Emperor Gaozu of the Han Dynasty had done to the persons who had established great contributions. After I ascended the throne, I have always tried my best to preserve those who have contributed greatly and hoped that they will pass their titles and wealth to endless generations. You are now in a very high position but you are prone to commit acts against the laws. From what happened today, I can see that it was not wrong for the Emperor Gaozu of the Han Dynasty to kill persons who had made great contributions and he did not kill Han Xin and Peng Yue for no reason. The most important thing for an emperor is to grant rewards and give punishments. I cannot always show special grace on you. You'd better behave yourself, or you will come to regret it." Yuchi Jing De was afraid and did his best to behave himself.

Li Ji had been instrumental in defeating the enemies of the Tang Dynasty; he commanded the Tang Army that destroyed the Eastern Turkic Khanate and the Tuyuhun Khanate; and he defeated the army of the Xueyantuo Khanate. Then, in 641, Li Ji suddenly fell seriously ill. The doctor wrote out a prescription in which some hairs of the beard of a man were needed as a component of the medicine. When the Emperor heard about this, he cut some of the hairs from his own beard and asked a servant to take these hairs to Li Ji. Li Ji took the medicine and recovered. Then he went to see the Emperor and banged his forehead very hard on the ground in front of the Emperor to express his heartfelt thanks. He rapped his forehead so hard that it bled. The Emperor went forward to help him up, saying, "You need not express your thanks to me. I have done this for the sake of the whole realm."

In order to commemorate the persons who had made great contributions to the Tang Dynasty, in February of 643 the Emperor ordered Yan Li Ben, the most famous painter of that time, to paint the portraits of the following persons in Lingyan Pavilion which was situated beside Sanqing Hall in the southwest of Taiji Palace in Chang'an: Zhangsun Wu Ji, Duke of Zhao; Li Xiao Gong, King of Zhao Prefecture; Du Ru Hui, Duke of Lai; Wei Zheng, Duke of Zheng; Fang Xuan Ling, Duke of Liang; Gao Shi Lian, Duke of Shen; Yuchi Jing De, Duke of E; Li Jing, Duke of Wei; Xiao Yu, Duke of Song; Duan Zhi Xuan, Duke of Bao; Liu Hong Ji, Duke of Kui; Qutu Tong, Duke of Jiang; Yin Kai Shan, Duke of Xun; Chai Shao, Duke of Qiao; Zhangsun Shun De, Duke of Pi; Zhang Liang, Duke of Xun; Hou Jun Ji, Duke of Chen; Zhang Gong Jin, Duke of Tan; Cheng Zhi Jie, Duke of

Lu; Yu Shi Nan, Duke of Yongxing; Liu Zheng Hui, Duke of Yu; Tang Jian, Duke of Ju; Li Ji, Duke of Ying; Qin Shu Bao, Duke of Hu.

66. Li Cheng Qian Is Deprived of the Title of Crown Prince; Li Zhi Is Made Crown Prince

Emperor Li Shi Min had fourteen sons: Empress Zhangsun gave birth to Li Cheng Qian, Li Tai and Li Zhi; Concubine Yang (who was the daughter of Emperor Yang Guang of the Sui Dynasty) gave birth to Li Ke and Li Yin; Concubine Yin gave birth to Li You; Concubine Yan gave birth to Li Zhen and Li Xiao; Concubine Wei gave birth to Li Shen; Concubine Yang gave birth to Li Fu; Lady Yang gave birth to Li Ming; Lady Wang gave birth to Li Yun; a lady in the imperial harem gave birth to Li Kuan and Li Jian.

Li Cheng Qian was the eldest son of Emperor Li Shi Min. When Li Shi Min ascended the throne of the Tang Dynasty in 626, Li Cheng Qian was appointed Crown Prince, the successor to the throne, at the age of eight. He seemed to be a very bright boy. Emperor Li Shi Min loved him very much. When the Emperor was out of Chang'an on a tour, Li Cheng Qian would stay in the capital to take care of the state affairs. But as he grew up, he indulged in sex and pleasures. He was afraid that his father would find out his misconducts, so he did his best to cover up all his incorrect behaviors. Whenever he held court and attended to the state affairs, he would talk about the doctrines of loyalty and filial piety. But after court, he did all kinds of immoral acts with base persons in the Palace for the Crown Prince. Some courtiers found out his misconducts and tried to admonish him against incorrect behaviors. Then Li Cheng Qian would sit solemnly and pretended that he was ready to accept the criticism. He even made some self criticism so as to give the impression to others that he would give up all the incorrect practices.

Li Cheng Qian had a brass oven of eight feet tall and a big cauldron with six legs built. He employed those run-away slaves to steal cows from the people. Li Cheng Qian personally cooked the cows and shared the cooked meat with his attendants and servants. Li Cheng Qian liked to speak the language of the Turks and wear the clothes of the Turks. He selected those who had the appearance of the Turks as his attendants. He divided his attendants into groups of small tribes each of which was composed of five people. They made their hair into braids like the hair style of the Turks. They wore the clothes made of sheep skins. Then they drove the sheep to the grassland; all the flags had the picture of five wolf heads on them. They set up tents and Li Cheng Qian lived in one of the tents. They caught the sheep and killed them and cooked them. When the sheep were cooked, they used their daggers to cut the meat and eat it. Li Cheng Qian said to his followers, "I now pretend that I am the khan. Now I am dead. You should follow the customs of the Turks to hold a funeral ceremony." Then he lay on the ground pretending that he was the dead khan. All of his followers cried loudly. Then they mounted their horses and rode around the dead khan. They cut their faces with their daggers following the customs of the Turks. After a long time Li Cheng Qian jumped up happily and declared, "When I become the emperor to rule over the empire, I will command over thirty thousand cavalry to the west of Jincheng to make a hunting trip. Then I will loosen my hair in the hair style of the Turks. Then I will go to Ashina Simo, the khan the Eastern Turks, and ask him to make me a Shad."

Li Yuan Chang, King of Han, was Emperor Li Shi Min's younger brother and Li Cheng Qian's uncle. He was unruly, and often did acts against the laws. The Emperor sent envoys to blame him for his misconducts. So he had a grudge against the Emperor. But Li Cheng Qian was very close to this uncle. They often went on trips together. Li Cheng Qian divided his attendants and guards into two teams. Li Cheng Qian and Li Yuan Chang each commanded a team. They wore amours made of felt and held bamboo spears and swords. The two teams were deployed in battle formations and then attacked each other. Some of them were wounded and shed blood. Li Cheng Qian got pleasure from these bloody games. Those who would not join in the games were seriously beaten. Some of the attendants and guards were killed in these games. Li Cheng Qian said, "If I am the emperor today, I will make a camp of ten thousand men in the royal garden tomorrow. I and King of Han each will command an army. It would be a great pleasure to watch the two armies fight in real battle." He also said, "When I ascend the throne as the emperor, I will do what I like to do and enjoy all kinds of pleasures. If anyone tries to persuade me to stop playing games, I will kill him. After several hundred of them have been killed, no one will dare to try again."

Li Tai was the fourth son of Emperor Li Shi Min. He was very good at writing when he was young. He was made King of Yidu in 620. In 621 he was promoted to King of Wei. In 627 he was made King of Yue. In 636 he was made King of Wèi. The Emperor loved him because Li Tai liked to study literature. The Emperor let him establish a literature study center and let him select literary scholars to this literature study center. Li Tai was very fat with a very big belly. He had difficulty to make a bow. The Emperor allowed him to go to the court by a small cart. In 638 Su Xu, a subordinate of Li Tai, suggested to Li Tai that he should ask the Emperor to let him compile Journal of Geography because in Chinese history many kings became very famous by compiling books. After getting permission from the Emperor, Li Tai summoned Xiao De Yan, Jiang Ya Qing and Xie Yan, who were men of letters, to his office to compile Journal of Geography. In 641 the compilation of the great work of Journal of Geography was completed. This book had five hundred and fifty volumes. It described the changes of the names of all the counties in China in history, the jurisdiction of the counties, the mountains and rivers, the cities, the historical sites and the mythologies and legends and important historical events in these counties. Li Tai presented this great work to the Emperor. The Emperor was very glad and ordered to keep this work in the royal library. The Emperor granted Li Tai ten thousand bolts of silk. The Emperor also granted Xiao De Yan, Jiang Ya Qing and Xie Yan many bolts of silk and other things. Later the Emperor ordered to increase the monthly supplies to Li Tai. The monthly supplies to Li Tai were more than those provided to Li Cheng Qian, the Crown Prince. The Emperor showed special favor to Li Tai and asked Li Tai to move into Wude Hall of the Taiji Palace. But Wei Zheng presented a memorandum to the Emperor stating that it was improper for Li Tai to live in Wude Hall which was situated to the west of the Palace for the Crown Prince. The Emperor accepted Wei Zheng's advice and gave up the plan to let Li Tai to live in Wude Hall.

Li Cheng Qian was lame and had difficulty in walking. In 643 Li Tai had a secret plan to take over the title of the crown prince from Li Cheng Qian. Li Cheng Qian saw that Li Tai was a great threat to him because the Emperor showed special favor to Li Tai. He was afraid that his father would deprive him of his title of Crown Prince and let Li Tai become the crown prince. So Li Cheng Qian and Li Tai each formed a clique of his own against each other.

Li Cheng Qian was especially fond of a young male musician of the band for the ceremonies of offering sacrifices to the ancestors. This young boy was about thirteen years old and looked like a pretty girl. He was so pretty that Li Cheng Qian called him "Chengxin (Sweet Heart)." Chengxin was very good at singing and dancing. Li Cheng Qian slept with Chengxin and had sex with him. When the Emperor heard about this, he was in a thunderous rage. He immediately ordered to arrest Chengxin and had him killed. Several persons of the Palace of the Crown Prince were involved in this incident and were all killed. Li Cheng Qian speculated that it was Li Tai who had revealed this to the Emperor. So he hated Li Tai all the more. Li Cheng Qian grieved for Chengxin. He had a small room built in the Palace for the Crown Prince in which a figure of Chengxin was placed. In front of the figure there were small artificial carriages and horses. He ordered the servants of the Palace for the Crown Prince to mourn for Chengxin in the morning and in the evening. Li Cheng Qian went there several times and cried bitterly. Then he had a small grave built inside the palace and set up a stone tablet in front of the tomb. From then on Li Cheng Qian did not go to the court held by the Emperor for several months. Li Cheng Qian employed assassins Zhang Shi Zheng and Hegan Cheng Ji to assassinate Li Tai. But they did not get the chance to do it. So they stopped the action.

Helan Chu Shi, Hou Jun Ji's son-in-law, was a body guard of Li Cheng Qian. In 643 Li Cheng Qian asked Helan Chu Shi to invite Hou Jun Ji to the Palace of the Crown Prince. When Hou Jun Ji came, Li Cheng Qian asked Hou Jun Ji for his advice as to how to preserve his title of the Crown Prince. Hou Jun Ji saw that Li Cheng Qian was actually a fool. Hou Jun Ji wanted to help him to overthrow Emperor Li Shi Min and then get the power from Li Cheng Qian. So he proposed that Li Cheng Qian should start a rebellion against the Emperor. He held up his own hands and said to Li Cheng Qian, "I will give this good pair of hands of mine to Your Highness to help Your Highness to get the power." He also said to Li Cheng Qian, "Now Li Tai is a favorite of the Emperor. I am afraid that you will meet the same fate as that of Yang Yong, the former Crown Prince of the Sui Dynasty. If you are summoned by the Emperor, you should be secretly on guard against danger." Li Cheng Qian agreed with him and gave him a lot of gifts. Li Cheng Qian also bought Li An Yan, the commander of the guards of the palace of the Emperor, with a lot of gold and silver. Li Cheng Qian asked Li An Yan to inform him of the intentions and movements of the Emperor.

Li Yuan Chang, King of Han, also seduced Li Chang Qian to hold a rebellion against the Emperor. He said to Li Chang Qian, "Recently I saw that there is a beauty standing by the side of the Emperor. This beauty can play the lute very well. When you succeed in getting the power, please give that beauty to me as a reward." Li Cheng Qian promised to give that beauty to him. Du He, Du Ru Hui's son, was also a member of Li Cheng Qian's clique. Du He married Princess Chengyang, the Emperor's daughter. So he was the Emperor's son-in-law. Du He said to Li Cheng Qian, "If there is a change in astronomical phenomena, you should immediately take action so as to respond to the change of the astronomical phenomena. You may pretend that you have fallen seriously ill and that you are going to die. Then the Emperor will come to see you. We will seize the chance to kill the Emperor. Then your cause will succeed."

Du Zheng Lun, who had been recommended by Wei Zheng, was in charge of the important and confidential matters of the palace of the Emperor and the palace of the Crown Prince. At that time Li Cheng Qian, the Crown Prince, had difficulty in walking and could not go the see the Emperor. He was very close to bad people. The Emperor said to Du Zheng Lun, "My son is ill. You may go to serve him. But my son does not have good reputation. I have never heard that he is close to good people and that he is doing good deeds. Most of his friends are villains. You may go and find out the facts. If he does not repent himself, you must come and tell me about it." Du Zheng Lun went to the palace of the Crown Prince. Du Zheng Lun tried many times to persuade the Crown Prince to give up his bad practices, but the Crown Prince refused to listen to him. Du Zheng Lun had to convey what the Emperor had said to him to the Crown Prince. Li

Cheng Qian wrote a memorandum to the Emperor to tell what Du Zheng Lun had said. The Emperor summoned Du Zheng Lun. The Emperor asked Du Zheng Lun, "Why have you revealed what I have said to you to the Crown Prince?" Du Zheng Lun said, "I tried very hard to persuade the Crown Prince to repent himself. But he would not listen to me. So I wanted to scare him by the words of Your Majesty. I hope that would help and the Crown Prince would repent himself." The Emperor was very angry and sent him to Guzhou (now Xin'an, Henan Province) as the governor of that prefecture.

Li You was the fifth son of Emperor Li Shi Min. He was made King of Qi and was appointed commander-in-chief of the army in the area of Qizhou (now Jinan, Shangdong Province) in 636. His uncle Yin Hong Zhi suggested to him, "Your Highness has many brothers. When His Majesty passes away, Your Highness should have many warriors to protect you." Li You agreed with him. Then Yin Hong Zhi recommended his brother-in-law Yan Hong Xin to Li You. Li You was very glad. He gave Yan Hong Xin a lot of gold and asked him to recruit warriors secretly. The Emperor sent Quan Wan Ji to assist Li You. The Emperor granted Quan Wan Ji the right to report all the unlawful acts of Li You to the Emperor. Li You liked hunting very much. He was very intimate with many base persons. Quan Wan Ji tried many times to persuade Li You to give up all his illegal practices, but Li You refused to take his advice. Quan Wan Ji had to report all Li You's wrong doings to the Emperor. The Emperor sent letters to reproach Li You. But Li You did not correct his faults. Then the Emperor sent Liu De Wei, the minister of law, to carry out an investigation. It was revealed through the investigation that Li You had committed all the illegal acts reported by Quan Wan Ji. The Emperor ordered Li You and Quan Wan Ji to go to Chang'an together. Li You refused to go. But Quan Wan Ji started his journey to Chang'an alone. Li You hated Quan Wan Ji very much and sent Yan Hong Liang, Yan Hong Xin's elder brother, to lead twenty cavalrymen to run after Quan Wan Ji. They caught up with Quan Wan Ji and killed him by arrows. In March 643 Li You held a rebellion in Qizhou.

When Li Cheng Qian got the information that Li You had held a rebellion, he decided to take action. He said to Hegan Cheng Ji and the members of his clique, "The wall on the west of my palace is just twenty feet away from the palace of the Emperor. We may attack the Emperor easily in such a short distance. We have the advantage that King of Qi does not have."

The Emperor sent Li Ji to suppress Li You's rebellion with an army. But before Li Ji's army entered the area of Qizhou, Li You was already captured by Du Xing Min, a sergeant of the army under Li You. Li You was brought back to Chang'an, and was ordered by his father to kill himself.

The Emperor ordered to carry out an investigation into Li You's rebellion. Through the investigation, it was found out that Hegan Cheng Ji was involved in the rebellion. So Hegan Cheng Ji was arrested and thrown into jail. He was sentenced to death. On April 1 Hegan Cheng Ji presented an urgent secret memorandum to inform the Emperor that Li Cheng Qian was going to stage a rebellion. The Emperor was shocked. Then he appointed Zhangsun Wu Ji, Fang Xuan Ling, Xiao Yu, Li Ji and the head of the Supreme Court to investigate into this matter. Investigation and interrogation showed that Li Cheng Qian had really plotted a rebellion.

On April 6 the Emperor issued an imperial order to deprive Li Cheng Qian of the title of crown prince and demote him to a commoner. Li Yuan Chang was ordered to kill himself by taking poison. Hou Jun Ji, Li An Yan, and Du He were all beheaded.

Since Li Cheng Qian had been deprived of the title of crown prince, Li Tai tried his best to take over the title of crown prince. He went to the palace to wait upon the Emperor every day. The Emperor promised to make him crown prince. But Zhangsun Wu Ji strongly recommended making Li Zhi the crown prince. One day the Emperor said to the attendants around him, "Yesterday Blue Bird threw himself to my bosom and said, 'I have at last become your son today. Today is the day on which I have been reborn. I have only one son. On the day when I die, I will kill my only son for Your Majesty and pass the throne to my younger brother Li Zhi.' As a man, who does not love his own son? When I heard his words, I felt sorry for him." Blue Bird was the nick name of Li Tai when he was a child. So Blue Bird was referred to Li Tai. Chu Sui Liang, the senior advisor, said, "What Your Majesty said is wrong. I beg Your Majesty to consider this matter carefully. I hope Your Majesty will not make any mistakes any more. When Your Majesty passes away and Li Tai becomes the emperor, is it possible for Li Tai to kill his own son and pass the throne to his younger brother? In the past Your Majesty had made Li Cheng Qian crown prince, but Your Majesty showed special favor to Li Tai. The honor and the supplies of materials for Li Tai exceeded those for Li Cheng Qian, the Crown Prince. This led to the disaster today. This incident has just occurred recently. It can serve as a warning. If Your Majesty makes Li Tai crown prince, Your Majesty must think of a way to ensure the safety of King of Jin." When the Emperor heard these words, he burst into tears and said, "I can't find any way to ensure the safety of Li Zhi."

Li Tai was afraid that his father would make Li Zhi crown prince. So he threatened Li Zhi by saying, "You were very friendly with Li Yuan Chang. Now Li Yuan Chang has been ordered to kill himself. You'd better mind yourself." Li Zhi became very worried. A worried expression was visible on Li Zhi's face. The Emperor was surprised and asked Li Zhi why he looked so worried. Li Zhi told the Emperor what Li Tai had said. The Emperor felt sorry for Li Zhi and regretted that he had promised to make Li Tai the crown prince. The Emperor summoned Li Cheng Qian to his palace and reproached him. Li Cheng Qian said, "I was already the Crown Prince. I would not ask for more. But Li Tai was trying secretly to take the title of crown prince from me. So I had to discuss with my subordinates to find a way to prevent Li Tai from taking the title of crown prince from me. Some bad people induced me to rebel against Your Majesty. If Your Majesty makes Li Tai crown prince, he will get what he schemed to get."

After Li Cheng Qian was deprived of the title of crown prince, the Emperor held court in Liangyi Hall which was situated behind Taiji Hall of Taiji Palace on April 6. After court the Emperor asked Zhangsun Wu Ji, Fang Xuan Ling, Li Ji and Chu Sui Liang to stay. After all the other ministers and generals had left, the Emperor said to them, "My three sons and a younger brother have done such things. I really feel disheartened." The Emperor threw himself on the bed and cried bitterly. Zhangsun Wu Ji, Fang Xuan Ling, Li Ji and Chu Sui Liang all rushed forward and helped the Emperor up from the bed. Then the Emperor drew out his sword and wanted to hurt himself. Chu Sui Liang took away the sword from the hand of the Emperor and handed it to Li Zhi. Zhangsun Wu Ji asked the Emperor to tell them of his intension. The Emperor said, "I intend to make Li Zhi crown prince." Zhangsun Wu Ji immediately said, "We will follow the order of Your Majesty. I now ask permission from Your Majesty to kill those who oppose this decision." The Emperor said to Li Zhi, "Your uncle has agreed to make you crown prince. Now you should kneel down to express your thanks to your uncle." Then Li Zhi knelt down and expressed his hearty thanks to his uncle. The Emperor said, "You all have agreed with me in making Li Zhi crown prince. But I don't know the opinions of the other ministers and generals." Zhangsun Wu Ji said, "King of Jin is benevolent, honest, kindhearted and filial. The people of the realm endorse him. Your Majesty may summon all the ministers and generals to the court and ask them to express their opinions. If any of the ministers and generals disagrees with this decision, it means that I am deceiving Your Majesty. I am willing to be put to death." Then the Emperor held court in Taiji Hall. He summoned all the officials above Rank Six to the court. The Emperor said, "Li Cheng Qian has committed illegal acts. Li Tai is ruthless and treacherous. Neither of them can be made crown prince. I intend to select one of my sons as the crown prince. Whom do you think is suitable to be made crown prince?" All of them said, "King of Jin is kindhearted and filial. He should be made crown prince." The Emperor was very glad to hear that. On that day the Emperor sent Li Tai into house custody in Beiyuan which was situated to the north of Taiji Palace.

On April 7 the Emperor issued an imperial order to make Li Zhi Crown Prince. The Emperor said to the ministers and generals attending around him, "If I made Li Tai crown prince, it would be telling the world that the position of crown prince could be obtained by treacherous schemes. From now on if the crown prince commits any unlawful acts and another prince is scheming to obtain the position of crown prince, then both of them will be dismissed. This should be a rule for the generations to come. Furthermore, if Li Tai became crown prince, both Li Cheng Qian and Li Zhi would be killed by him when he ascended the throne. If Li Zhi becomes crown prince, Li Cheng Qian and Li Tai will be safe."

Portrate of Chu Sui Liang

On 10 April 643 the Emperor issued an imperial order to appoint Zhangsun Wu Ji as the Grand Preceptor of the Crown Prince, Fang Xuan Ling as the Grand Tutor of the Crown Prince, Xiao Yu as the Grand Guardian of the Crown Prince and Li Ji as the official in charge of the general affairs of the Palace of the Crown Prince and commander of the left army of the guards of the Crown Prince. The Emperor said to Li Ji, "My son has newly been made Crown Prince. In the past you were a general under me. Now I have entrusted the safety of the Crown Prince to you. This is the reason why I have made the appointment. This appointment would be a degradation of your rank. I hope you will not mind." In a banquet held by the Emperor, the Emperor said to Li Ji, "You are the best choice for me to entrust my young Crown Prince in your care. I can't find a better man for the job. In the past you were still faithful to Li Mi when Li Mi was in an unfavorable situation. I am sure you will not fail to live up to my expectation." Later in that banquet, Li Ji was so drunk that he put his head on the small table in front of him and fell fast asleep. The Emperor put his robe on Li Ji to keep him warm.

In September 643 Li Cheng Qian was sent into exile in the area of Qianzhou (now Pengshui, in the southeast part of Sichuan Province). He died in exile in 645.

In September 643 Li Tai was sent into exile to Yunxiang County (Yunxian, Hebei Province). He died there in 652 at the age of thirty-five.

In this incident, two persons, that is, Du Zheng Lun and Hou Jun Ji, were involved. These two persons had been strongly recommended by Wei Zheng. Wei Zheng had told the Emperor that these two persons had the ability to be premiers. But it turned out that Du Zheng Lun had been dismissed from his original office and sent to Guzhou and Hou Jun Ji had been executed for his crime. The Emperor began to suspect that Wei Zheng had been ganged up with these two persons. The Emperor was so angry that he ordered to destroy the tombstone of Wei Zheng's tomb the characters on which were written by the Emperor.

67. The Emperor Personally Leads an Expedition against Koguryo

In the area to the east of the Liao Shui River (now Liao He River which flows from north to south in the middle part of Liaoning Province) and the area of the Korean Peninsula, there were three kingdoms: the Kingdom of Koguryo in the area to the east of Liao Shui River and the northern part of the Korean Peninsula; the Kingdom of Paekche in the southwest part of the Korean Peninsula; and the Kingdom of Silla in the southeast part of the Korean Peninsula.

The capital of the Kingdom of Koguryo was Pyongyang which was situated to the southeast of Yalu River (which runs from northeast to the southwest between the border of Jilin Province, Liaoning Province of China and the North Korea). During the reign of Emperor Li Yuan of the Tang Dynasty, the king of the Kingdom of Koguryo was Gao Jian Wu. In 619, Gao Jian Wu sent an envoy to Chang'an to have an audience with Emperor Li Yuan of the Tang Dynasty. In 621 Gao Jian Wu sent envoys to escort tributes to Emperor Li Yuan of the Tang Dynasty. In 624 Emperor Li Yuan sent Shen Shu An, Minister of Justice, to Pyongyang with an imperial order to make Gao Jian Wu King of Liaodong Prefecture and King of the Kingdom of Koguryo.

In the expeditions against Koguryo carried out by Emperor Yang Guang of the Sui Dynasty, many of the soldiers of the Sui army were killed. The Koguryo soldiers stacked the dead bodies of the Sui soldiers up and sealed the high stacks of the dead bodies of the Sui soldiers with mud to make high towers of the dead bodies to show off their victories over the Sui Dynasty. In 613 Emperor Li Shi Min ordered General Zhangsun Shi with an army to go to Liaodong area to destroy such towers and collect the bones of the Sui soldiers and bury them properly.

Gao Jian Wu was afraid that the Emperor of the Tang Dynasty would send an army to attack Koguryo. So he ordered his soldiers to build a long wall from Fuyucheng (now Siping, Jilin Province) in the north to the sea in the south. In 640 Gao Jian Wu sent his son Gao Huan Quan, the crown prince, to Chang'an to present tributes to the Emperor of the Tang Dynasty. The Emperor of the Tang Dynasty asked Gao Huan Quan to convey his best regards to Gao Jian Wu, King of Koguryo.

Quan Gaisuwen, the governor of the eastern part of the Kingdom of Koguryo, was a very fierce and brutal man. He did a lot of unlawful acts. Gao Jian Wu, King of Koguryo, and his ministers secretly planned to get rid of him. Quan Gaisuwen found out their secret plan and decided to act first. He declared that he was going to carry out a military examination of the troops under his command in a place to the south of the city of Pyongyang. He prepared a grand banquet to entertain all the guests who would come to watch the examination. He invited all the ministers to attend the banquet. On that day, more than a hundred ministers and officials came to attend the banquet. At the banquet Quan Gaisuwen ordered the soldiers under him to kill all the ministers and officials who attended the banquet. Then he rode quickly to the palace in the city of Pyongyang and killed Gao Jian Wu, the King of Koguryo. He cut Gao Jian Wu in pieces and threw his dead body in a ditch. Quan Gaisuwen put Gao Zang, the son of Gao Jian Wu's younger brother, to the throne of the Kingdom of Koguryo. He made himself the greatest premier and minster of war. All the power was in the hands of Quan Gaisuwen. He carried out a despotic rule.

In November 642 Zhang Jian, the commander-in-chief of the Tang army in Yingzhou (now Chaoyang, Liaoning Province), reported this incident in Koguryo to the Emperor. When the Emperor got the information, he felt sad for Gao Jian Wu, the former King of Koguryo. He sent an envoy to Pyongyang to mourn for the death of Gao Jian Wu. Some of the ministers suggested to the Emperor that he should send an army to carry out an expedition against Koguryo. The Emperor said, "Gao Jian Wu, King of Koguryo, has paid tributes every year. Now he has been murdered by his subordinate. I feel very sad for him. But if I attack Koguryo at the time when the King of Koguryo has just died, even if we win, it is not an honorable act on our part. And at present, the situation in the area to the east of Xiaoshan Mountain is not prosperous. I shall not be hard-hearted enough to mobilize an army." In June 643 the Emperor sent an envoy to Koguryo to make Gao Zang King of Liaodong Prefecture and King of Koguryo.

In September 643 the King of Silla sent an envoy to Chang'an to tell the Emperor of the Tang Dynasty that the Kingdom of Koguryo had colluded with the Kingdom of Paekche and was ready to attack the Kingdom of Silla. The Emperor sent Xiangli Xuan Jiang, the minister of agriculture, to Pyongyang with a letter by the Emperor to demand Koguryo to stop the action against Silla. When Xiangli Xuan Jiang arrived at Pyongyang in January 644, the army of Koguryo under the command of Quan Gaisuwen had taken two cities of Silla. Gao Zang, King of Koguryo, sent an envoy to call Quan Gaisuwen back to Pyongyang. When Quan Gaisuwen came back, Xiangli Xuan Jiang conveyed the order of the Emperor of the Tang Dynasty to stop the attack on Silla. Quan Gaisuwen said, "When the army of the Sui Dynasty attacked Koguryo, Silla took the chance to occupy two hundred square kilometers of our territory. If Silla does not return the territory, the war against Silla will not stop." Xiangli Xuan Jiang said, "We should not mention the past. In the past the area to the east of Liao Shui River belonged to China and the cities in this area were counties and prefectures of China. The Emperor of the Tang Dynasty has not demanded you to return this area to China. How can you demand Silla to return the land to you?" But Quan Gaisuwen would not listen to him and insisted on attacking Silla. In February 644 Xiangli Xuan Jiang came back to Chang'an and told the attitude of Quan Gaisuwen to the Emperor. The Emperor said, "Quan Gaisuwen has murdered his king and killed more than a hundred ministers and officials. He suppressed the people of Koguryo. Now he has gone so far as to go against my order. He has invaded his neighboring kingdom. Now we may carry out an expedition against him with justifiable reasons. And it will be very easy for us to kill him." Chu Sui Liang said, "Your Majesty has pacified the whole realm of China and has conquered the barbarian tribes around China. Your Majesty enjoys great prestige. Now Your Majesty is going to cross the Liao Shui River to carry out an expedition against a small barbarian state. If Your Majesty wins, it will be all right. But in case of unexpected failure, it will do great harm to the prestige of Your Majesty. Now Your Majesty has decided to carry out an expedition out of a sudden anger. It will be very difficult to predict the outcome of the expedition." The Emperor thought that there was something in what Chu Sui Liang had said and was ready to accept his advice. But Li Ji said, "Last time the Xueyantuo Khanate invaded our border area. Your Majesty decided to send an army to pursue the invading army of Xueyantuo. But Wei Zheng was strongly against this decision. Your Majesty adopted Wei Zheng's advice and gave up the chance. If the wise decision of Your Majesty had been carried out at that time, no soldiers of the army of Xueyantuo could have gone back alive. And there would have been peace in the northern border area for fifty years." The Emperor said, "This was really a mistake made by Wei Zheng. This time I will insist on my correct decision." The Emperor decided to command the expedition personally. Chu Sui Liang presented a memorandum to the Emperor which read, "The whole realm is like a human body. The two capitals are the hearts of the human body. The prefectures and counties are the limbs of the human body. As for the remote barbarian tribes and states around China, they are external things that are not physically connected with this human body. Koguryo has really committed a serious crime and should be punished. But Your Majesty may send two or three fierce generals with an army of fifty thousand men to carry out an expedition. With the mighty reputation of Your Majesty, they will surely be victorious. The Crown Prince has newly been made. He is still young and needs protection from Your Majesty. Now Your Majesty has decided to abandon the safety of Your Majesty and cross the Liao Shui River and go to a dangerous place. Your Majesty is the supreme ruler of the people of the whole realm. For the benefit of the people, Your Majesty should not go to such a remote and dangerous place. As a minister under Your Majesty, I am really worried about the safety of Your Majesty." But the Emperor would not listen to his advice.

In July 644 the Emperor ordered Zhang Jian, the commander-in-chief of the Tang army in Yingzhou (now Chaoyang, Liaoning Province) to command the Tang army in Yingzhou and Youzhou (now the area around Beijing) and the armies of the Tribes of Khitan, Xi and Mohe as the vanguard of the whole army to march to the area of Liaodong (the area to the east of Liao He River, Liaoning Province). At that time a scout of Koguryo was caught. He revealed that Quan Gaisuwen would come to the area of Liaodong. Then the Emperor ordered Zhang Jian to command the army to intercept Quan Gaisuwen. When Quan Gaisuwen got the news, he did not dare to go to the area of Liaodong.

In September 644 Quan Gaisuwen sent envoys to escort a lot of silver to Chang'an to present to the Emperor of the Tang Dynasty as tributes. Chu Sui Liang said to the Emperor, "Quan Gaisuwen has murdered his king. This is a crime which is not acceptable even to the uncivilized barbarian tribes. Now Your Majesty is going to carry out a punitive expedition against Quan Gaisuwen. Quan Gaisuwen has sent this silver to Your Majesty as a bribe. It will be immoral to accept this bribe. In the early period of Spring and Autumn, the State of Song destroyed the State of Gao and took the big tripod of Gao which was the treasure and symbol of the State of Gao from the ancestral temple of the State of Gao to the State of Song. Later Hua Du, a minister of the State of Song, murdered Duke Shang of the State of Song. In order to quell the condemnation from other states, Hua Du presented the big tripod of Gao to Duke Huan of the State of Lu as a bribe. Duke Huan of the State of Lu accepted the bribe and put it in the ancestral temple of the State of Lu. This act of Duke Huan of the State of Lu has been condemned in Chinese history." The Emperor accepted his advice and said to the envoys, "You served Gao Jian Wu and got your positions. Now Quan Gaisuwen has murdered Gao Jian Wu, your king. You do not revenge your king. You have come to work for Quan Gaisuwen to deceive me. You have committed a serious crime." So the Emperor ordered to throw them into jail for further investigation.

In October 644 the Emperor appointed Zhang Liang, the minister of justice, as the commander-in-chief of the army of Pyongyang Route to command forty thousand soldiers to cross the sea on board of five hundred war ships from Laizhou (now Laizhou, Shandong Province). Generals Chang He and Zuo Nan Dang were appointed deputy commanders-in-chief of this route of the Tang army. Generals Ran Ren De, Liu Ying Xing, Zhang Wen Gan, Pang Xiao Tai and Cheng Ming Zhen were commanders of this army. The Emperor appointed Li Ji as the commander-in-chief of the army of Liaodong Route to command sixty thousand soldiers of the Tang Dynasty and soldiers of the Tribe of Qibi and the Eastern Turkic Khanate to march to the area of Liaodong. Li Dao Zong, King of Jiangxia, was appointed deputy commander-in-chief of this route of the Tang army. Generals Zhang Shi Gui, Zhang Jian, Zhishi Sili, Qibi Heli, Ashina Mishe, Jiang De Ben, Qu Zhi Sheng and Wu Hei Ta were commanders of this route of the Tang army.

In February 645 the Emperor commanded the generals to start from Luoyang. He ordered Xiao Yu to stay in Luoyang to attend to the affairs in Luoyang. In March the Emperor, accompanied by Li Zhi, the Crown Prince, reached Dingzhou (now Dingzhou, Hebei Province). The Emperor was to march north and the Crown Prince was to stay in Dingzhou to attend to the state affairs. The Crown Prince was sad and wept for several days. The Emperor said to the Crown Prince, "You are to stay to attend to the state affairs on behalf of me. I have appointed wise ministers to assist you. You should show your great ability in handling the state affairs so that the people of the realm know that you are a successor to the throne with great ability. The most important thing in ruling an empire is to promote the wise and virtuous ministers and keep out of the villains; to reward the persons who have done good and virtuous deeds and to punish those who have done evil acts. You should do your best to put my advice into practice. It is not necessary to weep like that." The Emperor appointed Gao Shi Lian as the grand tutor of the Crown Prince. Liu Ji, Ma Zhou, Zhang Xing Cheng and Gao Ji Fu were also appointed by the Emperor to assist the Crown Prince in handling most important and confidential matters. Then the Emperor started his march to Liaodong. Zhangsun Wu Ji, Cen Wen Ben and Yang Shi Dao accompanied the Emperor. The Emperor said to the ministers attending him, "The area of Liaodong originally belonged to China. The Emperor of the Sui Dynasty carried out four expeditions against Koguryo trying to recover the land. But he failed. Now I am carrying out an expedition against Koguryo to avenge the Sui soldiers who were killed in Liaodong. I also carry out this expedition to revenge Gao Jian Wu who has been murdered by Quan Gaisuwen."

In late March 645 Li Ji commanded his army to start from Liucheng (the headquarters of Yingzhou, now Chaoyang, Liaoning Province). He ordered some troops to march towards Huaiyuan Town (now Liaozhong, Liaoning Province) showing to the enemies that the Tang army would cross Liao Shui River from that part of the river. All the enemy forces concentrated in that part to prevent the Tang army from crossing Liao Shui River from that area. But he ordered the main force to march secretly to the north. On April 1 Li Ji reached Tongding (now Xinmin, Liaoning Province) where the Tang army crossed Liao Shui River (now Liao He River, Liaoning Province). When the Koguryo generals knew that the Tang army had crossed Liao Shui River, they shut the gates of their cities tight. On April 5 Li Dao Zong, the deputy commander-in-chief of the Tang army of Liaodong Route, commanded several thousand soldiers to Xincheng (now Gao-ershan City which is situated in Gaoershan Hill to the north of Fushun, Liaoning Province). Cao San Liang, a field captain, commanded about ten cavalrymen to go to the foot of the city wall to challenge for battle. But the Koguryo soldiers did not come out to fight.

At the same time, General Zhang Jian, the commander-in-chief of the Tang army in Yingzhou (now the area of Chaoyang, Liaoning Province) commanded the Tang army under him to cross Liao Shui River and march southward to attack Jian'an City (now Yingkou, Liaoning Province). A battle was fought outside the city. The Tang army defeated the Koguryo army. Several thousand Koguryo soldiers were killed.

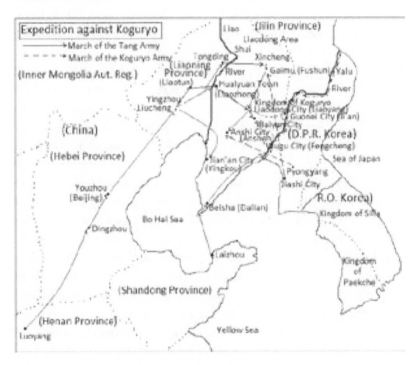

On 15 April Li Ji and Li Dao Zong commanded the Tang army under them to attack Gaimu City (now Fushun, Liaoning Province). On 26 April, the Tang army under Li Ji and Li Dao Zong took Gaimu City. They captured twenty thousand Koguryo soldiers and got more than 275,000 bushels of grain.

In this month, the Tang army under Zhang Liang sailed from Laizhou and crossed the Bo Hai Sea. They landed in a place at the tip of Liaodong Peninsula. Then they attacked Beisha City (now Dalian, Liaoning Province). This city was built on a mountain with precipices on three sides. This city was accessible from the west gate. On May 2 General Cheng Ming Zhen commanded the troops under him to reach the west gate at night. They started an attack and took the city. They captured eight thousand Koguryo soldiers. Then Zhang Liang sent General Qiu Xiao Zhong to lead an army to march towards Yalushui River (now Yalu River) to threaten Pyongyang, the capital of the Kingdom of Koguryo.

Having taken Gaimu City, Li Ji marched his army to Liaodong City (now Liaoyang, Liaoning Province).

On May 3 the Emperor reached the marsh area of Liao Shui River. On March 5 the Emperor and his army crossed the Liao Marsh (which lay between Liaotun and Liaozhong, Liaoning Province) with great difficulty and reached the west bank of Liao Shui River.

On May 8 forty thousand Koguryo soldiers were sent from Guonei City (now Ji'an, Jilin Province) to reinforce Liaodong City. The generals said that the Koguryo troops were greatly outnumbered those of the Tang army and they should dig deep ditches and build high towers around their camps to prevent the attack by the enemies; they should just stay inside the camps and wait for the Emperor and the main force to come. Li Dao Zong, King of Jiangxia, said, "Our enemies look down upon us because they are greatly outnumbered us. They have come from afar and they are very tired. If we attack them in such a time, they will surely be defeated. Now we are the vanguards of the whole army. Our task is to clear the way for the Emperor. Why should we leave the enemies for the Emperor to deal with?" Li Ji agreed with his idea. So the Tang army went out of their camps to fight against the coming enemies. Ma Wen Ju, a field captain, shouted loudly, "If I don't meet the strong enemies, how can I show that I am a brave man!" Then he urged his horse to dash at the battle formation of the enemies. Wherever he went, the enemies dispersed. The battle went on fiercely. General Zhang Jun Yi could not stand the attack by the enemies and retreated. The Tang army suffered some setback. Li Dao Zong collected the defeated Tang soldiers and reorganized them. Li Dao Zong went up a high ground and watched the fighting. He found that the battle formation of the Koguryo army was in disorder. So he commanded over forty cavalrymen to dash at the enemy formation. They fought through the enemy battle formation from front to the back several times. Li Ji commanded the rest of the army to press on the enemy battle formation. The Koguryo army collapsed. More than one thousand Koguryo soldiers were killed.

On May 10 the Emperor and his army crossed Liao Shui River. They marched to Liaodong City. When the Emperor reached Liaodong City, he stationed his army in Mashoushan Mountain (Now Shoushan Mountain which is situated to the southwest of Liaoyang, Liaoning Province). The Emperor rewarded Li Dao Zong for his great contribution in the battle to defeat the Koguryo army. He promoted Ma Wen Ju to the position of general. He ordered to execute Zhang Jun Yi who had retreated under the attack by the Koguryo army. Then the Emperor personally commanded several hundred cavalrymen to Liaodong City. When he saw that the soldiers under Li Ji were carrying soil to fill the deep ditch around Liaodong City, the Emperor helped the soldiers by carrying their heavy load of soil on his horseback. When the followers of the Emperor saw that the Emperor carried the heavy load of soil on his horseback, they all carried bags of soil on their backs to fill the ditch. When the ditch around the city had been filled, Li Ji ordered the soldiers to push the equipment for attacking the city across the ditch to the foot of the city wall. Li Ji ordered to line up the stone launchers around the city. A stone launcher could throw a big stone of 150 kg for a distance of half a kilometer. The defenders built fences of logs of wood on the top the city wall to protect their buildings inside the city. But these fences were destroyed by the big stones launched by the stone launchers and the houses inside the city were destroyed and the people were killed by the big stones. The Emperor commanded more than ten thousand cavalrymen to join in the attack of Liaodong City. The Tang army surrounded the city in many rings and attacked the city day and night. The sound of drum beating shook the sky. On May 17 a strong wind rose from the south. The Emperor ordered the soldiers to climb up to the top of the watch towers made of wood to shoot fire arrows into the city from the south. Very soon the south part of the city was on fire and the south wind blew the fire to the north part of the city. Then the whole city was on fire. The soldiers of the Tang army climbed up to the top of the city wall on the south. The Koguryo soldiers could not stand the attack by the Tang army. Very soon Liaodong City was taken by the Tang army. In this battle ten thousand Koguryo soldiers were killed; ten thousand Koguryo soldiers and forty thousand people were captured. The Emperor ordered to turn Liaodong City into Liaozhou.

Twenty-five kilometers southeast to Liaodong City, there lay a city named Baiyan. The governor of that city was Sun Dai Yin. When Liaodong city fell into the hands of the Tang army, he sent an envoy to see the Emperor and promised to surrender when the Tang army reached Baiyan City. On May 28 the Tang army marched to Baiyan City (now a place 25 kilometers southeast to Liaoyang, Liaoning Province). But when the Tang army reached Baiyan City, Sun Dai Yin went back on his promise and refused to surrender. The Emperor was very angry and issued an order that when the city was taken, all the properties and people in that city would be distributed to the officers and men of the Tang army as rewards for their hard fighting. On May 29 the Tang army began to attack Baiyan City. In the battle General Ashina Simo was wounded by an arrow. The Emperor sucked the blood from Ashina Simo's wound with his mouth to prevent poison from coming into Ashina Simo's body. When the generals and soldiers heard about this, they were all deeply moved. Ten thousand Koguryo troops were sent from Wugu City (now Fengcheng, Liaoning Province) to reinforce Baiyan City. General Qibi Heli commanded eight hundred cavalrymen to fight with the advancing Koguryo army. Qibi Heli dashed at the enemy formation and fought bravely. Unfortunately he was wounded by a spear by the waist. Xue Wan Bei (Xue Wan Jun's younger brother) rode into the enemy formation single handedly, saved General Qibi Heli and brought him back. The Emperor personally treated and dressed Qibi Heli's wound. After his wound was dressed, Qibi Heli went back to the battlefield. He and the cavalry under him fought very bravely and defeated the Koguryo army. They gave a hot pursuit to the enemy and killed more than a thousand Koguryo soldiers. On June 1 Li Ji commanded the Tang army to attack the city wall from southwest. The Emperor personally went to the northwest side of the city wall to supervise the attack. Sun Dai Yin, the governor of Baiyan City, sent an envoy out of the city gate to see the Emperor and told the Emperor that the governor of Baiyan wanted to surrender but some of his subordinates would not, and that he would send the signal of surrender by dropping swords and spears out of the city wall. The Emperor gave some flags with the characters of "Tang" on them to the envoy and said, "If the governor has decided to surrender, he should put up these flags on the top of the city wall." The next day when the Tang army was attacking the city, Sun Dai Yin put up the flags of Tang. When the Koguryo solders saw that the flags with the characters of Tang were flying on the top of the city wall, they all thought that the Tang soldiers had climbed up to the top of the city wall. Then all the officers and men followed Sun Dai Yin to surrender. When Li Ji saw that the Emperor had accepted the surrender, he went to see the Emperor and asked the Emperor to distribute the properties and people to the officers and men as he had promised. Li Ji said to the Emperor, "The offices and men were fighting bravely against the rain of arrows and stones because they thought that when they took the city by storm they would get the properties and people of the city as their rewards. Now we are going to occupy the city by attacking the city. Why should Your Majesty accept their surrender? This will make the officers and men disappointed." The Emperor got down from his horse and apologized by saying, "What you have just said is true. But if we let the officers and men to kill the men in the city and take their wives and sons and daughters as their trophies, I am not hardhearted enough to let my officers and men to do that. I intend to use the money in the national treasury to reward all the officers and men under you who have established great services in this battle so as to redeem the city." Then the Emperor ordered to set up a big tent by the river. The Emperor sat in that tent to accept the surrender of Sun Dai Yin. He turned Baiyan City into Yanzhou, and appointed Sun Dai Yin as the governor of Yanzhou. He ordered to find out the Koguryo officer who had wounded Qibi Heli and handed over that man to General Qibi Heli and let Qibi Heli to kill that man with his own hands. But Qibi Heli said, "This man fought bravely amongst sharp broad swords and spears and wounded me in the battlefield. He was doing this for his own master. He is a man of devotion. We don't know each other. There is no personal hatred between us." So he let this man go.

When the Tang army was attacking Gaimu City, Quan Gaisuwen sent seven hundred Koguryo soldiers from Jiashi City (now a city to the southwest of Pyongyang, D.P.R Korea) to station in Gaimu City. When Li Ji commanded the Tang army to attack Gaimu City, all the seven hundred Koguryo soldiers were captured. When the Tang army was attacking Liaodong City and Baiyan City, they offered themselves to take part in the attack of these cities. But the Emperor said to them, "Your families are now in Jiashi City. If you fight for me, Quan Gaisuwen will surely kill your wives and children. I am not hardhearted enough to get the help from you at the sacrifice of your families." On June 2, he set all the seven hundred Koguryo soldiers free and let them go back home.

On June 11 the Emperor commanded the Tang army to leave Liaodong City. On June 20 the Tang army reached Anshi City (now Anshan, Liaoning Province) and began to attack the city. On June 21, Gao Yan Shou, the commander-in-chief of the Koguryo army in the northern part of Koguryo, and Gao Hui Zhen, the commander-in-chief of the Koguryo army in the southern part of Koguryo, commanded one hundred and fifty thousand Koguryo soldiers and three thousand soldiers of the Tribe of Mohe to rescue Anshi City. The Emperor said to the generals around him, "As I see, Gao Yan Shou may have three stratagems: he may command his army to fight straight forward and link up with Anshi City, establish his camp just beside the city wall and build a strong fortress in the favorable grounds and get food from the city and let the Mohe soldiers to loot the cows and sheep of my army; then we cannot take the city in a short time, and if we want to retreat back to China, it will be difficult for us to go back because the marshes along the Liao Shui River are now flooded by the river, then we will be trapped here; this is his best stratagem. He may retreat together with all the army in the city back to Koguryo. This is his second best stratagem. He may fight with our army head on. This is his worst stratagem. I can tell that he will adopt the worst stratagem. Then he will be captured by us." In Gao Yan Shou's army, there was an old official who knew a lot about China. He said to Gao Yan Shou, "When Li Shi

Min was the King of Qin, he overcame many strong enemies and conquered the northern tribes. He is now a very capable emperor. Now he has come to Liaodong with a great army. We cannot fight head on with him. Our stratagem should be just to stay inside our camps and not to fight with his army. Then the Tang army and our army will be in a stalemate. If this situation lasts for a long time while we will send detachments to cut the food transportation line of the Tang army, then he will run out of food. He will be in a very awkward situation: he cannot fight with us and he cannot retreat either. Then we will surely win." But Gao Yan Shou would not listen to him. He marched his army to a place twenty kilometers away from Anshi City. The Emperor was afraid that Gao Yan Shou would hesitate and not come to fight with the Tang army. So he sent General Ashina She'er to command a thousand Eastern Turkic soldiers to lure the Koguryo army. When the two armies engaged, General Ashina She'er pretended that he was defeated and retreated with his army. Seeing that the Tang army retreated, the Koguryo officers thought that the Tang army would be easily defeated. So they marched forward boldly to a place four kilometers to the southeast of Anshi City and pitched their camps on a hill. The Emperor rode up a hill with Zhangsun Wu Ji and other officers and observed the mountains and rivers and topography of that area and tried to find out suitable places to lay an ambush and routes through which they could attack the Koguryo army. The Koguryo army and the army of Tribe of Mohe had been lined up in a battle formation of twenty kilometers long. Li Dao Zong, King of Jiangxia, said to the Emperor, "Nearly all the soldiers of Koguryo have come here to resist our army. The defense of Pyongyang must be very weak. I hope Your Majesty would assign me five thousand men to occupy its capital. Then these Koguryo troops will surrender without a fight." But the Emperor ignored his suggestion. At night, the Emperor summoned all of Generals and officials to his tent. He ordered Li Ji to command fifteen thousand foot soldiers and cavalrymen to line up in battle formation on a hill to the west of the camp of the Koguryo army; he ordered Zhangsun Wu Ji to command eleven thousand soldiers as a surprise attack party; they should secretly move to the back of the enemy and come out from the valley in the mountain to the north of the enemy camps. The Emperor himself would command four thousand cavalrymen carrying drums and rolled up banners to go up the mountain to the north of the hill where the Koguryo troops had pitched their camps. He ordered that all the troops should start fighting when they heard the beating of the drums and the blowing of the horns. He also ordered the officials concerned to set up a big tent for the ceremony of accepting the surrender of Gao Yan Shou. On June 22 Li Ji deployed the troops under him in battle formation against the Koguryo army under Gao Yan Shou. Gao Yan Shou saw that only fifteen thousand Tang troops under Li Ji were facing his great army. So Gao Yan Shou was about to order his men to attack the battle formation of the Tang army. Standing at the top of the mountain, the Emperor saw that dust rose high in the valley and he knew that the Tang army under Zhangsun Wu Ji was marching quickly to the rear of the Koguryo army. The Emperor ordered to beat the drums and to blow the horns. All the Tang troops began to attack the Koguryo army with loud war cries. Gao Yan Shou was afraid and wanted to send detachments to resist the Tang army attacking from all sides, but his battle formation was already in great confusion. At the same time there was thundering and lightening. A soldier name Xue Ren Gui, dressed in white, rode very quickly at the Koguryo battle formation with loud war cry. He was invincible wherever he went. The Tang army took this advantage and fell upon the Koguryo soldiers. The Koguryo army was defeated. Zhangsun Wu Ji commanded the troops under him to attack the rear of the Koguryo army. The Emperor personally commanded four thousand cavalrymen to charge from the top of the mountain. More than twenty thousand Koguryo soldiers were killed. Gao Yan Shou and the remaining Koguryo army had to retreat up to the hill and defend themselves. The Emperor ordered his army to surround the enemy. The Emperor had seen how bravely Xue Ren Gui fought in the battlefield and promoted him to the position of a general. Zhangsun Wu Ji ordered the troops under him to destroy all the bridges over the rivers so that the Koguryo army could not go back to Pyongyang. On June 23 Gao Yan Shou and Gao Hui Zhen with over one hundred thousand troops surrendered. The Emperor picked out three thousand men who were the chiefs of the sub tribes and high ranking officers and appointed them as officials of the Tang Dynasty and sent them to China. He granted Gao Yan Shou a high ranking position in the ministry in charge of foreign relations, and he appointed Gao Hui Zhen a high ranking position in the agriculture ministry. He released all the rest and let them go back to Pyongyang. All the Koguryo soldiers knell down and touched their heads to the ground and shouted loudly to express their thanks to the Emperor. The Emperor renamed the mountain he had stayed during the battle as Zhubi Mountain meaning the mountain in which the Emperor had stayed.

On June 5 the Emperor moved his army to the mountain to the east of Anshi City and ordered the Tang army to pitch camps there. On August 9 the cavalry scouts of the Tang army captured a spy sent by Quan Gaisuwen. The spy's name was Gao Zhu Li. He was brought before the Emperor. The Emperor untied the spy and asked, "Why are you so thin?" Gao Zhu Li said, "I had to go through secret paths. I have not had any food for many days." The Emperor ordered to provide food for Gao Zhu Li and said to him, "You are a spy. You should go back to Pyongyang quickly and report what you have found out to Quan Gaisuwen. You may tell Quan Gaisuwen that if he wants to know the information of my army, he may send someone directly to me. It is not necessary for him to send any spies who have to take the trouble of going through secret paths." The spy was barefooted because his shoes had been worn out during his secret travel. The Emperor granted him a pair of straw sandals and sent him back to Pyongyang.

When the Tang army had taken Baiyan City, the Emperor said to Li Ji, "I hear that Anshi is a city with favorable natural defense and the soldiers defending the city are picked troops. The governor defending the city is very brave. When Quan Gaisuwen murdered his king and usurped the power, the governor of Anshi City would not submit to the power of Quan Gaisuwen. Quan Gaisuwen commanded an army to attack the city trying to bring the governor of the city to submission. But Quan Gaisuwen could not take the city and had to leave. The Koguryo troops in the city of Jian'an are weak and they do not have enough food supply. If we carry out a surprise attack on the city of Jian'an, we will surely take that city. We may attack Jian'an first. Then Anshi City will surely be taken by us later. It is written in the book of arts of wars that some cities may be left untaken." Li Ji said, "Jian'an City is situated to the south of Anshi City. All the food supplies of our army are stored in Liaodong City. If we leave Anshi City untaken but attack Jian'an City in the south, our enemy may cut the transportation route of our food supplies. Then what shall we do? We'd better attack Anshi City first. If Anshi City is taken, then we can march south to take Jian'an to the beating of the drums." The Emperor said, "I have appointed you commander-in-chief of my army. You have the power to make the final decision. Now do what you think is right." Then the Tang army began to attack Anshi City. When the Koguryo soldiers saw the banner of the Emperor and the carriage of the Emperor, they all went up to the top of the city wall and shouted insulting words against the Emperor. The Emperor was furious. Li Ji said, "When the city is taken, all the people, no matter men or women, will be put to death." When the people of Anshi City heard about this, they were all the more resolute to defend their city. The Tang army attacked Anshi City for a long time but could not take it. Gao Yan Shou and Gao Hui Zhen said to the the Emperor, "We have submitted ourselves to Your Majesty. We will be devoted to Your Majesty. We hope that Your Majesty will succeed in defeating the enemies of Your Majesty as soon as possible. Then we will be able to meet our wives and children. The people of Anshi City are resolute to defend their families and fighting bravely. It is not easy to take the city in a short time. Now that the great army of over a hundred thousand men under our command has been defeated, the whole Koguryo is shocked. The commander-in-chief of the Koguryo army of Wugu City is old and does not have the ability to defend the city of Wugu. We suggest that Your Majesty should march the Tang army to that city. Then if the Tang army attacks the city in the morning, the city will be taken in the evening. Then the Koguryo armies in the small cities on the way to Pyongyang will all run away. Then Your Majesty will surely occupy

Pyongyang." All the generals agreed with Gao Yan Shou and Gao Hui Zhens' suggestion and said that Zhang Liang was at that time in Beisha City (now Dalian, Liaoning Province) and if he was summoned by the Emperor he would arrived in Anshi within one day and one night; and that the Tang army might take Wugu City (now Fengcheng, Liaoning Province) and then the Tang army might cross Yalushui River (now Yalu River, the border river between Jilin Province, Liaoning Province of China and D.P.R. Korea) and occupy Pyongyang. The Emperor was about to agree with their suggestion when Fang Xuan Ling said, "Now this expedition is directly under the command of Your Majesty. This expedition is different from other expeditions commanded by other generals. The victory of this expedition must not depend on chance. Now there are one hundred thousand Koguryo troops in Jian'an and Xincheng. If we march to Wugu, they will follow us and attack our rear. I think it would be better to take Anshi City, and then take Jian'an. After that, we may march to Wugu. This is an absolutely safe measure." Then the Emperor gave up the idea of marching to Wugu City. The Tang army stepped up the attack of Anshi City. One day, the Emperor heard the sound of pigs and chicken being killed. The Emperor said to Li Ji, "The city has been surrounded for a long time. The food of the defenders of the city has run low. Now we heard the sound of pigs and chicken being killed. The commander of the city must be treating the soldiers with good food so that they will carry out a raid on our army at night. We should be prepared for their attack." That night, several hundred Koguryo soldiers came out from the city with ropes and baskets. When the Emperor got the information, he went to the foot of the city wall and summoned soldiers to combat with the Koguryo soldiers. Over thirty of the Koguryo soldiers were killed and the rest turned back to the city. The Tang army tried to smash the city wall with wall-smashing machine and stone launchers. Some upper parts of the city wall were destroyed. But the Koguryo soldiers immediately built frames made of logs of wood in the destroyed parts of the city wall. Li Dao Zong, King of Jiangxia, was in charge of building a high hill to the southeast of the city wall so as to threaten the city. The Tang army built the hill day and night. Over 8,000 Tang soldiers worked for nearly sixty days to build this hill. The top of the hill was just about ten meters away from the top of the city wall. Li Dao Zong sent General Fu Fu Ai to command soldiers to stay at the top of the man-made hill to resist the attack by the Koguryo troops. One day, the hill suddenly collapsed to the side of the city wall and destroyed that part of the city wall. Incidentally General Fu Fu Ai had left the troops under his command for some personal matters. Several hundred Koguryo soldiers took the chance to occupy the man-made hill and dug deep ditches to defend the hill. The Emperor was so angry that he ordered to put General Fu Fu Ai to death. He ordered the Tang troops to take back the man-made hill. The Tang army attacked the man-made hill for three days but could not take it. Li Dao Zong took off his hat and his shoes and went to the Emperor. He knelt down in front of the Emperor and asked the Emperor to punish him. The Emperor said, "You have committed a crime which deserves death penalty. In the past Emperor Wu of the Han Dynasty killed Wang Hui for their failure of ambushing the King of the Huns. In the period of the Warring States, Duke Mu of the State of Qin spared Meng Ming for his defeat by the army of the State of Jin and again appointed him commander of the army of the State of Qin to attack the State of Jin. I prefer to adopt the policy of Duke Mu of the State of Qin and use Meng Ming again. You have contributed greatly in the attacks on Gaimu City and Liaodong City. This is the reason why I have spared you."

It was already late August and it was very cold in Liaodong area. The grass in that area had become withered. It would be very difficult for the Tang soldiers and the horses to stay in that area for long. The food supply of the Tang army was running low. On September 18 the Emperor issued the order to withdraw the troops back to China. The Tang army in Liaozhou and Gaizhou with all the people in those two cities left first. They crossed the Liao Shui River. Then the Emperor ordered all the troops surrounding Anshi City to line up in front of the city to say farewell to their enemy. The Koguryo soldiers all stayed within the city wall. The governor of Anshi City went up to the top of the city wall to say farewell to the Emperor. In order to praise the governor's resolution to defend Anshi City, the Emperor granted a hundred bolts of silk to the governor of Anashi City. The Emperor ordered Li Ji and Li Dao Zong to command forty thousand men to bring up the rear. On September 20 the Emperor reached Liaodong City. On September 21 the Emperor crossed Liao Shui River. On October 1 the Emperor reached Pugou (a place in Liao Marsh which lies between Liaotun and Liaozhong, Liaoning Province) and stayed there. He personally supervised the construction of a path to cross the Bocuo Shui River (a river in Liao Marsh which lies between Liaotun and Liaozhong, Liaoning Province). It happened that there was a snow-storm when the Tang army was crossing the river. Many soldiers died in this bitterly cold weather. In this expedition, the Tang army took ten cities including Gaimu, Liaodong, Baiyan and Beisha. Seventy thousand people of Liaozhou, Gaizhou and Yanzhou were moved into China. In this expedition, the Tang army killed about forty thousand enemies, but about two thousand Tang soldiers died in these battles. Seven or eight out of ten horses died in this expedition. The Emperor thought that this expedition was a failure and he regretted having carried out this unsuccessful expedition. He exclaimed, "If Wei Zheng had been still alive, he must have stopped me from carrying out this expedition." Then he ordered some officials to rebuild the tomb of Wei Zheng which had been destroyed under the order of the Emperor, and offered sacrifices to Wei Zheng.

68. Emperor Li Shi Min Passes Away

General Li Jun Xian was from Wu'an (now Wu'an, Hebei Province). At first he was an officer in the army of Wang Shi Chong. He resented Wang Shi Chong. So he came over to the army of the Tang Dynasty under the command of Li Shi Min. He became one of the officers of the guards of Li Shi Min. He took part in the expeditions against Liu Wu Zhou and Wang Shi Chong. In every battle, he would ride at the head of the whole army and attack the enemy battle formation. He made great contributions in wartime. Li Shi Min granted him many rewards. When Li Shi Min became Emperor of the Tang Dynasty, Li Jun Xian was made Duke of Wulian Prefecture. He was appointed to guard Xuanwu Gate of the Palace.

In May 647 the star of Venus often appeared in the sky at night. The official historian predicted that a female emperor would come to power. A book entitled "Secret Records" began to spread among the people. The book prophesied, "After three generations of the emperors of the Tang Dynasty, a female emperor by the name of Wu will take over and rule over the whole realm." The Emperor resented this prophecy.

One day the Emperor held a banquet in the palace to entertain all the generals. During the banquet, they played a drinkers' betting game. The game provided that each drinker should tell what his nickname was when he was a child. When it was Li Jun Xian's turn, he said that his nickname was "Wu Liang Zi" (meaning the Fifth Lady). The Emperor was surprised to hear that and said with a laugh, "What a strong and brave lady you are!" But inwardly, he resented Li Jun Xian because here was yet another word "Wu" linked to him, in his nickname, when he already had "Wu" in his official title "Wu Wei Jiang Jun" (meaning General of Military Guards), his title of dukedom "Wu Lian Jun Gong" (meaning Duke of Wulian Prefecture), and in the county of Wu'an where Li Jun Xian was from. That was enough "Wus" to make an emperor nervous, given the prophecy.

A man named Yuan Dao Xin claimed that he could survive without eating and drinking, and that he was very knowledgable about Buddhism. Li Jun Xian believed him and had several secret talks with him. The legal minister reported to the Emperor that Li Jun Xian was associating with bad people to plot a rebellion. In July 647 the Emperor ordered Li Jun Xian be put to death.

The Emperor consulted the prophecy in the "Secret Records" with Li Chun Feng, the official historian. The Emperor asked Li Chun Feng, "Do you think that the prophecy in Secret Records will really come true?" Li Chun Feng answered, "I have studied astronomical phenomena at night and read the records of the calendars. I realize that the person predicted in the prophecy is now in the palace of Your Majesty. She is a very close relative of Your Majesty. Thirty years from now, she will become emperor of the whole realm. She will kill nearly all of Your Majesty's grandchildren. The prophecy will come true." The Emperor said, "What if we kill everyone who could be suspected?" Li Chun Feng answered, "This is the will of Heaven which cannot be violated. And if the person has been appointed by Heaven, she will not be killed. If the persons under suspicion are all killed, this will lead to the massacre of many innocent people. Thirty years from now, that person will be old. Maybe she will become benevolent. Although she will change the name of the dynasty, she will not do much harm to the grandchildren of Your Majesty. If Your Majesty finds out that person and kills her, another person appointed by Heaven will be born and she would be younger and stronger and will do greater harm. In that case she will kill all the grandchildren of Your Majesty and none of them will survive." The Emperor agreed with him and took no action to counter the prophecy.

On 2 April 649 the Emperor was staying in Cuiwei Palace, which was situated in Cuiwei Mountain south of Chang'an. The Emperor said to Li Zhi, the Crown Prince, "Li Ji is a very capable man. But you have never granted him any favor. I am afraid that he will not submit to you in the future. Now I will dismiss him from his present office and send him out of the capital. When I die, you may summon him back and appoint him as one of the premiers. If he hesitates and will not go, I will kill him." On May 15, the Emperor dismissed Li Ji from his office and sent him to Diezhou (now Têwo, Gansu Province) to be the commander of the Tang army there. When Li Ji received the order, he started the journey to Diezhou directly from the palace where he received the order without even going home.

In mid May the Emperor suffered from dysentery. He lay on the bed in Hanfeng Hall of Cuiwei Palace. The Crown Prince stayed beside the bed of the Emperor day and night. He was so worried that he did not eat anything for several days in a row. Some of his hair turned white. The Emperor shed tears and said, "You are such a filial son that I am satisfied, even if I should die." On May 24 the Emperor's illness took a turn for the worse. He summoned Zhangsun Wu Ji into Hanfeng Hall. Zhangsun Wu Ji sat by his bed. The Emperor reached out his hand to touch Zhangsun Wu Ji. Zhansun Wu Ji was weeping so bitterly that he could not speak. The Emperor wanted to say something to him, but Zhangsun Wu Ji was so sad that the Emperor could not speak. Then the Emperor had to let Zhangsun Wu Ji go out of Hanfeng Hall. On May 26 the Emperor summoned Zhangsun Wu Ji and Chu Sui Liang to Hanfeng Hall. The Emperor said to them, "I entrust to you two all the affairs which should be attended to after I die. The Crown Prince is benevolent and filial. You two know this very well. You should assist him and guide him." Then the Emperor said to the Crown Prince, "Now Zhangsun Wu Ji and Chu Sui Liang are here. You do not need to worry about state affairs." The Emperor said to Chu Sui Liang, "Zhangsun Wu Ji has always been devoted to me. I gained the power to rule over the whole realm with the help of Zhangsun Wu Ji. After I die, don't let anyone sow discord between the Crown Prince and Zhangsun Wu Ji." Then he ordered Chu Sui Liang to draft an imperial order. Later on that day, the Emperor died at the age of fifty-three. Clinging to Zhangsun Wu Ji's neck with both arms, the Crown Prince cried bitterly. He was crying so bitterly that he nearly fainted away. Zhangsun Wu Ji dried his tears and told the Crown Prince that he should control his emotions and take up the reins of the state. The Crown Prince could not govern his feelings and continued to cry bitterly. Zhangsun Wu Ji said, "The Emperor has entrusted the whole realm to Your Highness. Your Highness should not cry bitterly like an ordinary man."

Zhaoling Mausoleum

The death of the Emperor was kept secret. On May 27 Zhangsun Wu Ji asked the Crown Prince to go back to the palace in Chang'an. All the guards and generals of the late Emperor accompanied him. On May 28 the Crown Prince entered the capital. Then the carriage for the Emperor and the procession arrived. All the guards of the late Emperor were still on duty as before. On May 29 the Crown Prince announced the death of Emperor Li Shi Min in Taiji Palace and a memorial ceremony of the late Emperor was held in Taiji Hall of the Taiji Palace with the coffin of the late Emperor in the memorial hall. Then the imperial order of the late Emperor was read out. On June 1 the Crown Prince ascended the throne of the Tang Dynasty. On June 6, Emperor Li Zhi summoned Li Ji from Diezhou and appointed him commander-in-chief of the army in Luoyang. Very soon Emperor

Li Zhi appointed Li Ji as one of the premiers and asked him to participate in important and confidential matters of the whole realm. On June 10 Emperor Li Zhi appointed Zhangsun Wu Ji as the premier of the government and Minister of War. On August 4 the officials and generals proposed that the posthumous title of the late Emperor be Emperor Wen, and proposed that the temple title of the late Emperor be Taizong ("Supreme Ancestor").

The statue of Li Shi Min, Emperor Taizong of the Tang Dynasty

The six horses that carried Li Shi Min in various battles; the mountain behind them is Jiuzong Mountain, the tomb of Li Shi Min, Emperor Taizong of the Tang Dynasty

On August 18 the late Emperor was buried in Zhaoling Mausoleum in Jiu-zong Mountain, Liquan County, Shaanxi Province.

69. The Reign of Emperor Li Zhi and the Reign of Emperor Wu Ze Tian

After Emperor Li Shi Min died, his concubine Cairen Wu was sent to a nunnery named Ganye Nunnery and became a nun. Emperor Li Zhi paid a visit to that nunnery and found that she was very beautiful. In March 654 Cairen Wu was brought back to Emperor Li Zhi's imperial harem and became one of Emperor Li Zhi's concubines. Later she was given the title of Zhaoyi (rank five of all the concubines). In October 655 Emperor Li Zhi deposed his Empress Wang and made Zhaoyi Wu empress. In November 656, Empress Wu gave birth to a boy. This boy was named Li Xian. After 656, Emperor Li Zhi began to suffer such headaches he could not attend to state affairs properly. He trusted Empress Wu to read all the memorandums presented to the Emperor and make decisions. So Empress Wu held power as great as that of the Emperor.

In June 666 Quan Gaisuwen, the premier of the Kingdom of Koguryo, died. His eldest son Nansheng succeeded his father as the premier. But not long later he was driven out by his younger brother Nanjian. Nanjian became the premier of the Kingdom of Koguryo. Nansheng sent his son to Chang'an to convey his intention to surrender to the Tang Dynasty. Emperor Li Zhi sent General Qibi Heli to lead an army to help Nansheng. In October Emperor Li Zhi appointed Li Ji as commander-in-chief of the Tang army of the Liaodong Route to carry out an expedition against Koguryo. In September 668 the Tang Army under the command of Li Ji defeated the Koguryo army and took Pyongyang, the capital of the Kingdom of Koguryo. The Tang army captured Gao Zang, the King of the Kingdom of Koguryo, and his premier Nanjian. The whole Kingdom of Koguryo was conquered. There were one hundred and seventy cities and six hundred and ninety thousand households in this kingdom. The land of the Kingdom of Koguryo became part of the territory of China.

On 27 December 683 Emperor Li Zhi died at the age of fifty-six. The ministers suggested that his posthumous title should be "Tian Huang Da Di" (meaning the Great Heavenly Emperor) and his temple title should be "Gaozong." He was buried in Qianling Mausoleum which is situated in Qian Xian, Shaanxi Province.

Li Xian, the Crown Prince, ascended the throne. He respected his mother Empress Wu as Empress Dowager. But she held the power to rule the whole realm in her hands. In February 684 Empress Dowager Wu deposed Emperor Li Xian and demoted him to King of Luling. Empress Dowager Wu held a firm grasp on the power of the Tang Dynasty. She sat on the throne, held court and issued imperial orders as if she was the emperor. In January 686 Empress Dowager Wu issued an imperial edict to the effect that she would return the power to Li Xian, the deposed Emperor. But Li Xian suspected some trick, seeing that Empress Dowager Wu did not truly wish to turn the power over to him. So he declined the offer.

Li Zhen, King of Yue, was the eighth son of Emperor Li Shi Min. His eldest son was Li Chong, King of Langya. Li Zhen resented Emperor Dowager Wu. He wanted to overthrow her and take the ruling power back to the royal family of Li. He secretly conspired to carry out a rebellion against Empress Dowager Wu together with Li Yuan Jia, King of Han (who was the eleventh son of Emperor Li Yuan), Li Ling Kui, King of Lu (who was the nineteenth son of Emperor Li Yuan), Li Yuan Gui, King of Huo (who was Emperor Li Yuan's fourteenth son), Li Yuan Jia's son Li Zhuan, Duke of the State of Huang, Li Ling Kui's son Li Ai, King of Fanyang, Li Yuan Gui's son Li Xu, King of Jiangdu, Li Rong, Duke of Dongguan Prefecture (who was the fifth son of Li Feng, King of the State of Guo, who was Emperor Li Yuan's fifteenth son) and Li Zhen's own son Li Chong.

In late August 688 Li Chong, King of Langya, held a rebellion in Bozhou (now Liaocheng, Shangdong Province) against Empress Dowager Wu. He expected that the other persons who had taken part in the conspiracy would come along. No one but his father Li Zhen responded to him by holding an armed rebellion in September 688; he occupied the city of Shangcai (now Runan, Henan Province). Empress Dowager Wu sent General Qiu Shen Ji to suppress Li Chong's rebellion. Before General Qiu Shen Ji reached Bozhou, Li Chong was killed by the gatekeepers of the city of Bozhou on the seventh day of his rebellion. General Qiu Shen Ji cut off Li Chong's head and sent it back to Chang'an.

Empress Dowager Wu sent General Qu Chong Yu to lead an army of a hundred thousand men to suppress Li Zhen's rebellion. When the army under Qu Chong Yu reached a place twenty kilometers away from Shangcai, Li Zhen killed himself by taking poison. His youngest son Li Gui killed his mother and then killed himself. Li Zhen's rebellion had lasted only for twenty days. Their heads were cut off from their dead bodies and brought back to Chang'an. Li Zhen, Li Chong and Li Gui were expelled from the royal clan of Li and given the surname of "Hui" (Hui is the name of a kind of poisonous snake). Li Yuan Jia, Li Ling Kui, Li Zhuan, Li Ai, Li Yuan Gui, Li Xu and Li Rong were implicated in the conspiracy. Li Yuan Jia and Li Ling Kui committed suicide; Li Yuan Gui was sent into exile in Qianzhou (now Guizhou Province) and he died on his way there. Li Zhuan was executed. They were all expelled from the royal clan of Li and given the surname of "Hui." Their young sons and grandsons were sent into exile to the far south.

Portrait of Emperor
Wu Ze Tian

On 9 September 689, Empress Dowager Wu changed the dynastic name from Tang to Zhou and declared that she had ascended the throne of the Zhou Dynasty. She made herself "Sacred Divine Emperor." She gave her father Wu Shi Yue the posthumous title of "Emperor Xiao Ming." She made her elder brother's son Wu Cheng Si King of Wei; she made her nephew Wu San Si King of Liang; she made twelve of her cousins' sons kings of different prefectures.

Emperor Wu stayed on the throne of the Zhou Dynasty for about fourteen years. On 23 January 705, Emperor Wu fell ill. She ordered Li Xian, the Crown Prince, to take charge of state affairs. On the same day Emperor Wu passed the throne to him, and she moved to live in Shangyang Palace. Four days later, on 27 January, Emperor Li Xian presented her the title of "Great Sacred Emperor Ze Tian." On 4 February the dynastic name was changed back to Tang.

Seven months later, on 16 September, Emperor Wu Ze Tian fell seriously ill. She issued an order to cancel her title as Emperor and ordered that she should be called "Great Sacred Empress Ze Tian." She died that same day, in Shangyang Palace, at the age of eighty-three. She was given the posthumous title of "Great

Sacred Empress Ze Tian." In May 706 she was buried in Qianling Mausoleum to rest forever with her husband Emperor Li Zhi.

Qianling Mausoleum

Made in United States
Troutdale, OR
11/27/2023

14968079R00137